NATHANAEL GREENE

NATHANAEL GREENE

A BIOGRAPHY OF THE AMERICAN REVOLUTION

GERALD M. CARBONE

NATHANAEL GREENE
Copyright © Gerald M. Carbone, 2008.
All rights reserved.

First published in 2008 by
PALGRAVE MACMILLAN™
175 Fifth Avenue, New York, N.Y. 10010 and
Houndmills, Basingstoke, Hampshire, England RG21 6XS
Companies and representatives throughout the world.

PALGRAVE MACMILLAN is the global academic imprint of the Palgrave
Macmillan division of St. Martin's Press, LLC and of Palgrave Macmillan Ltd.
Macmillan® is a registered trademark in the United States, United Kingdom
and other countries. Palgrave is a registered trademark in the European
Union and other countries.

ISBN-13: 978–0–230–60271–7
ISBN-10: 0–230–60271–1

Design by Newgen Imaging Systems, Ltd., Chennai, India.

Printed in the United States of America.

Book Club Edition

for Bonnie and Mary

CONTENTS

ILLUSTRATIONS

ACKNOWLEDGMENTS

*T*his book could not have been written without the former executive director of the Rhode Island Historical Society, Al Klyberg; Thomas Casey Greene (a collateral descendant of Nathanael Greene); and Tom's mother, the late Anne Greene. In deciding how best to spend some money raised to honor General Greene's memory, those three hit on the idea of gathering, transcribing, annotating, indexing, and publishing all of Greene's voluminous papers, a project that from inception took thirty-five years. The editors of those papers, Richard K. Showman, Dennis M. Conrad, and Roger N. Parks, provided first-rate scholarship in compiling and presenting the thirteen-volume series.

This book would not have been written without Joel Rawson, the executive editor of the *Providence Journal.* Joel recognized that Nathanael Greene's story is a great one, and he gave me the time to pursue it as a fifty-eight-part newspaper series that spawned this work. *Journal* publisher Howard Sutton also deserves credit for dedicating time and space to that work.

Mary Preziosi, my wife, made the book possible by formatting it and proved to be a diligent copy editor with a natural eye and ear for language. Friend Bill Malinowski introduced me to RLR Associates, where my agent, Scott Gould, was an enthusiastic supporter of this story, and he found a good home for it. Alessandra Bastagli, a senior editor at Palgrave Macmillan, saved the planet much waste by deftly suggesting ways to shorten and tighten the narrative.

In traveling the South to research this story I found a resurgent interest in Nathanael Greene, from South Boston, Virginia—where Ted Daniel, Barbara Bass, Anne Raab, and others are promoting the historic "Race to the Dan"—to Charleston, where Carl Borick and the staff of the Charleston Museum showed me some of South Carolina's many Revolutionary War battle sites. In between, Charles Baxley, David Reuwer, Joanna Craig, and George Fields took me for tours of Camden, Hobkirk's Hill, and Eutaw Springs. In Savannah, I found the staff of the Georgia Historical Society to be friendly and knowledgeable. They set me up with felt gloves and an original copy of Ban Tarleton's memoirs for an immensely satisfying afternoon.

Closer to my Rhode Island home, Gregg and Mary Mierka opened the Nathanael Greene homestead in Coventry to provide an off-season, behind-the-scenes look at Greene's house. Martha Koziara and Jean Di Bona arranged a private peek of the battleground on the Carnegie Abbey's property. Gwen Stearn and her staff at the Rhode Island Secretary of State's Archives Division—Tracy Croce, Ken Carlson, and Elliott Caldwell—seemed to sincerely enjoy finding and sharing archival information; and staff at the Rhode Island Historical Society, past and present, did yeoman's work in pulling Greene's papers together. Staff at the Redwood Library in Newport also cheerfully shared their special manuscripts collection.

Providence Journal editor Jean Plunkett deserves a medal for bearing with me during the publication of the aforementioned fifty-eight-day newspaper series.

Author/historian John Buchanan read the uncorrected proofs and caught some potential mistakes. And I owe a special debt to Dr. Lawrence Babits for reading a very early draft and saving me many embarrassments, though my mention of him here must not be construed as an endorsement as he has not seen the final draft, and I'm not sure whether it will win his approbation (though I hope it will).

Mike Chandley's excellent Rhode Island history collection at the Cellar Stories bookstore in Providence proved to be a treasure trove, from which I heavily drew. Friends and former colleagues who have published books—Mark Arsenault, Carl Borick, Edward J. Delaney, G. Wayne Miller, Mike Stanton, and Robin Young—offered useful information on how to get that done, and for that I am grateful.

Tobias Wolff gave me good advice while I was sorting through the nettlesome business of finding an agent, and he made me a better writer through meticulous editing in his fiction writing workshop at Stanford. And lifelong thanks to Jason Brown, the late Andre Dubus, Len Levin, John Yount, and my late uncle, Edward Jesby, who have also taught me a lot about writing.

PROLOGUE

R hythmically swinging their picks in an old graveyard, two men broke through the brick walls of a tomb; a stench soon tainted the springtime air. This red brick vault, like the other ten vaults they had knocked open, was squat, not tall enough for a man to kneel in. Both workmen crawled in on their bellies, illuminating the cramped, foul crypt with a sputtering lantern. Even though a hundred years had passed since 1801, when a body was last placed in that vault, the odor was strong enough to sicken the men.

In the lamplight, they saw a coffin with a name engraved on a metal plate: Sarah S. Wood, died 1801. This was not the corpse of the famous man they were seeking; the search had failed again.

The two workers crawled out into the fading light of a March day. They reported their finding to Col. Asa Bird Gardiner, a dignified Yankee in a high, black hat.[1] Gardiner was president of an exclusive club: the Rhode Island State Society of the Cincinnati, an organization only for descendants of military officers of the Revolutionary War. In January 1901, Rhode Island's chapter of the Cincinnati had voted to spend one hundred dollars—more than two thousand dollars today—to send Gardiner to Georgia on a mission: Find the forgotten bones of a great American hero, Major General Nathanael Greene.

Greene had died near Savannah, far from his Rhode Island roots, in 1786. Now, 115 years later, no one in that city could say for certain where his body rested. Some said that a woman loyal to the British crown had taken the

Revolutionary War hero's bones from her family crypt and tossed them into Negro Creek; others said that his bones had been exhumed from the old Colonial Park cemetery and reburied next to his widow out on Cumberland Island; one old man recalled that as a child he played on a hill said to contain Greene's bones over on Bull Street.[2]

The Society of the Cincinnati thought it shameful that the bones of "such a great patriot and soldier" should be interred in an unknown, unmarked grave. Gardiner had come to Savannah with his one hundred dollars and a firm resolve to find Greene's tomb.

Savannah's city fathers agreed that the search was an excellent idea; they loaned a crew from the Park and Trees Commission to do the dirty work of busting into the tombs in Colonial Park, a bygone graveyard in the city's downtown.

Naturally, the sight of men breaking into tombs in the heart of the city drew crowds. The *Savannah Morning News* of Sunday, March 3, 1901, described the search: "A morbid curiosity drew a crowd to the scene. Many of those attracted by the prospect of a peep at the remains of persons who died a century ago did not stay long, the one peep sufficing them, but there were others with no especial interest in the work who remained for hours."

After 115 years of decay, it would be hard to distinguish a particular pile of bones as Greene's without some sort of identifiers.

Gardiner knew that Greene had been tall for his time, about five feet-ten inches, so the bones would be bigger than most.[3] One of Greene's grandsons, George Washington Greene, had written of his grandfather: "His face was a well-filled oval, with all the features clearly defined, though none of them, except, perhaps, the forehead, large enough to arrest the attention at a first glance. . . . The eyes themselves were of a clear, liquid blue."[4]

The "well-filled oval" of Greene's face—the "full lips" of the mouth, those eyes of "liquid blue"—had long ago decayed to dust; but Gardiner hoped that Greene's distinctive skull, with a large forehead prominent in every known portrait of him, might yet be intact.

Gardiner hoped, too, that Greene's sword might still be at his side, and that fragments of his uniform—metal buttons or the gold-silk epaulets that decorated Greene's shoulders, might be recognizable.

As the sun set on Saturday, March 2, 1901, the workmen laid down their tools until Monday morning, when the search resumed. Again a crowd formed in the old cemetery framed with a fence of black iron spears.

The first tomb they knocked through that Monday was empty. In the second vault they found a well-preserved coffin; a silver coffin plate screwed into the lid said it contained the bones of a man who had died fifty-six years before. Then one of the workmen saw, on the other side of the narrow vault, fragments of a coffin rotted into the sandy soil. "Upon these [fragments] being removed," Gardiner wrote, "there appeared a man's skeleton quite intact, except some of the smaller ribs."

The two workmen, Charles Gattman and Edward Keenan, worked without a lamp now, near midday, while sunlight pierced their entry hole and illuminated the vault. Even from outside the crypt the bones within were visible. Edward Kelly, the supervisor of the two workmen, called out to Gardiner that the skull looked unusually big.

Kelly dispatched Keenan to the city greenhouse for a sieve to sift the moldy sand from the bones.

With Keenan gone, his partner, Gattman, poked through the skeleton's breast bones, searching for the coffin plate that should have sunk into the mold from the rotted lid. He found it. The silver was badly corroded; Gattman wiped it against the cloth of his shirt and held it up to a shaft of sunlight. He called out that he could decipher the figures: 1786.

The number must have set Gardiner's heart pounding; he knew that was the year of Nathanael Greene's death.

Keenan returned with the sifter and plunged into the sands of the tomb to see what he could find. He heard something clatter inside the sieve, and plucked from it three metal buttons with a patina of green. He wiped one button clean and saw the faint outline of an eagle.

Gardiner recognized these as buttons worn by officers of the revolution. Enlisted men wore buttons of wood covered with cloth; officers wore the eagle-stamped metal.

Keenan then found a French silk glove filled with finger bones. French silk had been a luxury during the Revolution; a glove like this was the kind of thing a high-ranking Frenchman such as Lafayette would have given to an American Army officer. Keenan found a second glove full of bones.

He then found a third glove, moldy and stiff with finger bones. Obviously more than one person had been entombed on this side of the vault.

For Gardiner, the intermingled sets of bones was additional evidence that they'd found the missing bones of Major-Gen. Nathanael Greene. After Greene died, his oldest son had swamped a homemade canoe and drowned in the Savannah River at age eighteen, and it had long been rumored that the son had been buried along side his famous father.

The workmen in the vault divided the skeletons into two empty soapboxes. The big skull crumbled beneath their touch, but its jaw bones stayed intact. The jaws still held thirty-two teeth, two of them filled with gold.

The soapboxes were taken to the police barracks, where they were held under guard. A police reporter for the *Savannah Morning News* saw the unmarked boxes in a sergeant's office. He gave one box a kick and asked a Sergeant Reilly what was in it. "Great heavens man," said the sergeant, "look out there, that's General Greene's body you are kicking."

From the Western Union office in the swank De Soto Hotel, Gardiner sent a telegram to Rhode Island Gov. William Gregory: "Have to announce to you and Rhode Island General Assembly that, after diligent search several days, committee appointed by Rhode Island State Society of Cincinnati from among eminent citizens Savannah discovered to-day remains Major-General Nathanael Greene in Colonial Cemetery."

The city parks crew constructed two boxes built of hardwood and lined with zinc; the next day the remains were transferred from the soap crates into the more dignified boxes. The *Savannah Morning News* reported: "Reverently the work was done, Col. Gardiner setting the example by removing his high hat when the chisel was used to open the soap boxes. Each bone was laid aside by the man making the transfer, and the members of the committee inspected them closely. Though a grewsome piece of work, it was not without interest."

The thigh bone of the large skeleton measured eighteen inches, indicative of a man about six feet tall.

The boxes were taken by a horse-drawn hearse to the Southern Bank of Georgia, where they were placed in a vault. Gardiner sent the corroded coffin plate north to a New York City museum to have it "scientifically" cleaned. After the silver plate was treated the engraved letters clearly read:

NATHANAEL GREENE
Obit. June 19, 1786
Aetat 44 years

Caisson bearing the remains of Major-General Nathanael Greene rolling to his reburial in Johnson Square, Savannah, Georgia, November 14, 1902. *Remains of Major-General Nathangel Greene*, 1903. Committee of the Rhode Island General Assembly. Providence: E. L. Freeman & Sons.

The coffin plate was mistakenly inscribed. Greene was forty-three years old when he died, not forty-four.[5]

Greene's bones remained in the bank vault while Rhode Island and Georgia haggled over where they should be buried for eternity. Members of the Greene family in both states had the final say; they decided that Savannah, where Greene lived the last days of his too-short life, was the proper place. After all, it was in the South that he made his reputation as a general of genius compared, not unreasonably, with Scipio, Caesar, and Napoleon.[6]

BOOK I

The North

ONE

War, War Boys!

From the deck of his sloop anchored in Narragansett Bay, Rufus Greene watched a two-masted ship armed with cannon bearing down on him. Rufus stood atop a valuable cargo stored in his hold: twelve hogsheads of West India rum, forty gallons of Jamaica spirits, and a barrel of brown sugar. Technically the cargo was contraband as it had not cleared the customs house in Newport, but by 1772 Rhode Islanders had grown accustomed to ignoring London's laws, and sporadic attempts to enforce them often excited violence.[1]

The cargo belonged not to Rufus but to the sloop's owners, Nathanael Greene & Co., his cousin's business on nearby Potowomut Peninsula. Rufus was twenty-three, brown-haired, tall, and slender. As young and strong as he was, he was no match for the armed boarding party bent on invading his ship, the *Fortune*.

The raiders were not pirates; they were British seamen in the King's Navy, sent into Narragansett Bay in the winter of 1772 to enforce the often-ignored customs laws. This was dangerous duty, for Rhode Islanders had been known to savagely beat customs collectors.

The British had sent a tough man for the job: Lt. William Dudingston, who had recently been sued for beating a Delaware River fisherman while a mate held the man helpless. From his ship, the revenue schooner *Gaspee*, Dudingston lowered a row boat into the still, winter-blue waters of Narragansett Bay. A Naval officer named Dundass rowed over from the *Gaspee*, climbed aboard the *Fortune*'s deck, and asked Rufus if he would carry some freight for the King's Navy.

Rufus said he would not.

"Unlay the hatches," Dundass said.

Rufus said that the hatches were already unlocked.

The officer ordered Rufus below decks. Rufus asked Dundass by whose authority did he order him about on his own boat.

With the whetting sound of steel on steel Dundass drew his sword.

"If you do not go into the cabin I'll let you know." He grabbed Rufus by the collar and shoved him below. Footsteps sounded on the deck above as a boarding party from the *Gaspee* invaded the *Fortune*. At swordpoint Dundass kept Rufus Greene confined below decks, and then let him up to watch as the boarding party marked the sloop's hatches with the letter "R," signifying that the *Fortune* and its cargo, valued at 295 pounds, now belonged to His Royal Highness, England's King George III.[2]

It would prove to be a costly seizure; arguably it cost the king the loss of his schooner, the *Gaspee*, and the colonies of South Carolina and Georgia. For in seizing the *Fortune*, the King's Navy had stoked the slumbering fires of its owner, Nathanael Greene.

Word of the *Fortune*'s seizure spread through every smuggler's port in Narragansett Bay. Within a week the *Newport Mercury* newspaper was reporting that the "piratical schooner belongs to King George the Third." When Rufus's cousin, Nathanael Greene, Jr., learned that the King's Navy had taken his ship he grew furious. Until that point in his life, Nathanael Greene had steered clear of the trouble brewing between England and her colonies. Now it was personal, and Greene became obsessed.

Nathanael Greene came from a family of influence. His great, great, great grandfather had been a contemporary of Roger Williams, fleeing with him from the theocracy of Massachusetts to begin a new colony of true religious freedom in 1620. By the time Greene was born, his family had been in Rhode Island for nearly 130 years. Greene's father had been the Quaker preacher[3] at the Greenwich Meeting House, and had built a prosperous business at the family's old homestead on Potowomut Peninsula.

The gabled, two-story house where Greene grew up with five brothers sat atop a hill that sloped gently to Hunt's River. The river splashed noisily over the Greene family's dam and gurgled through the sluiceway that turned the wheels of their mill and forge. Here in Potowomut the Greenes' mill wheels ground grain hauled there by ship and in the carts of local farmers. Here, too, the Greene brothers forged red-hot iron and banged it into massive fishermen's anchors that they shipped across the bay to Newport, a hub of international shipping. On nearly two hundred acres, Nathanael Greene & Co.

Birthplace of Major-General Nathanael Greene, Potowomut section of Warwick, Rhode Island. The house has been in the Greene family since the 1600s. *Home of Major-General Nathanael Greene*, 1903. Committee of the Rhode Island General Assembly. Providence: E. L. Freeman & Sons.

owned a wharf, warehouse, saw mill, and store, as well as the dam, sluiceways, forge, and anchor works. The Greene homestead was very much a man's world; Greene's mother, Mary, died when he was eleven, leaving the six boys under the tutelage of a loving but stern father who believed in hard work and plain living. Greene's father did remarry, to another devout Quaker named Mary a year later, but judging from the few references Greene made to "Mother Greene" in his voluminous correspondence, the relationship was more formal than loving.

The elder Greene and his six surviving sons also owned a forge at Coventry, a small inland village where they smithed more anchors, a staple in seagoing Rhode Island. Months before Greene's father died in 1770, he built a drafty, fourteen-room house at the Coventry forge so he could better manage his work-force of one hundred men there. Nathanael Jr. drew the job of moving out to Coventry to oversee the works.

Greene found Coventry a dismal place. It was a smoky, isolated village that essentially owed its existence to the Greene family's forge, where men from dozens of families toiled, stoking furnaces to smelt iron with rough ore and black sand to make a malleable metal for the smiths to hammer into big black anchors.

For companions in Coventry, Greene generally had only the unschooled, rough-handed men who wrestled his iron into anchors. In some ways Greene was a lot like his laborers; he had little schooling and was accustomed to hard work, having grown up stoking the furnaces of his father's forges, plowing his fields, and grinding grist in the mill at the family's main homestead in Warwick.

In other ways Nathanael Greene was very much different, not only from his laborers but from most men: He was richer, smarter, driven, and relentlessly curious. Although his father had discouraged reading as an idle waste of time, Greene was exceptionally good at it. Those who knew Greene best said that, "Nobody could get the substance out of a book as he could."[4]

In satiating his driven curiosity, Greene had amassed in his Coventry house an eclectic library of 250 volumes, an impressive collection in an eighteenth-century village. His shelves held the four thick octavos of the *Dictionary of Arts and Sciences*, Locke's *An Essay on Human Understanding*, Euclidian geometry, and Ferguson's *Essay on Civil Society*; he read Roman history, the novels of Swift and Sterne, and four quartos of Blackstone's *Commentaries on the Laws of England.* To help deal with the everyday details of running the family business he consulted *Book-keeping Methodized.*[5]

When he lost the sloop *Fortune,* Greene was single, closing in on thirty, rambling around a big, lonesome house in which every wall was painted white. He had recently been spurned in love by Nancy Ward of Westerly, a fair-haired woman with "soft eyes of bluish gray."[6]

Nathanael and Nancy traveled in the same social circle, so their meeting was inevitable. Nancy was one of six rich and pretty daughters of the eminent merchant Samuel Ward, a former governor; Greene was one of six brothers, excluding two older half-brothers who had died in their twenties. During Greene's stormy, on-again, off-again courtship of Nancy, he was introduced to her little brother, Sammy Ward, and a strange, strong, lifelong friendship blossomed between them. Greene may have begun writing to Sammy in order to ingratiate himself with Nancy. Sammy was fourteen years younger, but he had a classical education that Greene sincerely envied. Around the time of Greene's breakup with Nancy, Sammy became Greene's epistolary confidant, the one person to whom Greene confided his innermost thoughts on everything from theology to the latest gossip.

In April 1772, Greene took quill in hand to write Sammy from Coventry, with the loss of his sloop very much on his mind. Noah Webster's efforts to standardize spelling did not take root until the early nineteenth century, so as he wrote to Sammy, Greene was free to punctuate as he saw fit and to spell words with a Yankee drawl in the way he might pronounce them:

> *I ... have been engageed in the pursuit of a Searover who took into his Custody a quantity of Our Rum and carried it round to Boston (contrary to the Express words of the Statute) for Tryal and condemnation. The illegality of his measure together with the Loss sustaind createed such a Spirit of Resentment That I have devoted almost the whole of my Time in devising and carrying into execution measures for the recovery of my Property and punnishing the offender.*

What Greene had in mind for "punnishing" Lieutenant Dudingston, the *Gaspee's* captain, was legal action: His company's lawyer, James Varnum, was even then drafting a suit against Dudingston for illegally capturing the *Fortune*.

Others had different ideas about a just punishment for Lt. Dudingston. On June 9, 1772, five dozen Rhode Islanders served the *Gaspee's* commander and crew with the maritime version of vigilante justice.

On the morning of June 10, 1772, a young man paraded along the Great Bridge in Providence, wearing the gold-laced beaverskin cap he had stolen from a British Naval officer. He proudly told the story of the night before—how he and sixty others had burned the king's revenue schooner *Gaspee* while it lay aground on Namquid Point, until some older men warned him to hold his tongue.[7]

The story circulated to the Providence home of Darius Sessions, the deputy governor. Sessions smelled trouble. He saddled a horse and galloped the five miles south to Pawtuxet Village, where the *Gaspee* was still smoldering out on Namquid Point. He found the ship's commander, Lieutenant Dudingston, lying wounded in a small house by the shore. Dudingston's left thigh was wrapped tightly with a linen bandage, concealing the hole that a musket ball fired by the raiders had blown through his groin, spilling the first British blood of the American Revolution. Sessions asked Dudingston for his version of the night-time raid on the *Gaspee*, but the lieutenant would not say much. Sessions wrote:

> *Mr. Dudingston answered that he would give no account of the matter; first, because of his indisposition of body, and secondly, because it was his duty to forbear anything of the nature till he had done it to his commanding officer, at a court martial, to which, if he lived, he must be called, but if he died, he desired it might all die with him.*[8]

While Dudingston lay convalescing in Pawtuxet, the sheriff of Kent County came calling with a warrant for his arrest. Dudingston did not know it but the sheriff, Abraham Whipple, had actually led the sixty-man party that raided the *Gaspee*. Dudingston's condition was too critical for Whipple to haul him off to jail, but the sheriff left the warrant charging him to appear in court as a defendant in Nathanael Greene's lawsuit alleging illegal seizure.

Naturally, Nathanael Greene was a chief suspect in the torching of the *Gaspee*, but he had an alibi: On the night in question he had hosted his brother

Kitt, his cousin Griffin, and a woman named Mrs. Utter out at his big house of all-white walls.

"Mrs. Utter an Old Lady Sat up with me till near Twelve OClock," Greene wrote to Sammy Ward. "Kitt and Griff staid till 10 O Clock, Mrs Utter saw me go to Bed, and my People saw me get up, and Griff Saw me about Sunrise."[9]

On July 22, 1772, Greene saddled his favorite horse, a bay stallion named Britain, for the ride from Coventry to the courthouse in East Greenwich, where his lawsuit against Lieutenant Dudingston was being heard. During the trial he lodged at the East Greenwich home of William and Catharine Greene, his distant relatives, who happened to be Sammy Ward's aunt and uncle. Catharine Greene was then raising her late sister's child, Caty Littlefield, a sixteen-year-old girl who was blossoming into a true, dark-haired beauty. Caty was the antithesis of the fair-haired Nancy Ward in looks and in temperament; but something about her caught Nathanael Greene's eye.

The Greene brothers prevailed in their lawsuit, winning a judgment against Dudingston of six hundred pounds for the illegal seizure of their sloop, rum, and molasses.[10] Winning that judgment was likely the high point of Greene's summer. After winning the lawsuit he rode Britain back out to his lonely house in Coventry where, a month later, on August 17, 1772, the intense flames required to shape steel in the forge burned out of control. Fires were an occupational hazard of the forging industry, and this one burned the forge to its foundation. Greene wrote his young friend, Sammy Ward:

Your Letter reacht me the Morning after the Destruction of the Forge. I sat upon the remains of one of the old Shafts and read it. I was surrounded with Gloomy Faices, piles of Timber still in Flames, Heaps of Bricks dasht to pieces, Baskets of coal reducd to ashes. Everything seemd to appear in Ruins and Confusion.[11]

He then turned his attention to the blue-eyed Nancy Ward, Sammy's sister. Clearly, Greene still wanted to marry her; she, just as clearly, had no interest in marrying him. Greene wrote Sammy:

I have seriously considered the connexions between me and your Sister, the way it began and the manner it has been carried on, and if I was to consult my

Pride instead of my Reason, perhaps I might think I had a sufficient Cause to Lay a foundation for resentment.... It is your advice to stop our Correspondence. What can I say to it? If you was to see her last Letter perhaps youd be of a different opinion. To stop the Correspondence is to loos her for Ever; to continue it is to overwhelm myself with agreeable Distress and pleasant pains.[12]

The smoldering ruins of the forge aggravated Greene's asthma, a condition that plagued him for life; six days after the forge fire he wrote to Sammy's uncle, William Greene, down in East Greenwich: "I have had a most severe turn of the phthisc [asthma]; I have not slept six hours in four nights, being obliged to sit up the last two nights."[13]

Nathanael Greene could not breathe, nor could he sleep. And the family forge with which he'd been entrusted had turned to ashes.

⌘   ⌘

By January 1773, a rebuilt Coventry forge rose phoenix-like from the ashes, and its massive bell hammer was again banging out steel. "The Sound of the Hamer is once more heard in our Land," Greene reported to Sammy Ward.[14] But that year, in which he turned thirty-one, brought few improvements to Greene's life. He bought a lottery ticket and fantasized that if he won "I intend to turn Beau with my part of the Money, and make a Shining Figure amongst the Greenwich Bucks,"[15] the fancy folk of East Greenwich, the nearest village to the homestead where Greene grew up. Living outside the outskirts of town, Greene was always something of a country bumpkin, his shoulders and torso thick from hard work, his plain Quaker's clothes smelling of smoke from the forge. A chronic stiffness in one knee, which may have come from the hours spent working the huge, foot-powered bellows in the forge, lent him a stiff, ambling gait. His family held wealth and position, but he did not cut, to use his phrase, "a shining figure" among East Greenwich society.

In the summer of 1773, Greene and his cousin Griffin were suspended from the Quaker church that his late father had led for going to "a place in Conecticut of Publick Resort where they had No Proper Business."[16] A suspension was not as harsh as expulsion, but it generally required public atonement for readmission.

There is no way to ascertain exactly what Greene did to be "put out from under the care" of the meetinghouse. Whatever the specific violation was, Greene was drifting from the principles of his father's faith, and he had given the Society of Friends multiple reasons to suspend him. Suing a man in court violated the conduct of the Society of Friends, for they saw litigation as an act of violence. Not only had Greene sued Dudingston, but in the months before his suspension, Greene acted as a lawyer for a man in a lawsuit involving the Town of Coventry. In writing to his client about the lawsuit, Greene used martial terms: "You go fourth to battle armed with solemn instruments."[17] And Greene certainly was taking an interest in military affairs at this time, eventually agreeing in 1774 to serve on the state's Committee to Revise Militia Laws. Being seen either at a martial parade, as some said he was, or at a place of "publick resort" (a pub), or in a courthouse would have been the last in a string of transgressions that put Greene out of his father's faith.

Greene was an irreverent, practical, and funny man who was never much interested in the Society of Friends anyway. When he eventually parted ways with the Quakers in April 1775 it was his decision to leave, not theirs.[18] Greene held the Society responsible for his own lack of an education, something he truly desired.

"I lament the want of a liberal education," Greene wrote Sammy, who at fifteen graduated from Rhode Island College, now known as Brown University. "I feel the mist [of] Ignorance to surround me, for my own part I was Educated a Quaker, and amongst the most Supersticious sort, and that of its self is a sufficent Obstacle to cramp the best of Geniuses; much more mine."

Quakers in country churches, such as the Greenwich Meetinghouse, felt that reading was a waste of time. His father's church, Greene wrote Sammy, prohibited "all Books except the Holy Scriptures, Barckleys Apology, Fox Journal and a few others of the same tennor and date. That my Dear friend was the foundation of my education."[19]

The Scriptures, Barkley's, and Fox may have formed the foundation of Greene's education, but he built heavily upon it. He had some tutoring in East Greenwich from Adam Maxwell, a Scottish-born school master who taught Greene geometry, which he pursued on his own, and some Latin.[20] Greene became so familiar with the novel *Tristram Shandy* that he could make his brothers laugh[21] with a perfect mimic of a character, the "squat, uncourtly figure"[22] of Dr. Slop.

The Society of Friends wasn't the only religion that Greene found suspect. He believed in a universal God, but mistrusted overly pious people; he felt that the sanctimonious were not selfless do-gooders; rather, they acted out of self-interest to secure themselves a better seat in the afterlife.[23]

Despite his irreverence, between his suspension from the Society and his final break with it, Greene still occasionally attended the Quaker meeting. He wrote to Sammy in 1773:

> I have been to Meeting today. Our silence was interrupted by a vain con-ceited Minister. His Sermon made me think of a certain Diet cald Whistle Belly Vengeance: he that eats the most had the worst share. He began with asking us what could be said that had not been said. Much more, thinks I, than you ever thought off or ever will.[24]

❧   ❧

Nathanael Greene never could woo Sammy Ward's sister, but he had better luck with Ward's cousin, Caty Littlefield, the dark-haired teen he had met at William Greene's house during the *Gaspee* trial. She was just two years older than Sammy, and twelve years younger than Greene.

Caty Littlefield was born on Block Island, a hilly, isolated island of stonewalls and cart paths connecting the fifty families who lived out there, a dozen miles off Rhode Island's coast. She was just eight when her mother died, leaving a husband with five children. When she turned ten, her father, perhaps seeking a woman's influence in Caty's development, sent her to the mainland to live with her late mother's sister, Aunt Caty Ray Greene.[25]

Aunt Caty lived in a big house on a hill above East Greenwich with her hus-band, William Greene, Nathanael's distant relative. Aunt Caty was an attractive, dark-haired woman who as a young woman caught the eye of Ben Franklin. Franklin, in his fifties, had tried to seduce twenty-three-year-old Caty Ray on a winter carriage trip from Boston to Westerly.[26] Though she spurned the old man's advances she took no offense; they often wrote each other throughout their lives, and Franklin twice stayed in her house on the hill near Love Lane.

Nathanael Greene was twenty-two when ten-year-old Caty Littlefield moved in with her aunt and uncle. Their manse overlooking East Greenwich stood about two miles from the Greene homestead on Potowomut, and Nathanael paid occasional visits. By the time of the Dudingston trial, Caty looked a lot like the aunt who turned Ben Franklin's head. Her contemporaries described her as "a small brunette with high color, a vivacious expression, and a snapping pair of dark eyes" with a form "light and agile."[27]

Greene's courtship of Caty Littlefield must have been brief, secretive, or both. He never wrote word of it, not even to Caty's cousin and Greene's confidant, Sammy Ward. Sammy must have been shocked when, in July 1774, he received a fat envelope stuffed with wedding invitations and a brief note. Love and war were on Greene's mind, as he wrote Sammy: "Friend Samuel,—Please to deliver the enclosed Cards to your Sisters. On the 20th this Instant, I expect to be married to Miss Kitty Littlefield."[28]

Greene spent one paragraph on the wedding—the party would be small, at Aunt Caty's place on Love Lane, and Sammy was invited—then he segued into a rail against the four thousand British soldiers then occupying Boston.

British warships blockaded Boston, stopping all trade until Bostonians paid for three shiploads of tea they had dumped, as a protest, into the harbor. With no trade on its wharves, and four thousand troops patrolling its streets, Boston faced hard times. Greene wrote: "The Solders in Boston are insolent beyond measure. Soon very soon expect to hear the thirsty Earth drinking in the warm Blood of American Sons."[29]

❦   ❦

Nathanael Greene did not have to be clairvoyant to predict, in the summer of 1774, imminent bloodshed. England and the American Colonies had been plunging deeper and deeper into crisis since 1765, with the passage of the Stamp Act.

For England, the Colonies were more liability than asset. They required huge sums to protect them from constant threats, first by the French and their Indian allies in the Seven Years War (1756–1763), then from the Great Lakes and Ohio Valley tribes of Native Americans, who formed a loose coalition to stave off European invasion of their lands. Theirs was the most successful resistance of Native tribes in North American history. In what is known as Pontiac's War the tribes captured nine forts and killed 2,500 whites before the uprising's end in 1766.

By the late 1760s, England paid some 350,000 pounds per year keeping an army in the Colonies to fight these wars. The Stamp Act was designed to recover 60,000 pounds per annum, just a fraction of the cost. But it was an overly broad, draconian, and expensive tax. Printed matter of all kinds needed to carry a tax stamp, even legal documents. Twelve of the thirteen Colonies closed their courts rather than comply, the exception being Greene's native Rhode Island, which kept the courts running and openly defied the Stamp Act.

Response to the act was so virulent that Parliament quickly relented. But in 1767 it followed up with the Townshend Acts, again designed to raise money for defense of the Colonies. The Acts included a new set of custom commissioners charged with enforcing the Navigation Acts, taxing ship cargo, which had long been ignored through an official policy of Salutary Neglect.

Attempts to collect customs fees after ignoring them for so long caused violence on the docks. When agents in Boston seized John Hancock's ship *Liberty* for nonpayment of bond in 1768, a mob beat customs officials on the wharves and later threatened their homes.[30] Two regiments of British regulars—more than one thousand soldiers—were then sent to permanently garrison Boston, causing resentment that led to the so-called Boston Massacre of 1770.

Greene's sloop, the *Fortune*, was swept up through the new enforcement of the Navigation Acts in 1772. In the two years since then, Greene had only become more radical in his opposition to England's administration, and for good reason. The Tea Act of 1773 did not raise taxes on tea; it actually exempted the well-connected East India Tea Company from paying the British duty to ship tea into the Americas. This allowed the company to undercut other legitimate tea shippers, and to compete on a level field with the majority of shippers who ignored the British duty and paid only the American tax, or just smuggled in tea.

A general boycott of tea ensued. In Providence, the local Sons of Liberty held a "tea party" in which they torched three hundred pounds of tea; one "spirited son of Liberty" went through the streets with a paintbrush, blacking out the word tea on all of the store signs.[31]

Boston's Sons of Liberty held the grandest tea party of them all. On December 16, 1773, a mob of locals thinly disguised as Indians stormed aboard three tea ships waiting to unload in Boston Harbor, and threw 342 tea chests into the sea. The destroyed tea had a value of $90,000—an enormous sum.

In response the British Ministry passed what the Colonials called the "Intolerable Acts," a series of laws designed to force Bostonians to pay for the destroyed tea. The Boston Port Bill prohibited any ship from loading or unloading in Boston Harbor. As Boston was a peninsula served by only one narrow road, cutting off its water trade caused serious deprivation. A further drain on supplies was the British garrison at Boston; in May 1774 Gen. Thomas Gage arrived from New York with reinforcements, swelling the troops in Boston to four regiments—more than four thousand men who required food, soap, candles, all the goods that could not be shipped.

Boston was a place Nathanael Greene knew well. He sometimes went to Henry Knox's "London Book-Store" in Boston, where he bought several books about military matters to add to his large library at Coventry.[32]

Boston was just fifty miles from Providence, one hard day's ride. Moved by the suffering of the town's inhabitants, the freemen of East Greenwich started a fundraising drive to buy food for the hungry, besieged residents of Boston. Greene donated nearly three pounds, a sum topped only by his friend and lawyer, James Varnum. In mid-November 1774, the fundraisers sent a drover to herd forty-four sheep and four oxen along the Post Road into Boston for consumption by the people there.[33]

❦   ❦

With the British encamped in Boston, the men around East Greenwich decided that they had better form a militia company in case trouble spread to Rhode Island. Nathanael Greene was among the fifty-four men who chartered this company, but he had a problem: the Greene brothers were Quakers and had not fought in the French and Indian Wars. They were farmers, not hunters; Nathanael Greene had no gun. So he rode to Boston to get one.

There is no documentary evidence of Greene obtaining a musket in Boston; this would have been a black market transaction, not something to be set on paper. But Greene did get a gun. His grandson wrote that Nathanael bought his gun in Boston, likely from a British deserter. He then "prevailed upon a farmer to hide his musket in his cart"—some stories say beneath a cartload of hay—and smuggled it back to Rhode Island.

While in Boston, Greene convinced a British deserter to come to work as "drill master" for the newly formed militia. The veteran of the British system signed a contract to lead the local militia in drills "as taught in the English Army" and to "Engage Two lads to Beat the Drum."

Music played an important role in military maneuvers then, not so much on the battlefield, where fife and drum would be drowned by the boom of musket and cannon, but on the march and in camp. Drummers beat the troop in the morning to gather soldiers, the retreat at sundown, and the tattoo at dark to signal troops to douse their fires and candles and go to bed.

In October 1774, the militia made it official: They obtained a charter from the General Assembly to form the Kentish Guards, a colorfully costumed group that contributed mightily to the looming war. The Guards dressed in uniforms of red coats with green facings, white pantaloons, and white vests.[34] Accounts of East Greenwich merchants at that time show a run on red broad cloth, red tammy (a fine worsted), silver jacket buttons, tailed wigs and wig powder, knee garters, and three yards of a fabric called Nonesopritty.[35] The Kentish Guards did not come together just to look sharp on the parade field; their accounts show that they also bought cartridge paper and lead to make bullets.

The Guards conducted their meetings in democratic fashion, with a moderator instead of a commanding officer; their meetings at a member's house felt more like town meeting than a military tribunal.

At the urging of his friend and cousin, Griffin Greene, Nathanael Greene ran for lieutenant in the newly formed company. Certainly Greene had every right to expect a prestigious position in the Guards. Though he had no military experience, few did. He had served on the state's Committee to Revise Militia Laws, and he was a charter member of the Guards from a prosperous family.

When the votes for officers were tallied, Nathanael Greene lost out. His fellow members of the Kentish Guards did not have confidence that this asthmatic, gimpy, bookish son of a Quaker preacher had the stuff to lead them. Greene was mortified, both by the vote and by some of the discussions afterward. He wrote to the new captain, his friend and lawyer James Varnum:

I was informd the Gentlemen of East Greenwich said that I was a blemish to the company. I confess it is the first stroke of mortification that I ever felt from

being considered either in private or publick Life a blemish to those with
whom I assosiateed. . . .

If I concieve right of the force of the Objection of the Gentlemen of
the town it was not as an officer but as a soldier, for that my halting was
a blemish to the rest. I confess it is my misfortune to limp a little but
I did not concieve it to be so great: but we are not apt to discover our
own defects.[36]

Greene submitted his resignation from the Kentish Guards, effectively ending his military career before it had even begun. He urged Varnum to stay on,
and pledged his financial support of the militia:

I would not have the company break and disband for fifty Dollars. It would
be a disgrace upon the country and upon the town in particular. I feel more
mortification than resentment, but I think it would manifested a more
generous temper to have given me their Oppinions in private than to make
proclomation of it in publick as a capital objection, for nobody loves to be the
subject of ridicule however true the cause.

For unknown reasons (perhaps Varnum talked him into it), Greene soon
changed his mind about resigning; he swallowed his pride and stayed on with
the Kentish Guards as a private. Through that winter and spring of 1775 he was
one of the more faithful attendees, marching to the beat of fife and drum three
days a week as the British deserter drilled the Guards in martial maneuvers on a
frozen parade field.[37]

Greene figured that even if the Kentish Guards never needed to fire a shot
they could pass the time as "a pretty little society in our meetings where we
might relax ourselves a few hours from the various occupations of Life." It would
not be long before the men of this "pretty little society" would be grabbing their
guns and marching off to war.

❧   ❧

Spring came early to New England in 1775. By April 19, the grass on the
village green in Lexington, Massachusetts had already grown so tall as to

undulate in that morning's breeze.[38] At dawn, British troops marching out from Boston to destroy an American militia's arsenal at Concord approached the small, crossroads village of Lexington. Warned by mounted messengers Paul Revere and William Dawes before their capture by British troops, a band of 70 minutemen awaited the arrival of Smith's soldiers. Leading the minutemen was Capt. John Parker, at 45 a veteran of the French and Indian Wars. Fewer than 40 of Parker's men had ammunition with them; these 38 he formed in a line across the Lexington Green.

John Pitcairn, fifty-three, a major in the Royal Marines, led the advance guard as the British swept on toward the Lexington Green. Pitcairn ordered his men to form the battle line; his troops smartly moved into formation, pointing their muskets and yelling "Huzzah! Huzzah!"

The British major spurred his mount toward the small line of rebels; he drew up before them with his troops bristling at his back. "Lay down your arms, you damned rebels, and disperse!"

Captain Parker knew there was no way the thirty-eight farmers lined up across the Green could hold off a battle line of the British Army. He ordered his minutemen to leave. They began breaking up, but they refused Pitcairn's demands to drop their muskets. As the rebels left the field, someone's gun flared. No one will ever know for certain who fired this first shot. What is certain is that it touched off a storm of fire from the British lines. And when the shooting stopped, eight minutemen lay dead in the undulating grass of the blood-spattered green. Here at the North Bridge they met resistance.

The British rolled on to complete their mission in Concord, six miles away. On the return march to Boston, the British battled for eight hours through a gantlet of armed and angry minutemen. Nearly four thousand men fired at them during the march; the muskets of that time were wildly inaccurate, so the farmers and merchants of Massachusetts just kept firing and firing one-ounce balls of lead. They shot about 75,000 rounds in all, averaging more than a blast every second.[39]

The first wave of British troops that made it as far as Concord had to march sixteen miles back to Boston carrying sixty pounds of gear while the trees, stone walls, and houses around them exploded. On their return trip through Lexington the exhausted British found friendly faces formed in a wide battle line on high ground outside the town—a brigade that had been dispatched from Boston that morning as reinforcements.

A member of the reinforcing brigade, Lt. Frederick Mackenzie of the Royal Welsh Fusiliers, wrote: "We were fired at from all quarters, but particularly from the houses on the roadside, and the Adjacent Stone walls. Several of the Troops were killed and wounded in this way, and the Soldiers were so enraged at suffering from an unseen Enemey, that they forced open many of the houses from which the fire proceeded, and put to death all those found in them."[40]

By day's end, Mackenzie tallied 168 British soldiers wounded, and 68 dead.

Mounted messengers relayed the news to Providence, where the cry rang out: "War, war boys! There is war."[41] Along the town's single street the drum beat to arms; the message pulsated down Narragansett Bay and then out into the inland villages. Nathanael Greene, private in the Kentish Guards, heard the news that night, at his house in Coventry. He said good-bye to Caty, his twenty-year-old bride of nine months, saddled his horse, and thundered off to Guards headquarters in East Greenwich, stopping at a friend's house to borrow cash.[42]

The Kentish Guards set out at dawn on April 20, marching by foot into Providence as the morning light touched their new red, white, and green uniforms. A man named John Howland later wrote, "I viewed the company as they marched up the street, and observed Nathanael Greene, with his musket on his shoulder, in the ranks, as a private. I distinguished Mr. Greene, whom I have frequently seen, by the motion of his shoulder on the march, as one of his legs was shorter than the other."[43]

The Guard got as far as the Rhode Island state line in Pawtucket, where a messenger reached them with an order from their governor, demanding that they not cross into Massachusetts. The bulk of the Guard obeyed the order, but Greene, two of his brothers, and a fourth man ignored it. Determined to fight, they mounted horses and pressed on. En route, they heard that British troops had retreated into Boston, so they turned back for Rhode Island where, in the coming days, Greene received some surprising news.

In response to the open outbreak of war, Rhode Island's General Assembly called an emergency session on April 22 in the Providence Colony House, a brick building on a grassy hill overlooking the town. Here they voted to form a Rhode Island army of 1,500 men. This army needed a general to lead it. The

General Assembly passed over Gen. Simeon Potter, a veteran of the French and Indian Wars, and bypassed Greene's friend, James Varnum, captain of the Kentish Guards. The assembly reached way down into the ranks and chose as general a private, Nathanael Greene.

Greene certainly had political connections, and in Rhode Island that has always been important. He was a friend of Samuel Ward, Jr., whose father was a former governor and Rhode Island's representative to the Continental Congress; Greene himself had served in the General Assembly[44] and his brother, Jacob Greene, was deputy in the legislature. Greene had shown sufficient gravitas to be named to a Committee to Revise Militia Laws, along with three militia colonels and a major, Daniel Hitchcock.[45]

Nobody knows why the General Assembly passed over experienced men to pluck Private Nathanael Greene out of the Kentish Guards and install him as general of the state's army. But it really would not have taken a miracle for the Assembly to recognize ability, if not hidden genius, in Nathanael Greene. He had a reputation for being bookish and smart; he had been reading military works, reviewing militia laws, and training with the Kentish Guards. As the foreman of a forge with one hundred workers he was used to leading men. When the East Greenwich elite chartered the Kentish Guards in the fall of 1774, war was still a distant threat. Their choice of leaders was a popularity contest, and the Quaker boy raised out beyond the village limits had never cut a shining figure among that set.

But by April 1775, when Rhode Island's General Assembly was choosing a leader for their state's army, the war and the bloodshed were very real. In choosing a general, the Assembly was not seeking the most popular man, they were seeking the most capable, and they chose a strong, introspective, intelligent man with a demonstrated ability to lead.

TWO

Mad, Vext, Sick and Sorry

I n spring of 1775, Nathanael Greene found himself in a fine mess. Just months removed from being a private in the Kentish Guards, he now commanded the one thousand men in Rhode Island's Army of Observation—mostly raw recruits plucked from wharves and farms, men who straggled reluctantly into Greene's camp on one of the hills that nearly encircled Boston. The sum of Greene's military training had been just six months of thrice-a-week drills on the East Greenwich parade grounds with the Guards. He had never seen combat.

His enemy, the British encamped down in Boston, was one of the finest fighting forces the world had yet known. The contrast was not lost on Greene. From camp he wrote to Rhode Island's new governor: "I lament the want of knowledge in Generalship. But as we have all been cultivateing the arts of Peace, its no wonder that we are deficient in the Art of War."[1]

For the Rhode Island camp Greene chose a hill in Roxbury, a coign of vantage that he described as a "most excellent post for observation."

Greene demonstrated a knack for picking good ground. He laid out his army's camp on a sixty-acre estate seized from a British loyalist; the camp included a mansion, a pond for bathing, exotic plants, and a hothouse that the Rhode Island troops turned into a storage shed for their casks of gunpowder.

After laying out his camp, Greene returned to Rhode Island to recruit more men for what was supposed to be a fifteen-hundred-man army. The recruiting did not go well. Greene never did raise fifteen hundred men; it was more like a thousand, and most of them had little discipline and no training.

From Providence, as he prepared to return to camp at Roxbury, he wrote Caty to explain why, after just eleven months of marriage, he felt compelled to leave their home for an army camp:

> *It had been happy for me if I could have lived a private life in peace and plenty, enjoying all the happiness that results from a well-tempered society, founded on mutual esteem. . . . But the injury done my Country, and the Chains of Slavery forgeing for posterity, calls me fourth to defend our common rights, and repel the bold invaders of the Sons of freedom. The cause is the cause of God and man. . . . I am determined to defend my rights and maintain my freedom, or sell my life in the attempt.*[2]

On his return to Roxbury, Greene found the Rhode Island camp "in great commotion." Entire companies were threatening to march home, partly because of the corruption of merchants who had won contracts to supply the army's food. A Providence baker sent barrels of moldy bread. The beef was tainted with horsemeat; as hungry as his men were, they would not eat it.

On inspection, Greene found his troops ill-fed, dirty, poorly trained, and undisciplined. Greene cracked down. He drilled his troops on the parade ground daily, instructing them on the proper methods of moving in formation and of firing muskets. He insisted that they use hot water to scrub their firelocks, the mechanism in the musket that generates a spark, a chore for men who had to haul water buckets and kindle fires to fulfill the order. Greene ran his camp the way his Quaker father would have run his forge: no swearing; no card playing; clothes would be cleaned and faces shaved.

After stemming the insurrection in his camp, Greene again returned to Rhode Island in early June in hopes of mustering more troops. He found time to see Caty in Coventry, but after midnight on June 18 business called him from their bed. A courier carried the news that the British had marched from Boston and attacked the American's new position on Bunker Hill.

Greene rode all night, his horse's hooves pounding through Swansea, Dighton, and Taunton along the post road to Boston. At daybreak he arrived at camp; looking down from his hill at Roxbury he saw smoke and flames smoldering from Charlestown, where red-coated British regulars had torched the houses on their march toward Bunker Hill.

Greene missed the Battle of Bunker Hill, but he watched and heard the cannonading that went on after it. He wrote to Rhode Island officials: "The action began yesterday, continued all last night and Charlestown is burnt down, and they are now closely engaged today. The number of slain and wounded is not known, but very considerable."[3]

At the end of the day the British held Bunker Hill, but at an enormous price. The Americans lost 440 men killed or wounded; British casualties totaled at least 828 wounded and 226 killed, including 92 officers. Greene reported back to Rhode Island: "Tho our enemies has gain'd ground upon us, it is at too dear a rate for them to rejoice much at their success. As Marshal Saxe said once upon obtaining a victory being complementd on the Occasion, said a few such Victories would ruin him, so a few such Victories would ruin them."[4]

❦   ❧

George Washington, like Greene, missed the action at Bunker Hill. Just two days after the Second Continental Congress named him commander in chief, he got word of the battle as he rode north from Philadelphia to take command of the troops.

Washington arrived at Cambridge on July 2, 1775, wet from rain and tired from the long ride. There was no pomp to greet the arrival of the army's new commander in chief; a planned reception had been cancelled on account of the rain.[5]

The next day, Washington rode out to inspect the troops camped in a nine-mile arc west of Boston. He sat a horse well, and he rode wearing a blue coat with buff-colored facings, epaulettes on each shoulder, buff underdress, an elegant dress sword, and a black cockade pinned to his hat. The American Revolution was not driven by the poor. Its engineers were the wealthy, like Greene, Washington, and the rice kings of the South, men who had something to gain by getting King George III and his corrupt bureaucrats out of their pockets. Washington was a combat veteran of the French and Indian Wars—as a twenty-three-year-old officer at Braddock's Defeat he'd had two horses shot from under him and heard four musket balls whiz through his coat.[6] He was also among the richest men in America, with 54,000 acres, 100 slaves, and a $100,000 dowry from his marriage to Martha Custis. His instructions to a London tailor show that he stood six-foot-three inches tall, a head taller than most men of his time.[7]

"His excllency George Washington has arrivd and is universally admired," Greene wrote to his state's governor, Nicholas Cooke, on July 4, 1775. "The excellent Character he bears, and the promising Genius he possesses gives great spirit to the Troops."[8]

Washington's appearance may have boosted the morale of the troops, but the looks of the troops encamped about Boston did little to boost the spirits of Washington. In a letter to his cousin, Washington described the New Englanders in his command as "an exceedingly dirty and nasty people."[9] He had reasons for drawing this conclusion.

The Rev. William Emerson rode over from his Concord home to have a look at the army camps and described them to his wife as a motley assembly of broken-down shanties. Just a few of the tents, Emerson reported, "are the proper Tents and Markees that look as the regular Camp of the Enemy."[10]

This "proper" camp outfitted with marquees—large tents with canvas fringe for superior officers—was the camp "of the Roadislanders," Emerson wrote, "who are furnished with Tent Equipage . . . in the most exact english Taste."

Greene's Rhode Island camp, with its neat rows of tents holding troops who drilled daily and scrubbed their firelocks, must have been a welcome sight for Washington. Because of his clean camp and the deportment of his troops, Greene's stock began to rise among the other generals.

Of all his brothers, Greene was closest to Jacob, to whom he wrote in June:

My task is hard and fatigue great. I go to bed late and I rise Early. But hard as it is if I can discharge my Duty to my own Honor and to my country['s] satisfaction, I shall go through the Toil with Chearfulness. My own officers and Soldiers are generally well Satisfied, nay I have not heard one complaint.

The General officers of the Neighbouring Camps treat me with the greatest Respect much more than my Station or Consequence entitle me to.[11]

Greene's diligence earned him a commission as brigadier general in the Army of the United Colonies. Months after being deemed unsuitable as officer material by the Kentish Guards, he was now, at age thirty-two, the youngest general in the Continental Army.

Washington had a few battle-hardened generals in his camp: Col. William Prescott, a hero of the recent action at Bunker Hill; Col. John Stark, an Army Ranger in the French and Indian Wars; and Israel Putnam, or "Old Put," a 5-foot-6 inch dynamo. At fifty-seven years old, Putnam was already a legend; he too served as a Ranger in the French and Indian Wars, survived a shipwreck, and supposedly was once rescued just as tribal warriors were setting him afire while tied to a stake.

But Washington was a shrewd observer of character. As he looked over the officers at his command he favored two young, unseasoned men with increasing responsibilities—Nathanael Greene and Greene's big bibliophile friend, Henry Knox.

In late July 1775, the Rhode Islanders moved closer to the action, encamping on Prospect Hill, just a half-mile from the British troops holding Charlestown. Greene and his Rhode Islanders were placed under the command of Major General Charles Lee, an English aristocrat by birth whose behavior showed little of the upper class. He was tall, big-nosed, and thin; no matter how nice the uniform he could not keep clothes mended and clean; he traveled with a retinue of small yappy dogs, including at least one cub-like Pomeranian that he lavished with attention. Lee had fought in America in the French and Indian Wars. He reached the rank of major in the British Army before becoming a soldier of fortune in the Polish Army, where he fought against the Turks and rose to the rank of major general. When Lee joined their side in the struggle for independence, Greene and his fellow officers were impressed—here they had a former British officer with military knowledge and experience. But Greene soon realized that in Lee, they also had an odd duck.[12] Like Washington, Lee was often exasperated by the rawness of the troops under his command, but he too had praise for Greene and his Rhode Islanders.[13]

The siege of Boston was a nasty drawn-out affair that tried men's patience on both sides. Greene had to get on his men for "voiding their excrements about the fields," which raised a stench in the summer heat, and for failing to shovel dirt over the dug latrines when they did use them. Dysentery ran rampant through the American camp, and British soldiers, too, were dying at the rate of thirty men a week due to camp sickness.[14] The Americans didn't have enough troops to storm a fortified city, and, after the slaughter at Bunker Hill, the British didn't dare to venture out. So the two sides lived miserably day after day, spying on each other through telescopes.

Sometimes the British fired bombs into the American camps, though the shelling was sparsely returned; the American supply of gunpowder ran dangerously low. First returns told Washington he had 485 quarter casks of gunpowder, but in August he was told that there had been a mix-up: American stores of powder actually stood at thirty-five half barrels—enough to fire just nine rounds per man.

British shells lit the skies, shrieking like banshees, and shuddered to the ground, occasionally with effect. In late summer, Greene ordered a party of five hundred Rhode Islanders to join five hundred New Hampshiremen in fortifying the works on Plowed Hill, a redoubt overlooking the Mystic River. Among the "fatigue party" was Augustus Mumford of East Greenwich, a friend of Greene's who had led the fundraising drive to aide Boston residents left poor and hungry by the siege. A cannonball fired from the British's hard-won position on Bunker Hill scored a direct hit on Mumford's head.

Augustus Mumford became the first Rhode Islander to die fighting for the United States of America. This first death of one of his men so shook Greene that he sent a colonel home to personally break the news to Mumford's widow.

From his camp upon Prospect Hill, Nathanael Greene had a panoramic view of the British Army's camp on Bunker Hill, just a mile away. Beyond Bunker Hill he could see the houses and streets of Boston, and the blue waters of Back Bay. Washington had ordered Greene's Rhode Island Army to hold that heavily fortified post in July. Now, in the darkening days of late September,

Greene was pessimistic to the point of being depressed about the Continental Army's prospects. On a day so cold his fingers could barely feel his pen, Greene wrote to Jacob: "You'l do justice to my Family I doubt not when I am no more. If there is no News favorable for America in three weeks you may expect to hear something terrible. Be silent on this Head as it may be a Disadvantage to the Attempt. Hundreds will perish and I among the Rest perhaps."[15]

Whatever "attempt" Greene was worried about did not come to pass, but he had just cause to worry. Many of the troops, including most of his own, had enlisted only into December; their time would soon be up.

While the American forces were packing their bags to go home, the British were growing more aggressive in their will to prosecute the war. In a speech that fall, King George III declared America to be in open rebellion and pledged to carry on with plans to send twenty thousand new troops and naval forces to quash the revolution. The King told parliament he had received "friendly offers of foreign assistance"—but what he didn't say was that the assistance came at a price.[16] German dukes had agreed to rent the king armies of their formidable soldiers at seven pounds four shillings per man for the first group. Americans called these German mercenaries "Hessians," because more than half the soldiers came from Germany's Hesse region. When they crossed the King of Prussia's lands on their way to America, he taxed them at the same rate he charged for cattle going off to slaughter.[17]

News that King George would send foreign mercenaries to fight his own British subjects incensed Greene. On December 20, 1775, he wrote Jacob:

George the Third's last speech has shut the door of hope for reconciliation between the Colonies and Great Britain. There are great preparations going on in England, to prosecute the war in the spring. We have no reason to doubt the King's intentions. We must submit unconditionally, or defend ourselves. The calamities of war are very distressing, but slavery is dreadful. I have no reason to doubt the success of the Colonies, when I consider their union, strength, and resources. But we must expect to feel the common calamities which attend even a successful war. We are now driven to the necessity of making a declaration of independence.[18]

Greene is apparently the first to write the phrase "a declaration of independence," a term that the following summer would be on the tongues of many. He again used the phrase two weeks later in a remarkably prescient letter to Samuel Ward Sr., in which he predicted that due to a German state's aggression in the Mediterranean, France would soon be forced to attack Hanover, which would bring England into a European war on the side of the German states; then France and Spain would align themselves with nascent America against England. Greene wrote of the French and Spaniards:

> *Let us embrace them as Brothers. We want not their Land Forces in America; their Navy, we do. . . . Their military stores we want amazingly. . . . Permit me then to Recommend from the Sincerity of my Heart, ready at all times to bleed in my Countrys Cause, a Declaration of Independance and Call upon the World and the Great God who Governs it to Witness the Necessity, propriety and Rectitude thereof.*[19]

   ❧   ❧

On New Year's Eve of 1775, Nathanael Greene wrote to Samuel Ward Sr. from Prospect Hill: "[N]othing but confusion and disorder Reigns." Most enlistments expired that day, and men were leaving the army understaffed and low on powder, with a tenuous grasp of a tiger's tail. Greene complained:

> *I wish our Troops were better furnisht. The Enimy has a great Advantage over us.*
>
>   *We have suffered prodigiously for want of Wood. Many Regiments has been Obligd to Eat their Provision Raw for want of firing to Cook, and notwithstanding we have burnt up all the fences and cut down all the Trees for a mile round the Camp, our suffering has been inconceiveable. . . . The fatigues of the Campaign, the suffering for want of Wood and Cloathing, has made abundance of the Soldiers heartily sick of service.*[20]

For Greene, the suffering got even worse: He contracted such a case of jaundice that, from the sound of his letters to Jacob, he nearly died: "I am as yellow as saffron, my appetite all gone, and my flesh too. I am so weak that I can scarcely walk across the room."[21]

Greene grew so ill that his wife was sent for. Though it was winter and she had just given birth to their first child—a boy whom they named George Washington Greene—she rode from Rhode Island to see her sick husband.[22]

While Greene lay ill, his friend Henry Knox descended the eastern slope of the Berkshire Mountains at the head of a group of eighty oxen pulling forty-two sleds. The sleds were loaded with sixty cannons weighing an aggregate 119,000 pounds, ordnance that Knox and his men had taken from the recently captured Fort Ticonderoga on Lake Champlain.

Knox didn't get all of the cannon in Fort Ticonderoga, but darned near it. By boat and sled, across ice and through mountains, with oxen and with horse, Knox had hauled the cannons, plus 2,300 pounds of lead to make bullets and balls, plus a barrel full of new flints for the firelocks.

Washington rewarded Knox by making him commander of artillery. Knox, who had trained with the local militia's artillery since he was seventeen, still had to teach others how to use the stuff, but at least now they had it.

In a single night, working under cover of heavy bombardment from Roxbury and Cobble Hill, Washington's army fortified the cannon on the top of a hill on Dorchester Neck. From a perch of 112 feet, Knox's heavy siege cannon could lob twenty-four-pound balls smashing onto the British barracks below; they could with reasonable accuracy also strike the British fleet lying at anchor in Boston Harbor two miles away.

The British made one faint-hearted attempt to storm the hill, but bad weather—and memories of Bunker Hill still sapping the morale of the troops— drove them back.

On March 17 the British fleet weighed anchor and left Boston Harbor, taking with them the British Army and thousands of Tory refugees who fled in justifiable fear of retaliation. The city they left behind had been decimated—shelled, its trees chopped for firewood, its people starving and suffering an epidemic of smallpox. Greene had had the foresight to have himself inoculated against small pox, a procedure that put a cloudy blemish in his right eye. Washington placed the sickened city under Greene's command.

Greene enforced martial law in Boston for two weeks, much of that a tense time; British troops and sympathizers had boarded ships in the harbor, but the ships had not sailed, leaving Greene wondering whether they meant another invasion. Finally on March 27 the fleet sailed for the open ocean. Four days later, Greene warned his men to have their baggage ready, for the next day they would begin their march southward.

Just twelve months earlier, on the heels of fighting at Lexington and Concord, Greene had galloped toward Boston with borrowed money in his pocket and a ranking as private in the Kentish Guards. Now on April 1, 1776, he commanded five spirited regiments as they marched triumphantly from the freed city of Boston. He had as yet done nothing spectacular, but in the early days of George Washington's army, simple competence—the ability to keep a clean, well-regulated camp—stood out.

❧   ☙

Forcing the British to quit Boston felt great; but strategically it didn't mean much. Leaders on both sides believed that whoever held the City of New York would control the country. John Adams called New York "a kind of key to the whole continent,"[23] with the Hudson River serving as the key slot. Control of the water was pivotal. All of life's staples, from fish to flour, could not be moved in requisite bulk by ox teams over rutted roads. Anything that moved in large quantities had to move by ship. Whoever controlled the Hudson would have water access up to Lake Champlain and beyond, all the way into Canada.

If the British controlled New York, they could shut off the Hudson to shipping, neatly severing the rebellious provinces of Connecticut, Rhode Island, New Hampshire, and Massachusetts from the quieter regions to the south.

Tories—people loyal to the crown—were powerful in New York; by Greene's estimate they owned two-thirds of the city's property and commanded influence over public opinion. "If the tide of sentiment gets against us in that province," Greene wrote to Samuel Ward Sr., "it will give a fatal stab to the strength and union of the colonies."[24] The British commander in chief, Thomas Gage (who was on the outs in London and would soon lose that title), shared Greene's assessment. And the race was on to claim New York.

The American Army had a head start: Gage, hampered by thousands of Loyalist refugees from Boston, first sailed for Halifax to drop them there and await reinforcements promised by the king.

On their march toward New York, Washington's army passed through Greene's home state of Rhode Island. Naturally Greene wanted to make a good impression as he marched his brigades through Providence. In the orders that Greene dictated while in Providence he ordered two regiments

> *to turn out to morrow Morning to Escort His Excellency* [George Washington] *into town to parade at Eight O Clock. . . . And None to turn out Except those who are drest* [in] *uniform; And those of the Non Commissioned Officers and Soldiers that turn out, to be Washd both face and hands Clean, their Beards shavd of* [f]*, their hair combd and powdered, and their arms Cleand.*[25]

Two of Rhode Island's regiments cleaned up well enough to parade in Providence's welcome to Washington; one wore uniforms of a fringed brown frock, the other sported uniforms of blue faced with buff white. People sailed and rode into Providence from miles around to catch a glimpse of Washington and his army hopefully stepping off for New York.

Greene drove his regiments at a punishing pace of thirty miles a day; two days out from Providence they encamped in Norwich, Connecticut, where he issued orders to parade at sunrise for the final push to a transport fleet anchored off New London. The transports hoisted sail on April 10 for a hundred-mile cruise through Long Island Sound to New York. Greene warned his ship's captains to be alert for British warships trying to sink them, but the true hazard turned out to be the weather. The night he sailed, a late winter storm ripped through; each small transport ship had to fare for itself in frightful wind that blew a stinging sleet through the rigging; waves swept baggage from the decks of at least one ship; many turned back. In good weather, a run through Long Island Sound wouldn't take a day. Greene's boat didn't arrive in New York until April 17, 1776, after a week at sea.

And the British weren't far behind.

⚜   ⚜

George Washington recognized that as New York was the key to the country, Long Island was the key to New York. Whoever held the high ground there would control the East River, and the entire eastern flank of Manhattan. Washington wanted a good general to command on Long Island; he chose Greene for the job.

Greene pitched his camp in "Brook Land," now known as Brooklyn; it was then a village of eight houses on the back side of a cliff rising from the East River. An advance party had built five forts linked by trenches to form a mile-wide arc around Brooklyn. The forts kept the river open to Greene's rear, but put up a wall to block troops that might try to attack from the east over land. A six-mile ridge called the Heights of Guana stretched away from the linked forts, crossing all the way toward Long Island Sound. The ridge presented a formidable climb for an army attacking from the island's south beaches. All in all, Brooklyn was a relatively easy post to defend.

Washington reinforced Greene's veteran Rhode Island regiments with two other regiments that included the rowdy Pennsylvania riflemen. Greene parceled out rations of wood for cooking and straw for bedding. A tent city sprung up between the East River and the walls of the forts. Camp life on Long Island was similar to what it had been in Boston, with Greene constantly haranguing the troops to keep themselves and their latrines clean and orderly. New York City's "holy land"—an infamous red-light district—was just a ferry ride across the mile-wide East River to which the troops kept straying. In one order Greene mildly scolded his men:

> Complaints Having Been made by the Inhabitants Near the Mill Pond that Some of the Soldiers come there to swim in Open View of the Women and that they Come out of the Water and Run up Naked to the Houses with a Design to Insult and Wound the Modesty of female Decency. Tis with Concern that the General finds Himself under the Disagreeable Necessity of Expressing His disapprobation of such a Beastly Conduct. . . . Have the troops Come Abroad for No Other Purpose than to Render themselves both Obnoxious and Ridiculous?[26]

Greene was an uncompromising commander, always badgering his troops; but letters written from Long Island to John Adams, then a man of influence in Congress, show that Greene cared about the well-being of his men. Greene asked Adams to establish "a support for those that gets disabled in the army or militia. . . . Is it not inhuman to suffer those that have fought nobly in the cause to be reduced to the necessity of geting a support by common Charity?"[27]

Congress did, months later, agree to provide pensions to veterans who could prove that their wounds happened in war, but despite Greene's efforts, it did not provide any money for the widows and families of soldiers killed.

A British attack on New York was inevitable, but no one was sure where they would strike first: Manhattan or Long Island? Washington stayed at headquarters in Manhattan, while Greene held down the forts on Long Island. They developed an alarm system to signal when the sails of British ships first stood on the horizon: If six or fewer ships appeared, one large flag of red and white stripes would snap in the breeze on the Staten Island highlands; if six to twenty ships showed, two flags on two poles; for an armada of more than twenty ships, three striped flags on three poles.

On Saturday, June 29, all three flags flew red and white from the highlands. Ship after ship coasted into a sheltered bay south of Long Island, dropping anchor. A Pennsylvania rifleman in one of Greene's brigades peeped through the hole of an outhouse door and saw a forest of masts off Long Island, "something resembling a forest of pine trees trimmed. . . . I declare that I thought all London was afloat."[28] King George had pledged to send twenty thousand new troops to the Americas; now he was making good on that promise. The one hundred ships that sailed in from Halifax on the twenty-ninth were just the first of a larger fleet heading to New York bent on annihilating the American army.

On July 5, 1776, the day after the congress in Philadelphia formally adopted its Declaration of Independence, Greene got the best intelligence on the number of ships, guns, and troops that were in harbor, and what was yet to come. Through interrogation of four prisoners taken at the Narrows, the channel between Staten and Long Islands, Greene learned that England was sending seven generals, more than 270 ships, and thirty thousand men to take New York. And Nathanael Greene was encamped in the bull's eye of their target.

Washington and Congress thought this a good time to boost Greene's status to major general; at thirty-four he was the youngest of Washington's generals. What made Greene happiest about the appointment was that the title gave him a chance to name a few aides-de-camp who could deal with the paper-work—issuing passes to and from camp, answering requests for supplies, et cetera—that often bogged him down.

Greene named three aides, including fellow Rhode Islanders William "Fat Billy" Blodget and Ezekiel Cornell, known by the troops as Old Snarl. Blodget was a natural comedian who had been an actor before the war; Cornell was a dependable disciplinarian. For his third aide, Greene picked an odd Englishman named Thomas Paine. With a long, low-slung nose and keen, narrow eyes, Paine looked a bit like a puffin. In London he'd been a debtor and ne'er-do-well, but Ben Franklin met him there, was charmed by the man's intellect, and wrote him a letter of introduction to Philadelphia society. Now in 1776, Paine was the author of a famous pamphlet called "Common Sense," the greatest bestseller ever published in America. The pamphlet sold 120,000 copies, roughly one book for every twenty-five people in the country. To achieve that today, a book would have to sell more than eleven million copies. Virtually every literate man in the colonies had read "Common Sense," which stated persuasively and with passion the reasons for American independence.

Greene and Paine got along well. Indeed, some of Paine's arguments sounded like they'd flowed from Greene's own pen, such as France would never openly back America as long as there was a chance that it would reconcile with England. Paine joined the army in July 1776, and Greene scooped him up as an aide-de-camp.

While Greene drove his troops to strengthen the forts in expectation of attack, an epidemic of dysentery or "camp sickness" spread through the ranks. Greene tried to stem the sickness by requesting more bars of soap, by ordering his troops to use and clean latrines rather than going in the ditches in front of the forts ("a Practice that is Disgracefull to the last Degree"), and by eating more vegetables. Despite Greene's exhortations, the sickness spread. About ten thousand soldiers on Manhattan and Long Island were laid low by it. Gen. William Heath noted: "In almost every farm, stable, shed, and even under the fences and bushes, were the sick to be seen."[29]

Within a month of telling his troops to keep clean and eat their vegetables, Greene himself fell ill. The preparations for war had kept him busy rounding up suspected Tories, driving off cattle so British invasion forces could not eat them, and stacking unthrashed sheaves of grain into piles that could be easily torched in case retreat became necessity. In a letter to Washington, he mentioned as an afterthought, "I am confined to my bed with a raging Fever. The Critical situation of Affairs makes me the more anxious."[30]

The "Critical situation" was the arrival of eight thousand Hessian soldiers on Staten Island. They merged with three thousand British soldiers on eighty-five ships that ghosted up to the southern tip of Long Island. Clearly the combined British-Hessian forces were poised for attack, and here was Greene, now a major general commanding a most strategic post, confined to his bed.

The fever nearly killed him. Dr. John Morgan, the director general of hospitals who had treated Greene's jaundice at Boston, this time labeled Greene's condition as "dangerous." Morgan ordered Greene removed from Long Island to a doctor's "healthy, airy" house on Manhattan. Greene, in and out of delirium, was in no position to protest.

For Washington, Greene's incapacitation could not have come at a worse time. Two days after Greene's removal from command, the British began their long-awaited amphibious assault of Long Island, where the Americans were now under the command of fifty-eight-year-old Israel Putnam, an officer who was better at promoting his own exploits than he was at command, and who was in any event past his prime.

On a clear Thursday morning, five British ships of the line shook out their sails and stood through the Narrows, anchoring with their guns broadside to Long Island's rolling beaches. These guns covered the landing of British and Hessian troops. American troops began burning stacks of grain to keep them from falling into the hands of British troops, sending up plumes of smoke from the island. By noon, 15,000 troops with forty artillery pieces had landed, ready to storm the works up on Brooklyn Heights. These 15,000 were reinforced two days later with another 5,000 German grenadiers, bringing it to a total of 20,000 British and Hessian regulars set to attack less than 10,000 rag-tag militia and Continental troops. After camping in the Flatlands for a couple of days to get the lay of the land, General Howe's combined troops launched their attack on August 27, 1776.

The Battle of Long Island was a rout. Even if the American forces had been well led they would have lost; the fact that their leadership was abysmal made the British victory even more discomfiting.

Putnam—"Old Put"—had neglected to station forces at Jamaica Pass, a long narrow passage through the Guana Heights, the ridge that ran across Long

Island from Brooklyn to the Sound. The British sent ten thousand soldiers marching unmolested through Jamaica Pass, moving through the night slowly but as smoothly as a column of red ants. When they reached the top of the heights, they flanked Putnam's troops and easily ran them back into the forts outside Brooklyn. By two o'clock that afternoon British and Hessian forces had killed 312 Americans and taken nearly 1,100 prisoners, including generals John Sullivan and William "Lord Stirling" Alexander.

Gen. William Howe, commander in chief of the British forces in America (and an illegitimate uncle of King George III) had pinned the American rebels behind the walls of their forts, sandwiched between his twenty thousand troops and the East River. As soon as the wind turned, his brother, Admiral Lord Richard Howe, commander in chief of the British naval forces, could sail big ships of the line right up to the cliffs outside Brooklyn. In a vise between the land troops and the cannon of the ships, Putnam would have no choice but to surrender nine thousand men and their equipment, nearly half the American army.

"Everything seems to be over with them, and I flatter myself that this campaign will put a total end to the war," the British Gen. Hugh Percy wrote home to his father. "This business is pretty near over."[31]

All General Howe needed was a shift in the wind and his brother's ships could draw up for the end game. But in waiting for the wind to shift he was like a cat toying with its prey.

❧   ❧

All day on August 28, 1776, it rained; a chill northeasterly wind continued to blow and the Americans hemmed in behind the forts of Brooklyn spent a miserable day of it, nine thousand men crowded together, ankle deep in rain.

At headquarters across the river in New York, Washington decided that Brooklyn was now indefensible. He had to get those men back across the East River before the wind shifted, allowing the English ships to move up and cut off their retreat. Moving nine thousand men across a mile-wide river with twenty thousand enemy soldiers poised to attack from the front was risky. If the British knew that the Americans were turning their backs and fleeing they could attack their exposed flank. Washington hoped to use the cover of darkness to sneak his men off Long Island without the British knowing. He put John Glover in charge of the boats.

Glover, a stocky redhead from Marblehead, Massachusetts, led a brigade of fellow fishermen, men who had grown up catching cod from dories in the fog of Stellwagen Banks. Throughout the night they passed back and forth across the river's current, ferrying men, cattle, and cannon. Dawn's light almost blew their cover, but a change in the weather cloaked their retreat. The wind died, and the river valley filled with a fog so thick that you could not see twenty feet. Glover's men silently rowed boats full of men, horses, and cannon to the Manhattan shore.

The fog lifted. And Howe discovered that his prey had fled Brooklyn.

The Americans had lived to fight another day, but their narrow escape from Long Island brought no joy. A pastor called to New York on that day, August 30, 1776, noted the troops walking up from the ferry looked "sickly, emaciated, cast down etc.; the wet clothes, tents . . . and other things were lying about before the houses and in the streets to dry."

The "merry tones on drums and fifes had ceased."

❦   ❧

Nathanael Greene, who had nearly died of fever, was still bedridden and deeply distressed. He wrote to his brother, Jacob, on August 30:

> *Gracious God! to be confined at such a time. And the misfortune is doubly great as there was no general officer who had made himself as acquainted with the ground as perfectly as I had. I have not the vanity to think the event would have been otherwise had I been there, yet I think I could have given the commanding general a good deal of necessary information.*[32]

Greene was not always averse to touting his own talents, but this time he was too modest to say what others said for him: Had he been in command on Long Island, there was no way the British would have taken it so easily. With twenty thousand men vs. Greene's ten thousand, they would have succeeded in taking the island. But Greene made it a habit to study topography, and he did know the ground "perfectly"; he would not have left a pass through the highlands undefended. He might have made the British pay dearly for Long Island, the way the redcoats had paid a steep price for Boston's Bunker Hill.

John Adams wrote: "Greene's sickness, I conjecture, has been the cause [of the enemy's] stealing a march on us." Henry Knox concurred: "had General Greene been fit for duty I flatter myself things would have worn a very different appearance at present."[33]

The appearance things wore at present was ugly indeed. New York, surrounded by water, was impossible to defend without a navy, and America essentially had none. Greene wanted to withdraw from Manhattan and from all of New York Island; yet Washington resolved to defend the city. Greene tried to change his mind.

"I give it as my oppinion that a General and speedy Retreat is absolutely necessary and that the ho[n]or and Interest of America requires it," Greene wrote Washington from his sick bed on September 5. "I would burn the City and Subburbs."[34]

Washington agreed that if forced to retreat, the Americans should torch New York City to keep it from providing a winter haven to the British troops. Congress disagreed, and ordered "that no damage be done to the said city" by retreating troops.

No one was listening to Greene, still sick and mostly bedridden outside the city. He could not attend a September 7 meeting of the general officers where a majority agreed to try to hold New York with a force of five thousand men. Greene was so upset by this decision that he circulated a petition to reconsider what he felt was the folly of trying to hold off thirty thousand British with an army of five thousand.

In his petition Greene wrote: "The Situation of the Army under your Excellency's Command is, in our Opinion, so critical and dangerous that we apprehend a Board of General Officers should be immediately calld for the purpose of considering it." Greene was the only major general who signed the petition; still, Washington agreed to hold another council of officers to reconsider, and Greene forcefully stated his case: Outnumbered six to one, without control of the surrounding waters, it would be a foolish risk to defend the city.

Greene carried the argument by a vote of ten to three.[35]

Impressed by Greene's acumen, a member of New York's Committee of Correspondence wrote to Washington's aide-de-camp: "I am much mistaken if [Greene] is not possessed of that heaven born genius which is necessary to constitute a great general."[36]

After the vote, Washington told Congress he was now "fully convinced" that the city could not be defended; it was time to retreat from Manhattan.

The retreat did not go well. After dallying for weeks after his victory on Long Island, General Howe finally decided to press an offensive on New York at the same time the Americans had begun withdrawing from Manhattan. To cover his troops landing at Kip's Bay, Howe ordered a fierce bombardment from ships in the East River. American militia manning breastworks there fled in fear; their panic spread to the troops streaming north from the city, who dropped their baggage and ran. They left on the field sixty-seven cannon, half of Washington's artillery.

A Virginia colonel named George Weedon witnessed Washington atop his horse barking at his troops to keep calm, but in their panicked flight they ignored him. Weedon wrote that Washington "was so exasperated that he struck several officers in their flight, three times dashed his hat on the ground, and at last exclaimed 'Good God! Have I got such troops as those?'"[37]

Greene witnessed a similar scene, reporting back to Rhode Island's governor:

We made a miserable and disorderly retreat from New York, owing to the disorderly conduct of the Militia who run at the appearance of the Enemies advance Guard. This was General [John] Fellows Brigade. They struck a pannick into the Troops in the Rear, and Fellows and [Samuel] Parsons whole Brigade run away from about fifty men and left his Excellency on the Ground within Eighty Yards of the Enimy, so vext at the infamous conduct of the Troops that he sought Death rather than life.[38]

The Americans lost 350 men in their flight to the north, but they regrouped on Harlem Heights, a rocky highland near the northern tip of New York Island. Greene commanded three brigades, about 3,300 men, who formed the first of three lines encamped on the Heights near what is now 125th Street. On an unusually hot Monday in mid-September, an advance party of three hundred British marched on the heights. Brigades from Rhode Island and Massachusetts met the enemy head on, while the 3rd Virginia Regiment and 150 Connecticut Rangers snuck around the British and attacked from the flank. What began as a minor skirmish grew into four thousand troops firing on each other. Greene, fifty-eight-year-old Gen. Israel Putnam, and Washington's trusted aide, Joseph Reed, rode among their troops while bullets zinged.

"The fire continued about an hour and the Enimy Retreated," Greene reported to Rhode Island's governor, Nicholas Cooke. "Our people pursued them . . . advanced upon the plain ground without cover and Attackt them and drove them back."[39]

Reed conceded it was "rash and imprudent for Officers of our Rank to go into such an action,"[40] but they couldn't help themselves. Finally, after being routed on Long Island and chased across New York, the American commanders felt exhilarated at standing strong against the British forces.

By the strict accounting of body counts the skirmish at Harlem Heights was at best a draw: American casualties were around 30 dead and 100 wounded; the British and German forces lost 14 dead, 154 wounded. But for America, Harlem Heights was a much-needed victory. The sight of red coats turning and running from their guns lifted American morale at a time when it was desperately needed.

Although Congress had expressly forbidden retreating troops from burning New York City, a group of American rebels did it anyway. On September 20, 1776, the city suffered a conflagration rivaling 9/11 as the worst in its history: Some six hundred houses and several churches, steeples flaring high, burned at once.

"It is almost impossible to conceive a Scene of more horror and distress," wrote British Lt. Frederick Mackenzie:

> *The Sick, the Aged, Women, and Children, half naked were seen going they knew not where. . . . The terror was encreased by the horrid noise of the burning and falling houses . . . the rattling of above 100 wagons, sent in from the Army. . . . The confused voices of so many men, the Shrieks and cries of the Women and children . . . made this one of the most tremendous and affecting Scenes I ever beheld.*[41]

Nathanael Greene watched the conflagration from across the Hudson River in New Jersey, where Washington had sent him to take command of Fort

Constitution, which was quickly renamed Fort Lee in honor of the eccentric general. The fort stood three hundred feet above the Hudson, directly across from Fort Washington atop a similar cliff on New York.

Fort Washington commanded the highest point on all of Manhattan Island. American soldiers had built the two forts on bluffs at a narrows in the river, in hopes of shelling British shipping down in the Hudson.

A private stationed in Fort Lee noted that when Greene took over "There was immediately a great change with respect to the discipline of the troops which before was very lax."[42] Greene worked to form good soldiers out of militiamen who came and went on short-term enlistments, but now that he had been in battle and seen them panic, his patience with militia was spent. From his fort he wrote his brother, Jacob:

> The policy of Congress has been the most absurd and ridiculous imaginable, pouring in militia men who come and go every month. A military force established upon such principles defeats itself. People coming from home with all the tender feelings of domestic life are not sufficiently fortified with natural courage to stand the shocking scenes of war. To march over dead men, to hear without concern the groans of the wounded, I say few men can stand such scenes unless steeled by habit or fortified by military pride.[43]

Besides lacking the nerve to march over dead friends, militiamen fresh from their farms were just too fickle—they deserted in droves. "Great numbers of the Rebels desert to us daily," British lieutenant Frederick Mackenzie wrote in his diary. "Near 80 deserters came in one day recently. . . . By the most authentic accounts which we receive of the State of their Army in this neighbourhood, it is extremely sickly, and many desert."[44]

One of those deserters, Ensign William Demont, snuck out of Fort Washington on the cold night of November 2; he crossed into the British lines carrying a key document exposing the fort's strengths and weaknesses.

Greene wrote Washington in early November that three British ships had passed between the high guns of Forts Washington and Lee, and the guns had inflicted considerable damage. For General Washington the important news was not Greene's boast that the ships had been damaged, but the fact that they had passed the forts intact. If Fort Washington was not able to stop British shipping, he reasoned, then why risk a defense of that garrison? On November 8, 1776, he put this question to Greene:

> *If we cannot prevent Vessells passing up, and the Enemy are possessed of the surrounding Country, what valuable purpose can it answer to attempt to hold a post from which the expected Benefit cannot be had. I am therefore inclined to think it will not be prudent to hazard the Men and Stores on Mount Washington, but as you are on the Spot, leave it to you to give such Orders as to evacuating Mount Washington as you judge best.*[45]

Washington, in headquarters seventy miles north of Greene, placed a lot of responsibility on his young general. To be fair to Greene, his first instinct had been to pull every last soldier and cannon off of Manhattan Island as soon as Long Island fell in September.

Now in November, Greene was more sanguine about American prospects in Fort Washington, America's last hold out on New York.

On November 9 he wrote Washington: "Upon the whole, I cannot help thinking the Garrison is of advantage, and I cannot conceive the Garrison to be in any great danger. The men can be brought off at any time."[46]

For the rest of his life, those words would haunt Nathanael Greene.

❦ ❧

It's said that a general's education is paid for in blood. For Nathanael Greene, the tuition came due at Fort Washington. And the price was high.

On the morning of November 15, 1776—a day of fair, mild weather—a British drummer beat for a parley while his officer approached the foot of Mount Washington waving a white flag of truce. The officer, Col. James Patterson, had a proposal for the commander, a Pennsylvania rifleman named Col. Robert Magaw, a back-country lawyer before the war. Magaw sent an adjutant down to the river to hear the proposal, which was basically: surrender or die. Patterson revealed that the night before, thirty British flat boats had slipped up the Hudson River carrying troops, and that Mount Washington was now surrounded. If

Magaw was to be so obstinate as to insist on defending the fort, all the Americans in it would be put to the sword.

Magaw sent a message across the Hudson to Greene, up in Fort Lee on the Jersey shore. Patterson "waits for an answer," Magaw said. "I shall send a proper one. . . . We are determined to defend the post or die."[47]

Greene concurred with the decision. At 4 p.m. he sent a letter to Washington, now encamped but six miles away in Hackensack: "I have directed Col. Magaw to defend the place until he hears from me." Greene also sent reinforcements, swelling the number of men at Fort Washington to 2,900 regulars.

Dawn, November 16, brought the roar of cannon echoing through the Hudson River valley. British batteries opened up on Fort Washington. Later that morning eight thousand British and Hessian soldiers, schooled in using the bayonet, began a methodical climb up Mount Washington. On the steep north side of the mountain, four thousand Hessian soldiers, dressed in yellow breeches and blue coats, met stiff resistance; they fell by the dozens yet they continued to climb, pulling themselves up a near vertical slope by grabbing the roots of beech trees, scrabbling through a hail of shot.

Washington had ridden in from Hackensack to confer with Greene and two other generals—Israel Putnam and Hugh Mercer. From Fort Lee, the four generals could see and hear the British assault on Fort Washington; they decided to row over for a better look. They landed, and soon found themselves between an advancing party of Scottish Highlanders and another party of Hessians.

"There we all stood in a very awkward situation," Greene wrote. "We all urged his Excellency to come off. I offerd to stay. General Putnam did the same, and so did General Mercer, but his Excellency thought it best for all of us to come off together, which we did about half an hour before the Enemy surrounded the fort."[48]

In a reckless maneuver, the four generals stepped into a skiff and were rowed back to the Jersey shore, avoiding what would have been a disastrous capture. What they saw from Fort Lee was depressing; legend has it that Washington watched with tears in his eyes. The Hessians on the north side gained the top of the hill; then, with oboes blowing a spirited tune, they drove American defenders toward the fort's earthen walls.

All around Fort Washington the scene was the same: Americans retreating inside the walls till they were packed in there so thickly they could not even raise their muskets in defense. Around 1 p.m. the sounds of war fell silent; a Hessian captain approached the fort with a white flag and again demanded its surrender. Washington sent a message across the Hudson telling Magaw to try and hold out till darkness, but it could not be done.

At 4 p.m. the American flag flying over Fort Washington dropped; a white flag of surrender took its place. All of the Americans holding that fort—2,837— were killed or captured. Hessian soldiers, enraged at the deaths of fifty-eight comrades, wanted to slaughter every American with the bayonet, but their commanders would not let them.

The survivors streamed out of the fort between two lines of jeering Hessians, and laid their arms in a pile. British Lt. Frederick Mackenzie observed:

> *The Rebel prisoners were in general but very indifferently clothed; few of them appeared to have a Second shirt, nor did they appear to have washed themselves during the Campaign. A great many of them were lads under 15, and old men: and few of them had the appearance of Soldiers. Their odd figures frequently excited the laughter of our Soldiers.*[49]

This dirty, poorly clothed flock of boys and old men was herded down to Manhattan, where most were locked up in squalid warehouses or in dank prison ships rotting at anchor in New York Harbor. Nearly two thousand of the men captured at Fort Washington eventually died of disease while imprisoned.

Besides the loss of 90 officers and nearly 2,800 soldiers, the Americans left in Fort Washington thirty-four cannons, two howitzers, scarce ammunition, and enough food to feed thousands for a fortnight. This was the second- largest loss of men and materiel in the entire war, behind only the later fall of Charleston, South Carolina, and many laid the blame on Washington's youngest general, Nathanael Greene.

From across the river at Fort Lee, Greene wrote his friend Henry Knox: "I feel mad, vext, sick, and sorry. Never did I need the consoling voice of a friend more than now. Happy should I be to see you. This is a most terrible event. Its consequences are justly to be dreaded."[50]

After losing Fort Washington with all its men and materiel, Nathanael Greene found no time to lick his wounds. He still held Fort Lee, perched on a bluff on the Jersey side of the Hudson, but he now knew that this post was also indefensible.

General Washington ordered Fort Lee's evacuation, an order easier written than executed. Greene had been so optimistic about holding Forts Washington and Lee that he'd laid in enormous amount of stores on the Jersey side of the river. He'd planned on feeding and equipping 2,000 men at Fort Lee for five months; now he had to move most of his 3,100 barrels of flour, 3,100 barrels of pork, 300 tons of hay, and 10,000 bushels of grain, lest it all fall into the enemy's hands.

On November 18, 1776, two days after the fall of Fort Washington, Greene wrote Washington: "I am sending off the Stores as fast as I can get Waggons. . . . The Stores here are large, and the transportation by land will be almost endless. The Powder and fixt ammunition I have sent off by land as it is an article too valuable to be trust upon the water."[51]

Greene had been optimistic about holding Forts Washington and Lee, but he had not been stupid: While making plans to hold the forts for five months he'd also taken pains to lay in enormous stocks of flour, beef, pork, hay, and grain in magazines across New Jersey just in case the army had to march across that state to Philadelphia. The chain of supply depots stretched from the northeast corner of New Jersey southwest to Trenton.

Down in Manhattan, the British knew exactly what Greene was up to in his fort on a bluff across the river. In his diary, on a "Fine mild day," British Lt. Frederick MacKenzie wrote: "Tis said the Rebels have been withdrawing from Fort [Lee] these two last days."

Gen. Thomas Gage, who had missed chances to trap Washington's troops at Brooklyn and in Manhattan, decided that this time he would strike quickly.

On the rainy night of November 19, a couple of British battalions numbering five thousand men struck their tents and boarded flat boats for a half-mile row to the Jersey shore. They landed at Closter Dock, six miles north of Fort Lee; by noon the weather had cleared and the column of men marched single-file up a steep pathway to the top of the bluff, bent on storming Fort Lee.

Greene summoned Washington from his headquarters in Hackensack; Washington rode into Fort Lee, assessed the situation, and did not like the odds. He gave the order to flee the fort.

Washington's orders came just in time. By 1 p.m. the British marched to the beat of snare drums through the fort's outer walls; inside they found the Americans' breakfast still simmering over smoky camp fires. One British soldier wrote: "They have left some poor pork, a few greasy proclamations and some of that scoundrel Common Sense man's letters."[52]

The "rebels" also left 1,000 barrels of flour along with the aforementioned poor pork, 30 cannon, and 300 tents still standing for the comfort of British soldiers to sleep in that night. Most of the American soldiers—all but 90 of the 2,500—escaped, and Greene felt those 90 who were captured were just "a set of rascals that Skulkt out of the way, for fear of fighting."

With the fall of Forts Washington and Lee the Americans had lost, in just four days, more than 3,000 soldiers, 46 cannons, 8,000 cannon shot, 400,000 cartridges, and 2,800 muskets. They had also left behind almost all their entrenching tools so they could not even dig a simple foxhole while fleeing from advancing British troops across the flat plains of New Jersey.

"This is now the time to push these rascals," MacKenzie wrote in his diary, "and if we do, and not give them time to recover themselves, we may depend upon it they will never make head again."[53]

The British did indeed push the American "rascals," a wet, dirty, and dispirited bunch. A New Jersey resident recalled a scene of November 1776: "The night was cold, dark, and rainy, but I had a fair view of Greene's troops from the light of the windows as they passed on our side of the street. They marched two abreast, looked ragged, some without a shoe to their feet and most of them wrapped in their blankets."[54]

At Newark, the Americans burned their few remaining tents to keep them from falling into the hands of the British bearing down on them. Now everyone slept, or tried to, in the cold November rain, wrapped in wet blankets, many without coats or shoes. By day they slogged along cold, muddy roads toward Philadelphia.

❧   ❧

Along the route, Greene's aide-de-camp, Thomas Paine, began drafting his next pamphlet. Tradition has it that he wrote some of it by firelight on a drumhead: "These are the times that try men's souls. The summer soldier and the sunshine patriot will, in this crisis, shrink from the service of his country."

Paine wrote from experience; at Newark he saw two brigades announce that their enlistments had expired and they were going home. "Notwithstanding the Enemy were within two hours march and coming on," Greene wrote on December 4. "When we left Brunswick we had not 3,000 men, a very pitiful army to trust the Liberties of America upon."

That same day in Trenton he wrote his wife:

The situation this Army was in when I wrote you last must naturally alarm your fears. The Enemy has since prest us very hard from place to place. . . .

Seventy sail of the Enemies fleet saild a few days past, their destination unknown; but tis suggested by many they were bound for Rhode Island; but I rather suppose them to be going to the Southward. . . .

I am hearty and well amidst all the fatigues and hardships I endure. I hope you enjoy your health and the company of your friends about you. Be of good courage; don't be distressd. All things will turn out for the best.[55]

THREE

Their Eternal Honor

Inside the damp chill of an unfinished fieldstone house, Nathanael Greene scratched out a letter to his wife, Caty. He wrote from the Merrick House on the Pennsylvania side of the Delaware River, which was then beginning to freeze in mid-December 1776.

Greene and what was left of his army, fewer than three thousand men, had just crossed the Delaware from Trenton, New Jersey, barely escaping before British troops swept into that town. His spirits were understandably low; the British had routed him from New York at Fort Washington, hounded him clear across New Jersey, invaded and occupied Newport in his home state of Rhode Island, and were now in a good position to move on the capital city of Philadelphia. Congress was so concerned about a British invasion that it quit the capital city and moved the nascent nation's business to Baltimore.

As a brigadier general, Greene earned $125 per month, decent money when he was commissioned in the summer of 1775, but now even with a promotion to major general he earned just enough to cover expenses, with nothing left to support a family in Rhode Island. As the American army lost battle after battle, the Continental currency's paper dollar fell in value against the hard silver of British coin. In Philadelphia a dollar was worth half of what it had been, and was steadily plunging lower.

Greene told his wife about the evacuation of New Jersey: "the enemy have reduced us to the necessity to pass the Delaware," and about the fall of the dollar, "The Continental currency . . . is almost lost in the Jerseys, and much injured in this state."

And then he told her more bad news: Gen. Charles Lee, the most experienced officer in the American Army, had been captured.

"This is a great loss to the American states," Greene wrote, "as he is a most consummate general."

In December 1776, Lee's star stood at its zenith. Even Washington wrote that Lee was "the first officer in military knowledge and experience we have in the whole army."

Lee had recently returned from Charleston, South Carolina as a hero. He had been the titular commander of the Southern army that June, when it blasted the British Navy at Charleston. Lee's role at Charleston had mostly been confined to giving bad advice to the real hero of that action, Col. William Moultrie. Through bravery, British blundering, and sheer good luck Moultrie's men had held out through heavy bombardment and forced a fleet of the British Navy to turn tail back to New York.

Some of the laurels from Charleston fell on Lee's head and swelled it. Lee felt that with the victory he had proof that he was a better general than Washington. He began ignoring America's commander in chief.

Before retreating across New Jersey, Washington had left Lee with seven thousand troops at White Plains, above New York. Now with Philadelphia under threat of invasion, Washington wanted Lee to come south with those troops. Lee refused.

From the start Greene had respected Lee's experience, but he also mistrusted him. On December 7, 1776, Greene had warned Washington: "I think General Lee must be confind within the Lines of some General Plan, or else his operations will be independant of yours."

Lee finally did cross the Hudson into New Jersey, though his troop strength had dropped to three thousand; and he had no intention of bringing those remaining troops to aid Washington. From Morristown he wrote Gen. William

Heath that he planned to ignore Washington and fight Cornwallis in New Jersey.

Outside of Morristown, Lee's hubris brought him down. He decided to sleep the night of December 12 in White's Tavern, a lodging house owned by a widow in Basking Ridge, some three miles from the protection of his main army. The next morning, Friday the thirteenth, Lee lingered over a late breakfast while his army marched even farther away. Wearing an old blue coat with red facing and greasy leather breeches, he bent over the table, absorbed in writing a letter to fellow general Horatio Gates:

> *Entre Nous, a certain great man* [Washington] *is most damnably deficient. He has thrown me into a situation where I have my choice of difficulties: if I stay in this province I risk myself and army, and if I do not stay, the province is lost forever. . . . In short, unless something which I do not expect turns up, we are lost.*[1]

Just as Lee signed that letter, the hollow thunder of horse hooves sounded outside White's Tavern. A party of thirty horsemen wearing green hunting jackets crashed through the woods and surrounded the house. Leading the charge at the front door was young Banastre "Ban" Tarleton, twenty-two, a ruthless and aggressive officer out to make a name for himself in the American war. Tarleton threatened to burn the house; Lee skulked out.

For the British, capturing Lee was almost as good as capturing George Washington himself. The dragoons took their prize back to Brunswick, where they toasted the king till they got themselves, and Lee's horse, thoroughly drunk.

In his December 16 letter to his wife, Greene lamented Lee's capture: "Fortune seems to frown upon the cause of freedom; a combination of evils are pressing in upon us on all sides. However, I hope this is the dark part of the night, which generally is just before day."[2]

❦   ❧

Nathanael Greene had a secret. Something big was about to happen, an attack, but he had to keep it confidential. From the tone of his letters he was dying to tell about it. On December 21, 1776, the darkest day of the year, Greene wrote to his governor, Nicholas Cooke of Rhode Island:

> *We are now on the West side of the Delaware, our force small tho collected together, but small as it is I hope to give the Enimy a stroke in a few days. Should fortune favor the Attack Perhaps it may put a stop to General Hows progress. His ravages in the Jersies exceed all description. Men slaughterd, Women ravisht, and Houses plundered, little Girls not ten years old ravisht, Mothers and Daughters ravisht in presence of the Husbands and Sons who were obligd to be spectators to their brutal conduct.*[3]

There was truth to Greene's stories of rape and plunder by General Howe's troops as they crossed New Jersey. The Hessians in Howe's command had no stake in this fight, other than what little pleasure and plunder they could take out of it. Even Loyalists weren't exempt from rape and looting, because the hoards of Hessian soldiers sweeping across New Jersey didn't know enough English to distinguish Tory from Whig.

That December the future had never looked so desperate. The American Army had dwindled from 28,000 that summer to about 6,000 nearly naked, poorly fed men. Charles Willson Peale, as yet a little-known painter, saw one soldier along the banks of the Delaware "who had lost all his clothes, He was in an old, dirty blanket jacket, his beard long, and his face so full of sores he could not clean it." Only when the man greeted him warmly did Peale recognize that he was looking at his brother.[4]

General Washington knew that the enlistment period for most of his regulars would expire on December 31, 1776; if everyone whose enlistment expired opted to trade the misery of camp for the fireside of home, his army would fall to 1,400 men. Washington wrote to Congressman John Hancock on December 20, "ten days more will put an end to the existence of our army." To his brother, John Augustine, Washington was even more blunt. He wrote: ". . . I think the game is pretty near up."[5]

Washington steeled himself to make a last, desperate attack before his little army disbanded. Benjamin Rush, a Philadelphia doctor and signer of the Declaration of Independence, visited Washington at his headquarters on

December 23 and found him "much depressed. . . . While I was talking to him, I observed him to play with his pen and ink upon several small pieces of paper. One of them by accident fell upon the floor near my feet. I was struck with the inscription upon it. It was 'Victory or Death.'"[6] Over and over Washington wrote that phrase, Victory or Death; he'd give the scraps of paper to his officers as the new countersign—anyone challenged by a sentry was to repeat that shibboleth.

On Christmas Eve 1776, a procession of officers crunched across the crusty snow outside the Merrick House, the chilly, unfinished house where Greene lived. They came for a strategy session led by George Washington. The officers assembled in the Merrick House included Greene, two future presidents (Washington and James Monroe), a secretary of the treasury (Alexander Hamilton), and a secretary of war (Henry Knox). After they took their Christmas Eve dinner Greene asked his hosts, the Merrick family, to please leave for awhile; the officers needed to conduct their council of war. Greene and a few others were already privy to the plans that Washington then laid out: On Christmas Day the troops would cross the Delaware, march under the cover of darkness to Trenton, and attack a garrison of 1,400 Hessian soldiers. Once they took Trenton they'd move on and take Brunswick, where the King's troops kept a war chest of 70,000 pounds.

"This is an important period to America," Greene wrote to his wife, "big with great events."

Christmas Day 1776 dawned clear and cold, one of those blue winter days that looks nice but isn't. The temperature peaked at thirty degrees, cold enough to sting ungloved hands. Around noon the main part of the army, approximately 2,400 men, gathered in camp to begin the march to McKonkey's Landing on the Delaware. As they stood in the cold, Washington ordered an officer posted at the head of each unit to read aloud Thomas Paine's latest pamphlet, "The Crisis." In air cold enough to see puffs of breath the adjutants read:

> These are the times that try men's souls. The summer soldier and the
> sunshine patriot will, in this crisis, shrink from the service of his country;
> but he that stands it *now* deserves the love and thanks of man and

woman. Tyranny, like hell, is not easily conquered; yet we have this consolation with us, that the harder the conflict, the more glorious the triumph. What we obtain too cheap, we esteem too lightly: it is dearness only that gives everything its value. Heaven knows how to put a proper price on its goods; and it would be strange indeed if so celestial an article as FREEDOM should not be highly rated.[7]

One by one each unit marched off toward McKonkey's Ferry, so that by 3 p.m. the entire army was in motion. They crunched across week-old snow that had thawed and refrozen so now it wore a sharp glaze. A major, John Wilkinson, saw spots of the snow stained red, "tinged here and there," he wrote, "with blood from the feet of the men who wore broken shoes."[8]

The sun set early on Christmas; by 4:30 p.m. the sky was dark enough to conceal the river crossing, and at McKonkey's Ferry the embarkations began. The wind blew from the northeast, funneling down the Delaware Valley, driving before it large ice floes that had broken from the river's edge. As the wind increased, so did its sound, making communication difficult. Through the roar of the wind in the gathering dark, the bass voice of 280-pound Henry Knox rang out. It was tough work loading Knox's cannon, the horses that would draw them, and then the men in the wind and the dark of a slippery river bank. A full moon rose at sunset but already the storm clouds veiled and soon smothered it.

Greene's three regiments went first, stepping gingerly into the boats, big, black boats used in peacetime for hauling iron and pig ore from the Durham Iron Works. They were forty to sixty feet long, eight feet at the beam, and even fully loaded with fifteen tons of cannon, cattle, soldiers, and crew they sunk only thirty inches into water.

Washington had planned to have all his men across by midnight, but conditions made the crossing painfully slow. Col. John Glover's regiment of Marblehead fishermen poled and steered the freighted boats across the current, battling their way through big floes of ice that clunked heavily against their sides. Washington, wrapped in a cloak, went over around 7 p.m. to view the landing parties. Knox recalled Washington stepping over men in the boat till he at last reached the bench where Knox sat. He nudged Knox with his boot and said, "Shift that fat ass, Harry. But slowly, or you'll swamp the damned boat!"[9]

Once ashore, Washington sat on a box that had contained a beehive and watched for hours while his plans slowly went awry. Around 11 p.m. a heavy snow began. The northeast wind whipped snow and sleet into the faces of Glover's men as they battled the current and the ice floes; their poles and gunnels wore a glaze of ice. By the time everyone was across and ready to march the nine miles to Trenton it was 4 a.m., four hours behind schedule. There was no way the troops would be able to spring a surprise, pre-dawn attack on the Hessians quartered at Trenton. But there was no turning back; they'd have to fight by daylight.

The troops stepped off, thankfully putting the windblown sleet at their backs, and marched as quietly as they could. After two hours they reached the dark village of Birmingham; here they gobbled cold rations before splitting in two: Greene and Washington led a thousand men down Scotch Road, while Sullivan took his troops toward Trenton along the River Road.

Sullivan sent word to Washington that his men were complaining that their gunpowder was wet. Washington sent a messenger back with an answer: Use the bayonet. "I am resolved to take Trenton."[10]

Greene's column made the first contact with a Hessian outpost at around 8 a.m., driving the twenty men in it a half-mile back into town. About 1,400 Hessians were barracked on a block between Queen and King Streets. Knox quickly placed his cannon at the top of these streets and cut down the enemy troops as they poured from their barracks into the streets. There followed chaos, with German martial music playing to rally the troops, American artillery banging away down the main streets at the Hessians trying to rally in the sleet and snow, then Brig. Gen. Hugh Mercer's troops rushing in from the west, their powder wet but their bayonets sharp. Smoke from the cannon mingled with the swirling snow, creating a thick curtain of fog. By 9 a.m., the fighting was over. Cannon smoke slowly dissipated. Blood stained the slushy streets where Hessian soldiers lay in bloody garments, audibly dying. Col. Johann Rall, the Hessian officer who took the sword of surrender at Fort Washington, lay wounded in a church, two bullet holes in his side. Greene and Washington visited Rall, who asked that his men be treated kindly. Rall died later that day.

If Nathanael Greene wrote much about the Battle of Trenton it has been lost; all that remains is one paragraph to his wife, Caty, and one paragraph to Rhode Island's governor, Nicholas Cooke.

To Caty, Greene wrote:

We crost the River Delaware at McKonkees Ferry Eight miles above this place [Trenton] *on the 25 of this instant and attackt the Town by Storm in the morning. It raind, haild and snowd and was a violent Storm. The Storm of nature and the Storm of the Town exhibited a Scene that fild the mind during the action with passions easier conceivd than described. The Action lasted about three quarters of an hour. We kild, wounded and took Prisoners of the Enimy between Eleven and twelve hundred. Our troops behavd with great Spirit. General Sullivan commanded the right Wing of the Army and I the left.*

In another, understated letter to Cooke, Greene repeated the essentials—crossed the Delaware on the twenty-fifth in "one of the severest Hails and rain storms I ever saw"—captured six cannon and a large number of arms. "I was out 30 hours in all the storm without the least refreshment."

Greene's estimate of Hessians killed and captured was high: Actually 1,024 were taken—22 dead, 84 wounded, 918 captured. Only 300 to 500 escaped. Four Americans were wounded, including Lt. James Monroe, who took a ball in the shoulder.

Washington called a brief council of war. Two regiments that were supposed to cross the Delaware to the south had obviously not made the crossing, so their southern flank was exposed to Hessian reinforcements. Washington asked his officers whether they should still press on for Princeton and Brunswick.

Greene and Knox said they should, but they were outvoted. Not only were enemy reinforcements behind them, but their troops were cold, wet, and exhausted. At noon they marched out of Trenton, slogging along slushy roads the eight or nine miles to the river crossing. Again the crossing was made at night with a cold wind blowing ice floes down the valley; this time three men who boarded the Durham boats never made it alive to the other side. In crossing the Delaware they froze to death.[11]

Moving thousands of troops across a freezing river in a deadly storm was a desperate roll of the dice—but it worked. The attack at Trenton proved to the British and to the American people that the revolution still breathed life.

Yet as he surveyed his troops on December 27, 1776, George Washington was not satisfied. He had not planned on stopping at Trenton; his plans called for driving the British out of Princeton, then capturing the main force at Brunswick with its treasure of 70,000 pounds. He resolved to finish what he'd begun.

Returns of his own troops that Friday showed that 40 percent were still too sick and tired to fight; Washington knew they needed a day or two to refresh themselves. After giving his troops just three days of rest, on December 30 he again crossed the Delaware into New Jersey, a dangerous country that was still largely held by the enemy. The river crossing was even tougher this time; though it was daylight, the ice floes were thicker, and Henry Knox was now moving forty cannon and draught horses, twice as many as they'd landed before.

On December 31, 1776, George Washington brought his horse to a halt before a New England regiment of his veteran troops encamped in Trenton. These men looked less like soldiers than like refugees with ragged clothes stretched across bony frames. Washington told them that they'd done a good job; they were not the "sunshine patriots" of Thomas Paine's pamphlet, they were the loyal sons of liberty to whom all should be grateful. Washington told them that if they'd extend the terms of their enlistment for just six weeks, he would top their regular pay with a bounty of $10.

His regimental officers called for volunteers to step forward and a drummer beat a roll.

Not one man moved.

Frustrated, Washington wheeled his horse around in a circle and rode along his men. One sergeant recalled that he then said:

My brave fellows, you have done all I asked you to do, and more than could be reasonably expected. But your country is at stake, your wives, your houses, all that you hold dear. You have worn yourselves out with fatigues and hardships, but we know not how to spare you. If you will consent to stay but one month longer, you will render that service to the cause of liberty, and to your country, which you probably can never do under any other circumstances. The present is emphatically the crisis that will decide our destiny.[12]

Again the drum rolled. This time there were murmurs ("I will remain if you do") and gaunt veterans came forward till all but the lame and the nearly naked stood in a line.

About half of the 2,400 regulars who had taken Trenton agreed to stay on for six more weeks to help Washington rid the Jerseys of the British. And about half of those who remained were, like Greene, Rhode Islanders.[13] Greene wrote home to Rhode Island's governor: "God Almighty inclnd [inclined] their hearts to listen to the proposal and they engaged anew, happy for America. This is the greatest example of N[ew] E[ngland] virtue that I ever saw. Let it be remembered to their Eternal honor."[14]

Lord Charles Cornwallis was close to walking up a gangplank for a much-anticipated ocean voyage home on December 31, 1776, when he received an urgent command from Gen. Sir William Howe. Cornwallis could not go home. Washington had emerged from a blizzard and taken Trenton by storm; now Howe needed Cornwallis to take command of the forces in New Jersey and use them to stop Washington.

Cornwallis mounted a horse in New York and pushed across New Jersey, fifty miles in a day. While Washington was in Trenton planning on ridding New Jersey of the British, Cornwallis was bent on ridding New Jersey of Washington. The odds were with Cornwallis: He had 8,000 men, well trained, well equipped, and well fed. Washington had about 4,600 men, mostly untested militia; his 1,200 regular soldiers were worn out after a hard year.

Cornwallis quickly rolled his troops and twenty-eight cannon south toward Trenton; Washington anticipated this move. He took his stand on the banks of the Assunpink River, a waist-deep river that marked Trenton's southern border. The river could act as a moat to slow the advance of Cornwallis's troops, but it wasn't deep enough to stop them.

To the west, Washington's left, was the Delaware, wide and deep, cutting off all hopes of retreat. If he turned south or east, Washington would be in a vulnerable position with his flanks exposed to a larger, aggressive army. When the British reached the Assunpink, his men—outnumbered and outclassed—were going to have to stand and fight.

The new year 1777 began with a bang. On January 2, Washington sent an advance party of riflemen to scout the progress of eight thousand British troops known to be moving on his entrenched troops of about five thousand.

The riflemen were under the command of Col. Edward Hand, thirty-two, an Ireland-born Pennsylvanian. His riflemen wore loose white hunting shirts and carried long rifles with bored barrels instead of the muskets most soldiers carried. Compared to muskets, rifles fired with deadly accuracy; they were good for skirmishing or guerrilla warfare, but they fouled after repeated firings, which made them unsuitable for protracted battle.

At around 10 a.m. of a mild morning, Hand's men spied Cornwallis's vanguard outside Maidenhead, five miles north of Trenton. The Pennsylvania riflemen did what they could to slow the advancing British, firing from behind walls and woods, then dropping back.

Washington sent Nathanael Greene, leading a regiment of Rhode Islanders, to buttress the riflemen. One Rhode Island soldier recalled in his old age: "I remember [Greene] dashing up to the company I was in and calling out in a clear, loud voice, 'Push on, boys! Push on!'"[15] Greene's goal was to reach some high ground on the north side of Trenton. That would afford Washington's army some cover while they tried to stream out of town into the hills of northern New Jersey before the rest of Cornwallis' army could come up. "But the enemy got possession of these hills before us," recalled a Rhode Island captain, "and commenced a smart fire upon us. General Greene was at the head of our column and gave the word, 'retreat.'"

Greene's regiment and Hand's riflemen fell back through the streets of Trenton to the bridge crossing the Assunpink, running back to their side of the bridge. With the early sunsets of January, Hand's riflemen had done their job. They had delayed Cornwallis's vanguard for five hours. Darkness was falling now as the Americans parted to let the last of Hand's men cross. Then they reformed the line. Henry Knox had forty cannon ready for the British assault.

After three blasts from Knox's artillery, the bridge ran red with blood, and the British stopped coming.

While the last flames from musket barrels tongued the darkness, Cornwallis decided to postpone his attack on Washington's position until the next morning. His men were worn out from an eleven-mile march over miry roads that filled their boots and bogged down their cannon. He did not need to contest the bloody bridge—the next morning, when they could see the unfamiliar ground, his troops could ford the waist-deep Assunpink, attack Washington's right flank, and push the Americans into the Delaware River.

"We've got the old fox safe now," Cornwallis told his officers at a council of war. "We'll go over and bag him in the morning."

Still, Cornwallis's quartermaster, Sir William Erskine, felt they should attempt a nighttime attack. He told Cornwallis: "My Lord, if Washington is the general I take him to be . . . you will see nothing of them in the morning."[16]

All that night of January 2 into the next day, the American campfires burned brightly, fed by the dry wood of dismantled split-rail fences stolen from the local farmers. All that night, too, the sounds of hundreds of soldiers digging trenches spilled over from the American lines. The bright fires, the sounds of shovel and pick axe, these were all part of an elaborate ruse. For at a war council that night, Washington had studied his dilemma—fight a superior enemy or suffer a demoralizing, potentially disastrous retreat—and he'd found a third option.

A map hastily drawn with the help of a spy and the local knowledge of Gen. Arthur St. Clair revealed that a new road from Trenton to Princeton had recently been cleared. This road ran east, around the town well to the left of Cornwallis's troops. In fact it was so new that where it passed through the Pine Barrens the short stumps of the trees felled for the road had not yet been dug out. Washington, with the concurrence of his generals, decided to stealthily march his men along this road, giving them a good head start on a retreat from Cornwallis.

A crew of five hundred stayed behind to keep the campfires burning, while the rest marched under strict orders to hold their tongues. The "baggage train"—wagons full of belongings and blankets—was sent south to Burlington; the wheels of Knox's artillery were wrapped in rags to muffle their heavy roll. By luck, a brief January thaw broke that night and the temperatures fell far below freezing, giving the wheels good ground to roll on. With a last heaping of rail fence to flare the campfires the final five hundred silently stole off into the gin-clear night.

On January 3, 1776, the sun rose into a cloudless New Jersey sky. An American soldier noted the sky was "bright, serene, and extremely cold, with a hoar frost which bespangled every object."[17] At first light, Cornwallis and his officers surveyed the American lines; they saw fresh earthworks, smoldering campfires—and nothing else.

The old fox had fled the trap.

❧   ❧

The cold, nighttime march to Princeton had been a tough one—eleven miles on a dark, dirt road studded in places with tree stumps too short to see by starlight but tall enough to bruise shins. The artillery horse moved slowly, holding up columns of stumbling men, many wearing rags and hides for shoes; some fell asleep standing, until the order came again to march.

At sunrise, when Cornwallis was gazing on Washington's empty camp, an advance party of Americans neared a hill outside Princeton. Col. James Wilkinson—then on Nathanael Greene's staff though later a personal enemy of Greene's—saw a flash along the ridge, sun striking on the burnished steel of musket barrels.

It was enemy muskets that Wilkinson saw on that ridge: the barrels of 2 regiments, 50 cavalrymen, and 150 wagons led by Lt. Col. Charles Mawhood, who had just ridden out of Princeton, leading troops to reinforce Cornwallis at Trenton. He left behind about 500 men to guard that town. And was Mawhood ever surprised to see Washington's army at the door to Princeton, when he supposed that Cornwallis had them pinned against the Delaware River at Trenton. As Henry Knox later put it: "I believe they were as much astonished as if an army had dropped perpendicularly upon them."[18]

An advance party of Americans led by Brig. Gen. Hugh Mercer, a Scotsman by birth and a doctor by training, was the first to tangle with Mawhood's troops. After a skirmish in a winter-bare orchard on a snow-covered hill, the British troops charged downhill through the orchard, bayoneting the outmanned Americans, who turned and ran. Mercer's gray horse took a ball in the leg and fell thrashing to the ground. Now dismounted, Mercer swung wildly with his sword; British troops surrounded him, cracked his head with a musket butt, and seven times they ran him through with a bayonet. Before he passed out Mercer heard them say, "Damn him, he is dead. Let us leave him."[19]

Mercer's men ran, and untested militiamen saw them coming through the orchard, panicked, and ran with them. Nathanael Greene saw the beginnings of a panicky retreat as he approached the hill from the backside. As Greene charged, an officer at his side reined in his own horse to avoid a dead man.

"On sir," Greene said, "this is no time for stopping."[20]

Greene ordered an artillery captain, Joseph Moulder, to haul his two four-pound cannons to the left of the hill in an attempt to anchor the line of militiamen before they totally broke ranks. Though the militia ran, Moulder's men held their ground, firing cannon that staved off the charging British troops long enough for reinforcements to arrive.

Washington saw the fighting in the orchard and galloped over to calm the panicked militia. Above the roar of the cannon Washington yelled, "Parade with us my brave fellows! There is but a handful of the enemy, and we will have them directly."[21]

Behind Washington came Col. Daniel Hitchcock, a Yale-educated lawyer, leading two brigades of New Englanders flanked by regiments from Massachusetts and New Hampshire. Hitchcock, suffering from an advanced case of tuberculosis, formed his men in a wide line next to the Virginians, who stood next to the Pennsylvania militia now under Washington's direct command. Washington rode out in front of the long line and waved his hat, a signal to come on. He rode uphill, toward the line of British, their coats red against the snow in the morning sun. About thirty yards from the British lines, Washington turned in his saddle. "Halt!" he said. "Fire!"

From both sides muskets thundered, cloaking Washington in a fog of gunpowder. His aide, John Fitzgerald, could not watch. He pulled his hat over his eyes. When the cloud cleared he saw Washington, again waving his hat to advance.[22]

Hitchcock's New Englanders came on, pushing the left flank of the British lines while Moulder, still where Greene had directed him to set up, continued his cannon fire on the British right. The British broke and ran. From being the hunted at Trenton, Washington was now the hunter. As his army took off after the retreating British troops Washington followed on horseback, bellowing, "It is a fine fox chase boys!"[23]

❧   ❧

Walking the ground where the battles were fought, a doctor saw dozens of dead and heard the moans of many more wounded. A college student noted "a number of pale, mangled corpses," thirty-six of which were buried the next day in a common grave.[24] Among the dead and dying were a colonel, John Haslet, and two of Nathanael Greene's best friends, Hugh Mercer and Daniel Hitchcock.

For two hours the American forces grabbed what they could find to eat and drink in the largely abandoned town. Some had marched one night from Crosswicks to reach Trenton, and then with no sleep, marched sixteen miles again at night to Princeton. All were hungry.

By early afternoon they were on the move again. Washington had wanted to march on Brunswick, capture that post, and take the British war chest of 70,000 pounds; but now he knew his plan was beyond human endurance. Brunswick was a seventeen-mile hike away, and Cornwallis was again on Washington's trail, marching up from Trenton.

Nathanael Greene, riding a worn-out horse ("I am miserably off for want of a horse," he wrote two weeks later[25]), led an advance column northeast toward Morristown. After a night in which troops slept fitfully on frozen ground with no blankets or wagons, the American Army straggled into Morristown.

Morristown was meant to be a temporary camp, but the more the American officers saw of the place the better they liked it. The village was nestled in a natural castle: The sharp hills of the Watchung range threw up a wall toward New York; behind it the Passaic River acted as a moat between Morristown and a possible British invasion. War had not yet torn up the countryside, so the foraging was good. Washington decided to pass the rest of the winter here.

From the house of a reluctant Tory host, Greene wrote Caty about the sad effects of the Battle of Princeton:

I forgot to mention in my last the death of poor Col. Hitchcock who dyed of the Pleurisy at this place. He was buried with all the honnors of War as the last mark of respect we could show him. Poor General Mercer is also dead of the wounds he receivd in the Princetown action. He was a fine companion, a sincere friend, a true patriot and a brave general. May Heaven bless his spirit with Eternal peace. Several more brave officers fell that day. Particularly one Capt [Daniel] Neale of the [New Jersey] Artillery. The Enemy refusd him quarter after he was wounded. He has left a poor widow overwhelmed with grief. She is as fine a woman as I ever I saw; her distress melts the hearts of all around her. . . . Such instances paints all the horrors of war—beyound description.[26]

When Washington settled in at Morristown, his wife, Martha, came to camp, as did many of the officers' wives. Caty, however, could not make it. She had visited Nathanael on Manhattan, before the evacuation; now in January 1777 she was five months pregnant with their second child and in no shape to travel. He worried about her health.

"The great distance there is between us and the few opportunities I have to hear from you leaves me in a very disagreeable suspence," Greene wrote his wife in March from Morristown. "Eight long months have past amidst fatigue and toil since I have tasted the pleasures of domestick felicity."[27] Much had happened in those eight months—the deaths of friends; the rout at Fort Washington to revenge at Trenton and Princeton; and most recently Greene had been in Philadelphia, where Washington sent him to give a report of the army's state to Congress.

One subject Washington wanted Greene to discuss with Congress was prisoners of war, particularly the treatment of the captured American general, Charles Lee. Congress, fearing harsh treatment of Lee, was on the verge of retaliating against British prisoners of war. But Lee's treatment was far from harsh—he had spacious quarters in New York, one of his dogs, food, wine, and occasional liberty to entertain guests.[28]

By custom, enemy armies would negotiate swaps of their prisoners, an officer for an officer, or five lesser officers for one general, and so on; Washington wanted all matters concerning prisoners to be conducted on the "principles of justice and humanity." Greene agreed. He felt it was good public policy to treat prisoners humanely. He wrote John Adams in Congress:

The mild and gentle treatment the Hessian Prisoners have receivd since they have been in our possession has produced a great alteration in their disposition.

Desertion prevails among them. One whole Brigade refusd to fight or do duty and were sent prisoners to New York. . . . For these and many other reasons that will readily occur to you I would wish the resolution concerning Retalliation might be suspended for a time at least especially as General Lees confinement is not strict.[29]

For the most part, Greene did not like his brief stay in Philadelphia. He never had been a fan of cities, once likening them to storms as a necessary evil. Greene was also no fan of politicians. After enduring four hours of interviews with Congressional committees he wrote Washington: "There is so much deliberation and waste of time in the execution of business before this assembly that my patience is almost exhausted."[30]

Ever the tactician, Greene spent his free time in Philadelphia reconnoitering the city to determine how he could defend it in the face of an expected British attack. He concluded that it could not be adequately defended, writing Washington:

I have road round the City and up the Scuylkill [Schuylkill River] *and give it as my oppinion that it cannot be fortified to advantage. The approaches may be made so many ways that it would take a greater number of Troops to defend the Works than would be prudent to have shut up in the City.*[31]

While in Philadelphia, Greene also took a survey of the local women, reporting back to his wife:

The young ladies of Philadelphia appeared angelick. A few months Seperation more will put my virtue to a new tryal. If you don't wish to put my resolution to the torture, bless me with your company; that is, providing your health and other circumstances favors my wishes.[32]

On the day Greene wrote that letter, March 30, 1777, Caty's health and circumstances did not favor his wishes for a New Jersey visit. Unbeknownst to Greene, she had delivered their second baby some time around March 14, this time a girl. Greene got the news on April 8, when he wrote to Caty:

I was most agreeably surprisd by a letter from brother Kitt with an account of your being in Bed. Thank God for your safe delivery. I read the letter with a trembling hand. Some supersticious fears had been hovering round me for some time that something would happen to you. What gave rise to this troublesome train of visitants I cannot tell unless it was the extream anxiety I felt for you in your critical situation. Heaven be praisd for this second pledge of conjugal affection. When I shall see the poor little beggar God only knows.[33]

Greene wrote from comfortable quarters, something he rarely enjoyed throughout the eight years of fighting in the American Revolution. He stayed at the Basking Ridge estate of William Alexander, a fellow major general who preferred to be called "Lord Stirling." Alexander laid claim to being an English earl of Stirling, though England never recognized that claim.

Alexander married a woman named Sarah who hailed from one of New York's most patrician families, the Livingstons. The couple poured so much into their country estate at Basking Ridge that, with its fruit orchards and deer parks, it later bankrupted the family. But while Greene stayed there in the spring of 1777, it was a nice place; for companions he had three young ladies, the daughters of Alexander and Livingston. "Their manners are soft and exaggerated," he wrote to Caty. "They wish much to see you here, and I wish so too. . . . Pray my dear are you determined to Suckle your baby or not? On that depends your liberty."

While Greene was faring well in Basking Ridge, Caty was miserably off at the Greene family homestead on Potowomut. Even if she was not determined to nurse their baby she was not at liberty to leave; she was seriously ill.

Word of Caty's illness filtered back to Basking Ridge, but Greene could not learn any of the particulars for weeks. Greene's brother, Jacob (who capitalized nearly every word he wrote), provided this eighteenth-century diagnosis:

I . . . Was Much Mortified To Find Caty Poorly With A Soar Brest. If thiss Misfortune Had Not Befell Her She Would Have Been out in four Weaks. She Was A Little Two Much In A Hury in Drying away Her Milk, Did Not Have Her Breast Sufficiently Drawn, which Occasioned Her Milk to Cake In Her Breast But Happily She is Likely To Get Well Soon Without Her Breast Breaking Which is Contrary To All the old Womens Expectations And of Her own Likewise. This Misfortune Will Protract Her Intended Journey To The Camp A Considerable Time.[34]

It would be months before Caty could travel; Greene wrote to commiserate with her ("My dear creature, my Heart mourns the Absence of its counterpart"), then turned his thoughts to their new baby: "I am happy to hear you have such a fine daughter. As to her name I must beg to be excused from giveing her any name: that falls more immediately under your province. Mrs. Washingtons Christian name is Martha. I shall have no objection to that or any other name you think proper to give her."[35]

Caty settled on the name Martha Washington Greene, baby sister to George Washington Greene.

❧   ❧

John Adams called 1777 "The year of the hangman" because the three 7s evoked images of the gallows. Throughout the summer of that year, Greene and General Washington were constantly baffled by British troop movements. The British commander in chief, Sir William Howe, had an embarrassment of riches under his command: 16,000 troops in and around New York City; 8,500 troops under General John Burgoyne up in Quebec, waiting to spill down the Hudson River; and 6,000 troops under General Richard Prescott in Newport—in all more than 30,000 men.

With barely 7,000 soldiers fit for duty at Morristown, and another 2,500 holding Fort Ticonderoga on Lake Champlain, the Americans could not press an offensive; they had to react to whatever Lord Howe decided to do from his New York headquarters, where he carried on a highly publicized dalliance with a blonde, married beauty named Elizabeth Loring. Her husband, Joshua, tolerated the arrangement in exchange for the post of commissary of prisoners, a lucrative sinecure and something of a cruel joke; the prisoners received little from the commissary department and 11,000 died of disease.

Waiting for Howe to make his move drove Greene to distraction. His cluelessness about British troop movements was evident when he wrote Caty in early May:

> By some late Accounts from England we learn that Boston is to be attackt.
> The troops continueing so long at Rhode Island seems to favor the opinion.

General How[e] *still threatens Philadelphia. If he attempts it, it will be a bloody march. It is said* [General] *Carlton is crossing the Lakes* [Champlain and George]. *If that be true General How must be bound up the North River, notwithstanding all his Parade for the Southward.*[36]

With a wife and two children living on Narragansett Bay, just a dozen miles from British-occupied Newport, Greene's attention often turned toward those 6,000 troops at Newport.

Rhode Islanders were among the most rebellious people in the former British colonies, and they were livid that 6,000 British soldiers were able to occupy their state without serious challenge. That spring, the state's ornery General Assembly declared it a disgrace that no attack "hath, as yet, been made against the enemy." The assembly then set bounties on the capture of British soldiers, from $20 for a private to $1,000 for a general.[37] There was one man from Warren, a twenty-nine-year-old militia captain named William Barton, who opted to go after the big prize.

On July 9, 1777, Barton led a party of thirty-eight men on a stealthy, night-time row beneath the cannons of warships surrounding Newport. Once on the island they stole past sentries, kicked in a door, and captured Gen. Richard Prescott, commander of all British and Hessian troops on the island.

Even British Lt. Frederick Mackenzie, who kept a meticulous diary during the Newport occupation, gave grudging respect to Barton and his men for pulling off the capture: "It is certainly a most extraordinary circumstance, that a General Commanding a body of 4,000 men, encamped on an Island surrounded by a Squadron of Ships of War, should be carried off from his quarters in the night by a small party of the Enemy from without, & without a Shot being fired."[38]

Within a week, news of General Prescott's capture traveled on horseback from Providence to New Jersey, where Nathanael Greene had been reunited with his wife. Caty had left their two babies in Rhode Island with Greene's brother, Jacob, and had ridden a rickety coach to Greene's camp in New Jersey. Here she lodged at the elegant country house of Abraham Lott, a wealthy New York merchant who fled to his estate before the British invasion. "You may learn musick and French, too, there,"[39] Greene had told Caty while enticing her to move in there.

"Col. [William] Livingston has doubtless informd you of Lt Col Bartons noble exploit in captivating Major General Prescot, one of the boldest attempts of the War,"[40] Greene wrote from camp to his wife.

Now that they had Prescott, the Americans had a bargaining chip to win the release of their most highly ranked prisoner of war, the eccentric Gen. Charles Lee.

During his time as a British captive, General Lee proved to be a most accommodating guest. Over dinner with British officers Lee offered a critique of their campaign so far, observing that they if they had pressed their advantage in the Battle of White Plains they could have ended the war there. Lee crossed the line from observer to traitor when he advised the Howe brothers, Gen. William Howe and Adm. Richard Howe, on the best way to defeat Washington's troops: capture Philadelphia and occupy Maryland, thus cutting off the rich supply state of Virginia from the rebellious colonies in the north.[41] Within two months "not a spark of this desolating war" would burn "unextinguished in any part of this continent."

Whether the Howe brothers acted on Lee's advice is debatable, but late in the summer of 1777 they embarked 18,000 troops on 260 ships for an amphibious assault of Philadelphia. After a month at sea the British fleet dropped anchor at the head of the Chesapeake Bay on August 25. The long journey in summer heat had been tough on man and beast alike; 5,000 of Howe's men arrived too sick to fight, and 300 artillery horses had died or been tossed sick into the sea. The troops disembarked at a settlement called Head of Elk, Maryland, sixty miles south of the target city, Philadelphia.

The day after the fleet dropped anchor generals Nathanael Greene, George Washington, and their new teenage protégé, the Marquis de Lafayette, stood on a hill outside Head of Elk, spying on the British forces flocking ashore in their red coats.

❦ ❧

Marie Joseph Paul Yves Roch Gilbert du Motier, Marquis de Lafayette, Lafayette for short, sailed to this country from France, arriving in South Carolina in June 1777, a teenage nobleman with romantic ideals of revolution and revenge. His father, a colonel of the French grenadiers, had been killed by a British ball at Minden in the Seven Years War. His mother had died when he was thirteen; his grandfather died a few weeks later, leaving the young Marquis a wealthy orphan. At sixteen he married a woman as rich as himself.

Lafayette had sailed to America in hopes that its Congress would grant him an officer's commission; his request for a commission could not have come at a worse time. Philippe Tronson du Coudray, a French Army engineer who also had connections, had recently been promised a commission as major general in charge of the American artillery—an appointment that would make him superior to Greene's friend, Henry Knox.

At first, du Coudray's promised appointment only mildly irritated Greene; he felt that Knox had done a good job building the American artillery from scratch, and that if du Coudray had to be made a major general it should be in another department. But shortly after Lafayette's arrival, Greene learned that du Coudray's commission had been back-dated to the previous summer, so that du Coudray held seniority over Greene.

Greene was livid. He, Knox, and another major general who had been out-ranked, John Sullivan, each sent letters to Congress threatening to resign if it followed through on the promise to du Coudray. Congressmen then became angry at the American generals, accusing them of militarily attempting to usurp powers vested in the civil government. Congress passed a resolution calling for the three generals to apologize or resign, which they promptly ignored. On a more personal level, John Adams, who had enjoyed a warm friendship with Greene, wrote that if Greene could not apologize for his effrontery, he "ought to leave the service," thus ending correspondence between the erstwhile friends.

Congress compromised by giving du Coudray a major general's commission, but he was not given charge of the artillery or any line command, nor was his appointment back-dated.[42]

When Lafayette appeared before them in the summer of 1777, Congress and the Army had had their fill of French noblemen seeking commissions as high-ranking officers. But Lafayette was different. Even though he spoke almost no English, his sincerity and affability made a good impression on General Washington. In recommending Lafayette for a Congressional commission, Washington called him "sensible, discrete in his manners" and noted that he was trying hard to learn English.[43]

Greene met Lafayette on August 8, 1777, at an army camp outside Philadelphia; he found the young nobleman "a most sweet temperd young gentleman."[44]

Washington, Greene, and Lafayette—accompanied by "a large body of horse" for protection—split off from the rest of the army on August 26, 1777, in order to spy on the British coming ashore at the head of the Chesapeake. They rode within a few miles of General Howe's troops, peering down from Grey's Hill at the soldiers disembarking from long boats. A storm drove the trio, soaking wet, into a farmhouse owned by a family loyal to the British crown; there they spent an uneasy night, fearing that a tip to General Howe on the location of three high-ranking officers might lead to their capture. They rode off at dawn to join the main part of the army at Wilmington, Delaware, where Washington steeled to meet the British head-on when they marched toward Philadelphia.[45]

Strategically, Philadelphia was not that important to the defense of the United States; symbolically, it was critical. Philadelphia was, in 1777, America's biggest city, with a working waterfront and 30,000 people; it was also the most prosperous. Here the Continental Congress met in the State House, a two-story building of red brick capped with a bell tower.

When 13,000 British troops began their march toward Philadelphia on September 8, an understandable panic spread. "Here are some of the most distressing scenes immaginable," Greene wrote his wife on September 10 from a camp on the Brandywine River:

> *The Inhabitants generally desert their houses, furniture moveing, Cattle driving and women and children traveling off on foot. The country all resounds with the cries of the people. . . .*
>
> *I am exceedingly fatigued. I was on Horse back for upwards of thirty hours and never closd my Eyes for near forty. Last night I was in hopes of a good nights rest, but a dusty bed gave me Astma and I had very little sleep the whole night, but little as it was I feel finely refreshd this morning.*[46]

In that same letter, Greene told Caty: "A general action must take place in a few days." His timing was off; the action ensued the following day with the Battle of Brandywine.

❧   ❧

On September 11, 1777, the time came for Gen. George Washington to make his stand. With Gen. William Howe leading 13,000 troops toward

Philadelphia, the country's de facto capital, Washington had no choice but to defend America's biggest city.

To make his defense, Washington chose the ground behind Brandywine Creek at Chadd's Ford, Pennsylvania. The hills on each side were a patchwork of forest and farm, sloping steeply to crests two hundred feet above his camp.

Howe pitched his encampment at Kennett Square, six miles south. At 4 a.m. his men began moving toward the American lines, manned by 11,000 troops, six miles away. With nearly 25,000 men poised for battle, Brandywine shaped up to be one of the biggest fights of the American Revolution.

Howe had a plan that would make him look either very smart, or very foolish. He split his army in two unequal parts. He put the smaller unit of about 5,000 men under the command the Baron Wilhelm von Knyphausen and sent them marching east directly toward Washington's larger army at Chadd's Ford.

Howe and General Charles Cornwallis led the main group of 8,000 north to Jeffrie's Ford, where they hoped to cross the Brandywine, then surprise Washington from behind while he fought Knyphausen at his front. The plan held a major risk: If Washington realized that the army sent to attack his front was just a ruse to cover the larger army's flanking movement, he could annihilate that smaller army, then roll up Howe's 8,000 men. This is what military strategists refer to as a "defeat in detail."

The day dawned with a fog that dissipated beneath the sun, leaving oppressive humidity and heat. By 10:30 a.m. Gen. Wilhelm von Knyphausen was in position to attack Washington's front at Chadd's Ford. From high woods on both sides of the Brandywine the artillery banged its thunderous duet.

At headquarters in a Quaker's house a mile behind the lines, Washington waited for the British charge. None came, and he began to suspect that the artillery duel was just a feint to cover a march of the main army. Between 10 and 11 a.m. word came down the Great Valley Road, well west of the action, that "A large body of the enemy" had been seen marching north through that morning's fog.[47] Washington decided to go on the offensive: He would attack and destroy the smaller army before him, and Nathanael Greene would lead the charge.

Greene prepared to spur his horse across Brandywine Creek, a chest-deep river, into the teeth of the British artillery dueling with American artillery roaring from his rear. He led a division—about 1,300 men—of America's best soldiers, comprised mostly of veteran troops from Virginia. Before Greene could get his advance troops across the river, Washington cancelled Greene's attack after hearing from Gen. John Sullivan, stationed up on Brinton's Ford, that there were no British troops up in his quarter. That meant that the whole of the British forces must be marching straight toward Washington, and he could not afford to splinter his own forces for an offensive.

Unfortunately for the American cause, Sullivan's information was wrong. Most of the British army was up in his area, and had in fact marched beyond his position, putting them in place to attack him from his rear. Washington was now in the jaws of a trap: Cornwallis was marching down on him from the rear, while Hessian Gen. William Von Knyphausen was setting up a strong artillery park on hills across the Brandywine in his front.

Now Washington gave Greene's crack division a different mission: Instead of spearheading an attack, they would stay out of the action as a reserve force, ready to rush wherever the army might need them most.

After 4 p.m., the British sprung their trap. From headquarters Greene and Washington heard the thunder of cannon rolling to the north. This firing was the signal for Knyphausen to splash his five thousand troops across the Brandywine to assault Washington's front. Washington dashed off a hurried note to Congress back in Philadelphia, twenty miles away: "At half after 4 o'clock, the enemy attacked General Sullivan at the ford next above this, and the action has been very violent ever since. It still continues. A very severe cannonade has began here too, and I suppose we shall have a very hot evening."[48]

Around 5:30 p.m., with a hot sun sinking low into the September sky, Washington ordered Greene to march his division on the "quickest step" to aide Sullivan's men, a march of four miles. Washington also left the fighting at Chadd's Ford by horse to see what Sullivan was up against.

On reaching the fighting, Washington saw Sullivan's troops had formed along the face of the high ground known as Plowed Hill. The American line looked pitifully small against the enemy troops flanking it. Sullivan fielded about three thousand troops to fight a British army of eight thousand. As the British advanced, the left side of Sullivan's line began to break and run. Washington and Lafayette rode hard to try and rally the troops, and as they tried to turn their men to face the enemy, Lafayette took a bullet in the thigh.

Almost miraculously, a brigade of Nathanael Greene's division arrived right on Washington's heels. In summer-like heat Greene had somehow managed to march a brigade of Virginians, with each man bearing the weight of packs, bullets, and a ten-pound musket, nearly four miles in forty-five minutes. As Sullivan's troops ran, Greene's entire division formed a line to cover their retreat.

A British officer described the battle at Plowed Hill as "a most infernal fire of cannon and musquetry. . . . The balls plowing up the ground. The trees crackling over one's head. The branches riven by the artillery. The leaves falling as in autumn" dislodged by the grape shot.[49]

At Chadd's Ford the fighting was also fierce: "the [American] battery playing upon us with grapeshot . . . did much execution," wrote an officer with the Queen's Rangers, which waded through the Brandywine to attack. "The water took us up to our breasts and was much stained with blood."[50] But the Queen's Rangers prevailed, driving the Americans before them on the road toward Philadelphia.

But Greene's division never broke. From a crossroads his men managed to hold off the British and Hessian forces, the main body of troops coming down from Birmingham Meeting House and Knyphausen's men streaming east from Chadd's Ford. Finally darkness fell, mercifully ending the fighting for that day.

A local Quaker, Joseph Townsend, walked over the battlefield on Plowed Hill and reported that the scene "was awful to behold—such a number of fellow beings lying together severely wounded and some mortally."[51] Doors to a meetinghouse were torn off and pressed into service as stretchers to carry the wounded inside, where surgeons amputated limbs with no anesthetic stronger than brandy.

Washington never did tally his losses for that day, but they were significant. General Howe likely overestimated the American loss at 300 killed, 600 wounded, and 400 captured, a loss of 1,300 men. Howe's own loss stood at 89 killed, 488 wounded, and 6 missing.

Although they lost the ground, many of their cannons, and more than twice as many men as their enemy, the Americans did not see the Battle of Brandywine as a rout. In his first orders issued after the battle, Nathanael Greene wrote: "The Genl. Has the pleasure to Inform the troops, that notwithstanding we gave the Enemy the ground, the purchase has been at much blood."[52]

Writing about the Battle of Brandywine many months later, Greene was understandably immodest in his assessment of his own conduct that day. "I think both the general and the public were as much indebted to me for saving the army from ruin as they ever have been to any one officer in the course of the war."[53]

Greene was entitled to crow. At Fort Washington he had lost an army. At the Brandywine, he saved one.

While Washington was being knocked from pillar to post in Pennsylvania, the American Army in the north was faring far better. On Sept. 28, 1777, word filtered into Washington's camp that the Americans had beaten British Gen. John "Gentleman Johnny" Burgoyne outside Saratoga, New York. Unlike many rumors, this one turned out to be true: American forces had driven the British from the field outside Saratoga, killing, wounding, and capturing six hundred enemy troops while losing less than three hundred. This marked the second triumph of the northern army in a month—they had also killed two hundred Hessians near Bennington in what is now Vermont—and Washington ordered a celebratory thirteen-gun salute followed by a gill of rum per man. A gill measured four ounces; for its capacity to numb the pain of hard living, rum was a staple good for an eighteenth-century army camp. And on this day, the American troops got a good dose of it.

Washington openly envied the successes to the north, and lusted for a victory of his own. He was spoiling for a fight. On the same day that he ordered the thirteen-gun salute and a gill of rum for all, he again called a council of war to advise on whether he should order an attack on Germantown, a village of fieldstone houses five miles from British-occupied Philadelphia.

General Howe then camped most of his army in Germantown, about 12,000 men. Even with reinforcements from New York, New Jersey, and Maryland, the Americans could only muster about 11,000 men for an attack, 1,000 less than the British had; Nathanael Greene did not like those odds. He joined the majority of officers in telling Washington that the time was not yet ripe for an attack.[54]

Then things changed.

Communication between military encampments was always a risky business. Mounted couriers passing along wooded roads were often challenged by armed guards, and if they did not know the day's password they faced serious trouble. On October 2, 1777, the Americans intercepted two letters sent by British couriers; from these Gen. George Washington learned that the large British encampment at Germantown had just shrunk by 3,000 men. Gen. William Howe had peeled off those men from his main encampment of 12,000 and sent them across the Delaware to tackle an American fort at Billingsport, New Jersey.

Washington called another council of war to tell his officers: Howe's camp at Germantown was now down to 9,000 men; the Americans outside Germantown numbered 11,000. Did the generals now favor an attack? This time Greene joined every other general in voting yes.[55]

In a house atop a hill some fifteen miles from Germantown, the American officers hatched an elaborate plan. To take Germantown they would march 11,000 amateur soldiers, many of them barefoot, more than fifteen miles, at night, to attack 9,000 well-armed professionals neatly arrayed in a three-mile-wide front. Adding to the audacity of the plan was its complexity—Washington would split his troops into four "wings" that were supposed to march through the dark and arrive at Germantown simultaneously for the pre-dawn attack.

Before putting his troops on the march, Washington issued a rousing general order, without masking his jealousy over General Gates's recent triumph at Saratoga: "The main American Army will not suffer itself to be out done by their northern Brethren," Washington wrote. Covet! My Countrymen, and fellow soldiers! Covet! A share of the glory due to heroic deeds! . . .

"Our dearest rights, our dearest friends, and our own lives, honor, and glory and even shame, urge us to fight. And My fellow Soldiers! when an opportunity presents, be firm, be brave; shew yourselves men, and victory is yours."[56]

Greene's division formed on the east or left side of Washington's army. Its men had the farthest distance to march—seventeen miles one way—so they moved first, pulling out of camp at 7 p.m. into the darkness of October 3, 1777.

Greene had with him some 5,000 men, by far the biggest wing of the four-pronged attack. They got lost. The local man hired to guide them on a back route to Germantown could not find his way through the dark. When he finally did hit on the right route, Greene moved his men at "quickest step," making up about thirty minutes of lost time. Still, he arrived on the field a good hour after sunrise, just a half-hour late. Smaller wings on the extreme left and extreme right never made it to the field at all, leaving all of the early fighting to the troops under New Hampshire's Gen. John Sullivan.

Sullivan's men marched straight down the Germantown Pike toward the heart of the village, a two-mile stretch of widely spaced fieldstone houses; the fighting began at daybreak, and no sooner than it began a fog rolled over the village. Smoke from the muskets thickened the fog till men could see no more than thirty yards. At first this was good for the American attackers as it cloaked them from the British lined up behind rail fences waiting to cut them down as they advanced along the pike and through mature fields of buckwheat. What the British could not see they could not shoot; Sullivan's men kept coming through the fog, driving the British light infantry right out of their camp. Private Joseph Plumb Martin, who was then sixteen years old, observed in his memoirs: "They left their kettles, in which they were cooking their breakfasts, on the fires, and some of their garments were lying on the ground, which the owners had not time to put on."[57]

About 120 men from the 40th British Regiment fled from camp and into a solid brick house recently abandoned by Judge Benjamin Chew. Henry Knox, chief artillery officer, had done a lot of reading about military theory, and he knew that it was bad form to leave an armed "castle" in your rear.[58] He prevailed upon Washington to train the artillery on the thick walls of the Chew House.

For an hour or more Knox blasted away; the walls were impregnable to the three- and six-pound balls Knox fired. All the while the troops within trained their muskets on the Americans clustered outside. Fifty-three Americans fell dead on the spot.

As Greene's men arrived late through the fog to the field they could hear the commotion of cannon and musketry at the Chew House. Greene's westernmost troops were commanded by Gen. Adam Stephen, a man of dubious character who had once been seen "in open view of all the soldiers very drunk taking snuff out of the Boxes of strumpets."[59] Stephen was often drunk and had been drinking that night; without consulting Greene, Stephen marched his men toward the commotion at the Chew House.

Gen. Anthony Wayne also heard Knox's firing on the Chew House; and though his troops had advanced into Germantown, he turned them around to see what the blasting was all about. While marching back toward the Chew House, Wayne's men ran into the drunken Stephen's men advancing on it, and through the literal fog of war they began firing on each other. Knox's men were being picked off by sharpshooters barricaded in the Chew House; American troops under Wayne and Stephen were shooting at each other with great effect; Sullivan's most advanced troops called out that their ammunition was almost gone. Howe's troops heard the desperate cries for ammunition. Buoyed by the knowledge that their enemy was low on bullets, the British rallied; the Americans panicked, running past their officers along the Germantown Pike. They had a long march ahead of them. Washington gathered his fleeing troops and marched them twenty miles, five miles farther north than they had been that morning, a round trip of thirty-five miles. Greene may have had this retreat in mind when he wrote to his brother, Christopher: "If you could see a defeat, follow a long and tedious nights march, hear the screams of the wounded that are going of[f] the field, see the labour and difficulty of getting them off, have to march forty miles without victuals or sleep, you would hardly think your sufferings worth naming."[60]

Already the Army's supply systems had begun breaking down toward their utter failure that winter at Valley Forge, so the retreating troops had at best broken shoes, worn blankets, and no food.

After the battle, while riding up the Perkiomen Creek on a "dreary night," Greene and Adjutant Gen. Timothy Pickering stopped to let their horses drink. Around this time Greene's blue and buff uniform was in need of replacement: he had lost his brass pistol, rode on a badly worn saddle, and had but one spur for his two boots. That day he'd had a lock of his hair shot off by a musket ball.[61]

As the horses drank, Pickering, a Harvard-trained lawyer who'd argued against trying to storm the Chew House, said: "General Greene, before I came to the Army, I entertained an exalted opinion of General Washington's military talents, but I have since seen nothing to enhance it."[62]

Greene replied, "Why, the general does want decision; for my part, I decide in a moment."

Washington settled his troops at Pawling's Mill, where he counted losses of 1,111 men: 152 killed, 521 wounded, and 438 captured. The British lost half that many, 537 killed and wounded, and they held the field at Germantown, clearly a victory for them.

Yet, as evidenced by Greene's written orders after the battle, the Americans took this loss as a moral victory.[63] They had attacked the British and felt, for the first time since Greene's initial taste of combat on Harlem Heights, the momentary thrill of seeing the redcoats run.

❧   ☙

After two months of marching and fierce fighting at Brandywine and Germantown, the British now held Philadelphia, but the Americans held the water approaches to it—the Delaware and the Schuylkill Rivers. If the British could not soon evict the Americans from two forts controlling the Delaware then they would have to quit the city. As it was troops and civilians in the city were miserably off because they could not ship in supplies; the city had no flour and only poor beef. With control of the rivers, Washington had reasonable hopes of starving the British out.

The Rhode Island regiments that fought well at Trenton and Princeton were now marching south from Peekskill, New York, where they'd been stationed to prevent British forces from pushing down the Hudson. On October 7, 1777 Washington sent orders to the advancing Rhode Islanders: As soon as possible they were "to throw themselves into the fort at Red Bank upon the Jersey shore."

The fort at Red Bank, Fort Mercer, was a large earthwork of fourteen cannon, barracks, and a few outbuildings built on the Jersey side of the Delaware River. Directly across from it, on Mud Island, stood Fort Mifflin. Together these two forts, built to blast British shipping, represented Washington's last hope of driving the British out of Philadelphia. With winter coming, British Gen. William Howe could wait no longer to clear the Delaware of the American forts. A Hessian officer, Carl Emil Kurt von Donop, practically begged for the assignment of attacking the fort. Donop's Hessians had been humiliated in the Christmas day attack on Trenton; he wanted revenge.

On October 22, 1777 Donop led four battalions of Hessian veterans, some two thousand in all, on a march toward Fort Mercer. Many of Nathanael Greene's closest friends were in that fort, including his young confidant, Samuel Ward Jr., now a veteran of the Canadian campaign. All were under the command of Col. Christopher Greene, Nathanael Greene's third cousin. Colonel Greene strolled along the top of the fort's earthen walls, peering through his pocket spyglass at a detachment of twelve hundred Hessians marching on his four hundred men. He took note of the enemy's elaborate uniforms.

"Fire low men," he said; "they have a broad belt just above their hips—aim at that."[64]

Around 1 p.m., the Hessians sent a demand for surrender; Colonel Greene refused it, and twelve Hessian cannons opened fire from the edge of nearby woods.

"It made the gravel and dust fly from the top of our fort, and took off all the heads that happened to be in the way," recalled Capt. Stephen Olney. "They then instantly advanced in two solid columns."[65]

Colonel Greene had drawn his men into the fort's core, leaving the first trenches unmanned. When the Hessians found these trenches empty they thought the Americans had abandoned them in retreat. They broke into a trot, believing they were chasing defeated, demoralized men. When they were at the walls, the waiting Rhode Islanders opened fire, aiming at the enemy's wide belts. The shot cut down the advancing troops.

The Hessians regrouped and stormed the fort again; again they were dropped by heavy fire at close range. After forty minutes of disastrous assaults the Hessians retreated, their ranks thinned by more than 400: 50 captured, 153 dead, 200 wounded, many fatally, including Commander Donop. Legend has it that from his deathbed Donop said, "I die a victim of my ambition, and of the Avarice of my sovereign." Though this sounds suspiciously like the work of propagandists, Greene, who was with Donop near his death, noted, "he lamented before his death, his folly in being concerned in the American war."[66]

The Rhode Islanders that day lost fourteen killed and twenty-three wounded.

Adding to the rout, a British ship of sixty-four guns sent to bomb the fort grounded in the Delaware; Americans across the river fired hot cannon shot at it, setting the ship afire. Its powder magazine exploded with a boom heard for thirty miles. The British themselves torched a second ship that had run aground for a total loss of two ships and four hundred men.

Ebenezer David, a chaplain to the Rhode Island regiments, wrote: "It is the Opinion of Gen. Green[e] who was a Spectator from the Pensilvania shore that there never was more noble defence in America."[67]

In his memoirs of the war, Private Joseph Plumb Martin wrote that at Red Bank "brave Rhode-Island Yankees . . . fought as brilliant an action as was fought during the revolutionary war, considering the numbers engaged, Bunker-Hill notwithstanding. . . . But why it has not been more noticed by the historians of these times I cannot tell."[68]

After Red Bank, the Howe brothers—Gen. William Howe and Adm. Richard Howe—decided to bring all of their power to bear on clearing the American presence from the Delaware River. With Nathanael Greene skulking about dangerously close to their works to gather intelligence, the British fortified an island with nearly three dozen cannon. On November 10 they opened a barrage on Fort Mifflin, across the river from the stubborn Rhode Island regiments ensconced at Red Bank.

On November 14, 1777, following four days of bombardment, Greene reported to Washington: "The flag was [still] flying at Fort Mifflin at sunset this evening."[69]

Now it was a waiting game: Which would break first, the forts or the British will to remain in a besieged city?

Greene wrote Washington: "The enemy are greatly discouraged by the forts holding out so long and it is the general opinion of the best of the citizens that the enemy will evacuate the city if the forts hold out until the middle of next week."[70]

To keep the forts from holding out, Admiral Howe brought up a fleet of six 64-gun ships; a 36-gun frigate; a 24-gun ship, plus a sloop and galley of 6 guns each. Ashore he had six batteries of six guns each, and a bomb battery of three mortars. After sunset on the fourteenth, they all opened fire on little Mud Island.

Private Martin, who had moved into Fort Mifflin, recalled: "The enemy's shot cut us up; I saw five artillerists belonging to one gun, cut down by a single shot, and I saw men who were stooping to be protected by the works, but not stooping low enough, split like fish to be broiled."[71]

Fort Mifflin fell. Now the Howe brothers could focus all of their naval and land forces on Col. Christopher Greene and his Rhode Islanders in Fort Mercer. They sent Lord Cornwallis with nearly five thousand troops to march on the five hundred Rhode Islanders at Red Bank.

As the British advanced, Colonel Greene and Gen. James Varnum ordered men to strip the fort of any guns, balls, and food that they could carry off; then, when the fort was empty, they blew it up. The British now controlled the Delaware and Hudson Rivers. With the campaign of 1777 coming to a close they owned the cities of Philadelphia, New York, and Newport.

With winter coming on Howe sent to New York for his mistress, Mrs. Elizabeth Loring. Howe made comfortable quarters for Mrs. Loring, himself, and his troops in Philadelphia; Washington's troops, barefoot, half of them without breeches, the whole near starvation, marched off to find winter quarters.

FOUR

Sore with the Hardships

Valley Forge to Morristown

On December 10, 1777, eleven thousand men—some sick, all tired, hungry, wearing shredded clothes—marched out of an army camp at Whitemarsh, Pennsylvania, destination unknown. Their general, George Washington, had little idea of where he would house them for the winter, or how he would feed and clothe them until spring.

"The army was now not only starved but naked," recalled one of his men, Private Joseph Plumb Martin, who had just turned seventeen; "the greatest part were not only shirtless and barefoot, but destitute of all other clothing, especially blankets."

Before marching from camp, Martin scavenged a "small piece of raw cowhide and made myself a pair of moccasins, which kept my feet (while they lasted) from the frozen ground, although, as I well remember, the hard edges so galled my ancles, while on a march, that it was with much difficulty and pain that I could wear them afterwards but the only alternative I had . . . was to go barefoot, as hundreds of my companions had to, till they might be tracked by their blood upon the rough frozen ground."[1]

They arrived in a gloomy valley called the Gulph; Nathanael Greene had advised Washington against coming here, but he'd been outvoted.[2] Their first night in the Gulph it snowed, a few inches of wet slush. The army had left its tents on the eastern side of the Schuylkill, so they lay in the snow, many barefoot and without blankets.[3] From here they pushed on through a chill rain into the Valley Forge.

They reached the valley less than a week before Christmas. By spring 2,500 of them would be dead of exposure or disease, a death rate of more than 20 percent.[4] Martin recalled in his memoirs: "We arrived at the Valley Falls in the evening; it was dark; there was no water to be found, and I was perishing with thirst. . . . fatigue and thirst, joined with hunger, almost made me desperate. . . . I am not writing fiction, all are sobering realities."[5]

There had been something like a village in the valley—a few fieldstone houses clustered near Isaac Potts's iron forge. The American army had kept a supply depot here until after the battle at Brandywine, when victorious British troops marched out and captured the supplies—3,800 barrels of flour, 25 barrels of horseshoes, some kettles. The British also destroyed the forge.

Even Washington, who'd chosen the winter encampment, called Valley Forge "a dreary kind of place and uncomfortably provided."[6] Despite the dismal nature of the encampment, Washington's wife, Martha, traded in her palatial digs at Mount Vernon and came to the valley to join her husband.

Caty Greene also came to camp from the estate of Abraham Lott, where she'd lived since summer; she'd left their infant son George and three-month-old daughter Martha in Coventry with Jacob and his wife.

The camp at Valley Forge was pitched on a two-mile-wide wooded slope rising from the western banks of the Schuylkill to a peak called, ironically, Mount Joy. The only commodity this dreary land provided was trees, and Washington put them to use. He divided his men into teams of twelve with orders for each team to build its own log hut. He specified the dimensions—14 feet long, 16 feet wide, 6½ feet high—just 18 square feet per man. The team that built its hut "in the quickest and most workmanlike manner" would win a $10 bonus.

The army's diet was mostly "fire cake"—a paste of flour and water cooked on the hot rocks of open fires—not much food to fuel the hard work of chopping trees, sawing off branches, hauling logs, and chinking them together with clay. A month of chopping and sawing passed before every man had moved from tent to hut. This log-hut village of less than 11,000 covered two miles of the valley.

Moving into dark huts with leaky roofs did little to alleviate the misery of life in the Valley Forge. "Our Troops are naked, we have been upon the eve of starving and the army of mutinying," Greene wrote on January 27, 1778 to the Scottish-born Gen. Alexander McDougall. Though McDougall was a decade older than Greene, the two were good friends, and Greene shared more information about camp hardships than he would have with someone less familiar. "Our horses are dying by dozens every day for the want of Forage, and the men getting sickly in their Hutts for the want of acids and Soap to clean themselves."[7]

Then came the snow: For two days in early February it fell, filling the valley so that no wagons could move, stopping what little food deliveries there'd been. Men went without meat; then they went without bread; many went day after day with no food at all.

Days after the snowstorm, Col. William von Cortlandt complained that twenty of his men had no pants: "they are obliged to take their blankets to cover their nakedness," as many had "no shirt, stocking, or shoe." Even men with clothes would soon "be laid up, as the poor fellows are obliged to fetch wood and water on their backs half a mile with bare legs in snow or mud."[8]

The smoke of a thousand campfires hovered over a village of squalid huts; herds of skeletal horses nuzzled the muddy snow in vain; horse carcasses rotted in the snow; men, too, died by the hundreds. To deal with this crisis, Washington turned to Nathanael Greene. In a direct order delivered to Greene on February 12, 1778 Washington wrote: "it is of the utmost Consequence that the Horses Cattle Sheep and Provender within Fifteen or Twenty miles" be taken from their civilian owners "to supply the present Emergencies of the American Army."

Washington always took great pains to avoid impressing goods from civilians near his camp, for he knew that even those who supported American independence would turn against the cause if the army stole their food, forage, and horses. Even in this order, he first blamed the need for impressments on the possibility that the British were planning to raid the country, so the Americans might as well beat them to it; he also ordered Greene to make sure that locals were given IOUs for anything taken from them. In his impressments order he wrote Greene: "I do therefore authorize, impower, and Command you forwith to take, carry off and secure all such Horses as are suitable for Cavalry or for Draft and all Cattle and Sheep fit for Slaughter."[9]

Like Washington, Greene had been a stickler for treating civilians fairly; but he zealously carried out these orders for impressments. By the next day he'd ridden to Springfield Meeting House, where he would "collect all the cattle carriages &c &c" before moving the next day to Edwards Tavern for the same purpose. From Springfield he wrote his aide-de-camp, Col. Clement Biddle, that to prevent people from complaining that their horses and cattle would starve if soldiers took all their oats and hay, they also had to take all their horses and cattle. Greene wrote: "You must forage the Country naked."[10]

Starving soldiers swarming on isolated farmhouses caused some heartbreaking scenes. "The Inhabitants cry out and beset me from all quarters," Greene wrote Washington, "but like Pharoh I harden my heart."[11]

Five days of foraging yielded "near fifty Head" of cattle that Greene sent to the starving at Valley Forge; from New Jersey, Gen. Anthony Wayne drove beeves across the Delaware at Coryell's Ferry and then down into the valley, enough meat on the hoof to feed the troops for several days; Colonel Biddle reported he had forty wagons loaded with forage headed for camp.

Although he'd pledged to harden his heart to pleas for leniency, Greene did cave in to a petition from one Nathan Sellers, who begged for the return of his pregnant mare for she "is all of the Horse Kind" he owned.[12]

After foraging for nearly two weeks, a "very disagreeable" business, Greene returned to Valley Forge. From camp, Greene wrote Henry Knox in Boston:

The troops are getting naked, and they were seven days without meat and several days without bread. . . . The seventh day they came before their superior officers and told their sufferings in as respectful terms as if they had been humble petitioners for special favors; they added that it would be impossible to continue in Camp any longer without support. Happily relief arrivd from the little collections I had made and some others, and prevented the Army from disbanding. We are still in danger of starveing; the Commisary department is in a most wretched condition; the Quarter Masters, in a worse. Hundreds and Hundreds of our horses have actually starved to death.[13]

As if Washington and Greene did not have enough to worry about in a smoky valley with huts full of diseased, dying men and hundreds of horses turning skeletal, they also fretted about an internal coup against them. The threat to Washington's leadership—or what he and Greene perceived to be a threat—began the previous October, with what should have been good news: America's Northern Army captured Gen. John Burgoyne and all of his five thousand men in a second battle at Saratoga, New York.

The laurels for that capture fell on the head of Gen. Horatio Gates, a myopic, uninspiring leader known to his men as "Granny Gates." Greene believed that better men set the foundation for success at Saratoga and "General Gates came in just timely to reap the laurels and rewards."[14]

As the titular commander of the Northern Army, Gates got credit for flushing the British out of the upper Hudson River valley. As his army was conquering, Washington's army was floundering, losing at Brandywine, Germantown, and the Delaware River forts. Naturally there were those who felt Gates could do a better job than Washington. One of them was Major Gen. Thomas Conway, an Irish-born French officer who came over to help win the revolution. At first Washington liked him and the feeling was mutual. But after watching Washington's string of defeats, Conway wrote Gates: "What a pity there is but one Gates! But the more I see of this army, the less I think it fit for general action under its actual chiefs and actual discipline."[15]

One of Gates's aides saw that letter and mentioned it to an aide of another general; by the time Washington heard it Conway's letter had been twisted to say: "Heaven has been determined to save your Country; or a weak General and bad Councellors would have ruined it."

Washington wrote Conway a curt letter showing his annoyance with being called "weak"; Conway protested that he'd never said that. The affair might have died there, but Congress then promoted a trio of Washington's harshest critics to key posts, beginning with Gen. Thomas Mifflin—a Philadelphian who held Greene responsible for advising Washington against a strong defense of that city—who won appointment to the War Board. Mifflin successfully promoted Gates as president of that board, and Congress promoted Conway to inspector general of the army, with rank of major general, putting him in a position to oversee Washington and his staff at Valley Forge.

There may have been a "cabal" of disaffected officers who wanted to displace Washington, but the evidence is as strong that the whole affair was nothing more than vain men praising each other at Washington's expense. Nathanael Greene held no doubt of the existence of a "Conway Cabal" that had designs on deposing Washington. He wrote in confidence to General McDougall from Valley Forge:

> What will be done with Conway, I don't know. I think him a very danger-ous man in this Army; he has but small talents, great ambition, and without any uncommon spirit or enterprize, naturally of a factious make and of an intrigueing temper. . . . This gentleman is puffd off to the public as one of the greatest Generals of the Age; and that the Army is indebted to him for every judicious movement they have made; but by the bye this is done by a certain faction that is said to be forming under the auspices of General Gates and General Mifflin, to supplant his Excellency from command of the Army and get Genl Gates at the head of it.[16]

To join the War Board, Thomas Mifflin resigned from his job as quarter-master general, the person in charge of supplying an army. His resignation was a good thing, as he'd been doing a disgraceful job of running the quartermaster's department. Now in the winter of 1778, with many of its soldiers barefoot, with-out pants, and starving, the nascent nation needed a good quartermaster general. This was Congress's appointment, though Washington would have some say in the matter.

Both Congress and Washington turned their eyes toward Nathanael Greene.

Greene had proven his value to Washington both as a field general who could marshal men quickly to the right places, and as a strategist who helped plot the big picture before battles. But he was also very good at matters of supply: When Washington needed cartridges for his army at White Plains in the fall of

1776, Greene forwarded 80,000 of them;[17] when his troops were retreating across New Jersey they lived off stores strategically placed beforehand by Greene; when the men were starving at Valley Forge it was Greene who "forage[d] the country naked" to deliver fresh meat. Right now, Washington needed a quartermaster general more than he needed a good field general; both he and a committee from Congress that met at Valley Forge pressed Greene to take the job.

Greene did not want it. To Henry Knox he wrote in late February 1778: "The Committee of Congress have been urging me for several days to accept of the Q M Generals appointment; His Excellency also presses it upon me exceedingly. I hate the place, but hardly know what to do."[18]

Greene had good cause for "hating" the prospect of becoming quartermaster general. As the Committee of Congress pointed out "the Confusion of the Department, the depreciation of our Money, and the exhausted state of our Resources" combined to make this a nearly impossible job.[19] The Continental currency traded in Philadelphia that winter at one-third its face value. Only the most loyal patriot wanted to sell goods to the American Army's quartermaster when the British were paying in the hard coin of silver specie.

Yet Greene eventually relented, writing to General McDougall:

> I am appointed Q M General, and am vexed with myself for complying with the pressing importunity of the Committee and the General. They were at me Night and Day. . . .
>
> All of you will be immortallising your selves in the golden pages of History, while I am confind to a series of druggery to pave the way for it.[20]

To Washington, Greene later complained: "No body ever heard of a quarter Master in History."[21]

Once he accepted the post of quartermaster general, Nathanael Greene plunged into it.

"[T]here is not a moments time to be lost," he wrote on March 30 to Col. Clement Biddle, a quartermaster for Pennsylvania's militia; then Greene set out an ambitious plan for storing more than one million bushels of grain to feed draft horses. "Give all sorts of grain the preference to wheat," he noted. "Oats first, Corn next, Rye next, and so on."[22] The drudgery of overseeing the myriad wants of an army was offset to a great degree by his new rate of pay. For every

$100 of government money Greene spent on feeding and furnishing the army, he would get $1; this he would split three ways with his two primary assistants, Charles Petit and John Cox. Greene also retained his rank as a major general.

Greene claimed not to care about the huge pay raise that was coming his way. "I am not solicitous about the profits of the Office of QMG," he wrote to Col. James Abeel from Valley Forge. Abeel was Greene's deputy quartermaster in charge of buying the army's camp equipage. "If the publick business is but well executed, that will be all that I shall be solicitous about. . . . I wish Officers in every denomination and in every department was more attentive to the publick good and less so to their private gain."[23]

Still, Greene was not entirely unconcerned with making money—he couldn't afford to be. The company his father had left was not prosperous enough to support many growing families—his own and those of his brothers. With British warships blockading Narragansett Bay, there wasn't much business in the anchor trade.

"Money becomes more and more the Americans' object," Greene wrote Jacob from Valley Forge. "You must get rich, or you will be of no consequence."[24]

Like the Cowardly Lion of Oz, Friedrich Wilhelm Augustus von Steuben wore courage upon his chest. Von Steuben was a baron, a former Prussian officer, and a bit of a con man.

Steuben appeared one February day in Valley Forge, wearing a medal, clinquant with jewels, that covered the left side of his chest. He was accompanied by a little Italian greyhound and a seventeen-year-old boy who could translate the native German's French into English. Steuben himself knew no English, though he proved proficient at picking up the curse words.[25] He carried a letter from Ben Franklin introducing him as the Baron von Steuben, "a Lieutenant General in King of Prussia's service."

It was true that Steuben was a baron, and had been an officer in the King of Prussia's army, a formidable force; but now at age forty-eight he had not served in the army for fourteen years. He was not in fact a current lieutenant general but a penniless former captain, an unemployed foreigner needing a job.

General George Washington put Steuben to work drilling the troops.

As a former captain in Frederick the Great's army, Steuben truly did know how a crack eighteenth-century army operated. He chose one hundred of Washington's best troops and tried to teach them the innumerable details of the Prussian system, marching, forming the line, wheeling, firing, thrusting and parrying with the bayonet. He stood in the muck of Valley Forge's parade grounds thinking in German and speaking commands in French, which his translator barked out in English; often the commands did not translate, leaving the men stumbling about the drill field while the roly-poly baron with a huge medal on his chest cursed in German, "Gott damn!" His translator, Pierre Duponceau, remembered that Stueben's "fits of passion were comical and rather amused than offended the soldiers."[26]

His one hundred men learned the Prussian system of warfare; others learned from their example, and over the month of March the soldiers at Valley Forge drilled and drilled till even Steuben had to say: "My enterprise succeeded better than I had dared to expect, and I had the satisfaction, in a month's time, to see not only a regular step introduced into the army, but I also made maneuvers with ten and twelve battalions [some 7,000 men] with as much precision as the evolution of a single company."[27]

Nathanael Greene watched in disgust as wagons full of sick and dying men became bogged down in the ruined roads leading from Valley Forge to Lancaster and Reading; oxen and draft horses strained dangerously hard to haul wagons from the mire; this at a time when there was no money to pay troops and a good draft horse cost more than one hundred pounds.[28]

As quartermaster, Greene couldn't afford to lose horses to bad roads. Through a colonel he asked Washington for one hundred men to fix those roads; he ordered another colonel to send along tar needed to build wagon bodies. Within a month of accepting the quartermaster general's post Greene had more wagons rolling over rebuilt roads hauling food and forage, knapsacks and canteens.

The surviving soldiers at Valley Forge weren't living in luxury, but with wagons rolling again they were no longer starving; thanks to Steuben, they now moved on the parade ground with a smooth efficiency; and the hills above the valley were growing green, providing natural forage to fatten the horses.

Spring brought good news into Valley Forge: The young French King Louis XVI—impressed with victories at Saratoga and the aggressive attack on Germantown—had agreed to recognize American independence in treaties against Great Britain. The new United States—broke, with nearly no navy, could now count on support from the French treasury and from France's formidable navy.

News of the treaties took nearly three months to cross the Atlantic and roll into Valley Forge; when Washington learned of the pacts on May 1, 1778, he wrote: "I believe no event was ever received with more heartfelt joy."[29] On May 6 Washington ordered a "feu de joye"—fire of joy—provided by roaring cannon and by eight thousand muskets, fired down the line like falling dominoes. The thunder reverberated from the hills, filling Valley Forge with sound.

Another piece of good news came wandering into the valley that spring— the eccentric Gen. Charles Lee himself, along with what Nathanael Greene called his "usual train of dogs." The British had agreed to release Lee in a swap for their general, Richard Prescott, captured the previous June by William Barton's raid on Rhode Island.

The man sent to fetch Lee, Elias Boudinot, noted that the general had not changed much since his 1776 capture in New Jersey. After a feast at Washington's headquarters, Boudinot showed Lee to his quarters, right behind Martha Washington's sitting room.

"The next morning," Boudinot wrote, "he lay very late and breakfast was detained for him. When he came out, he looked dirty, as if he had been in the street all night. Soon after I discovered that he had brought a miserable dirty hussy with him from Philadelphia (a British sergeant's wife) and had actually taken her into his room by a back door, and she had slept with him that night."[30]

In a letter written from Valley Forge to his cousin Griffin, Nathanael Greene wrote of Lee's return: "I apprehend no great good. . . . He is undoubtedly a good officer and a great scholar. But he is not a little unhappy in his temper."[31]

❦   ❧

On May 17, 1778, from headquarters at Valley Forge, Gen. George Washington sent a mounted messenger to find Nathanael Greene; the courier found Greene in Morristown, New Jersey, where he'd gone on quartermaster's business.[32] Greene broke the seal on Washington's letter and read:

> *Every piece of intelligence from Philadelphia makes me think it more and more probable that the Enemy are preparing to evacuate it. . . . There are some reasons that induce a suspicion they may intend for New York. In any case it is absolutely necessary we should be ready for an instant movement of the army. I have therefore to request you will strain every nerve to prepare without delay the necessary provisions* [to support an army on the move].[33]

So the long months of encampment at Valley Forge were drawing to an end. The British—alarmed by the possibility of a French naval attack on New York City—were poised to move their eleven thousand troops in Philadelphia back into New York. The British troops had a new commander in chief, Sir Henry Clinton, a shy "smallish, paunchy" man,[34] who had led the successful invasion of Rhode Island.

Clinton could move his troops from Philadelphia to New York by land or by sea. He chose the land route, a direct march across New Jersey. Now this would be a real test: The last time the British Army marched through New Jersey in 1775 they breezed through with no opposition, chasing Washington and Greene's beaten troops like scared hares. Nathanael Greene vowed that this time would be different.

Clinton faced a logistical nightmare as he moved his eleven thousand men across the sandy plains of New Jersey. His wagon train held 1,500 wagons, a line of men, camp followers, and horses that stretched for twelve miles. The passage across New Jersey was slow going, with wagon wheels churning the sand into a floury mix, slowing the horse and the men; an oppressive heat wave draped New Jersey with humid air.

As Clinton rolled along, Washington's twelve thousand troops followed like a pack of predators looking for a weakness. They camped near ample supplies that Greene had had the foresight to lay in, at great expense, for this very scenario.[35] The American Army that marched from Valley Forge—eight thousand veterans plus four thousand new recruits—was much stronger than the one that had retreated there from Germantown. They were better disciplined, better fed, and backed by France.

As he dogged Clinton's steps Washington asked his own generals what he should do about the British Army's slow march through New Jersey. Nine of the twelve, led by Major Gen. Charles Lee, urged Washington to let Clinton's troops pass unmolested.

A minority of three, including Nathanael Greene, strongly disagreed. In protest, Greene told Washington:

> *If we suffer the enemy to pass through the Jerseys without attempting any-thing upon them, I think we shall ever regret it. . . . We are now in the most awkward situation in the World. We have come with great rapidity and we got near the Enemy and then our courage failed us. . . . People expects something from us and our strength demands it.*[36]

Washington agreed. Over the strong objections of General Lee, Washington ordered an attack on the British wagon train.

On the morning of June 28, 1778, George Washington rode a beautiful horse, a white charger given him by the governor of New Jersey. At noon, the sun, near the summer solstice, hung straight overhead, casting a harsh white glare. The temperature that day climbed to near 100 degrees Fahrenheit, without even a ghost of a breeze. From camp, Washington and Greene expected to hear the sounds of muskets blasting three miles away, where Gen. Charles Lee had been sent to attack the rear of Clinton's long wagon train. Although Lee had argued against the attack, he had accepted command of the 4,100 soldiers who were to begin it. "Great things was expected of this detachment," Greene wrote to Jacob of Lee's advanced troops.[37]

Greene waited with Washington and the main army of eight thousand men poised to march in support of General Lee once he began the attack.

Private Martin was with Lee's advanced troops under the command of a Rhode Island captain. "Now," the captain said, "you have been wishing for some days past to come up with the British, you have been wanting to fight,—now you shall have enough fighting before night."[38]

Martin recalled waiting at the edge of a field for the battle to begin. In the midday glare "the mouth of a heated oven seemed to me but a trifle hotter than this ploughed field; it was almost impossible to breathe."

At the main camp Washington and Greene could likely hear the big booms of artillery, but not much in the way of musketry; these were not the sounds of the attack that Washington had ordered. Tipped off by a young fifer that American troops were retreating, Washington rode his white charger through the heat toward Monmouth to see what was happening. Though he habitually affected a cool, diffident demeanor, Washington could flash a nasty temper. As he rode toward the line, Washington saw that his troops were not attacking, as ordered—they were, as the fifer said, retreating.

Private Martin watched as Washington "crossed the road just where we were sitting. I heard him" ask, "By whose order are the troops retreating?"

The passing troops answered: "By General Lee's."

Washington caught up with Lee and, according to Washington's aide, Tench Tilghman, asked him: What is the meaning of this?

Lee stammered, "Sir, sir," then allowed that the entire attack "was against [my] opinion."

Tilghman observed: "General Washington answered, whatever his opinion might have been, he expected his orders would have been obeyed, and then rode on to the rear of the retreating troops."[39]

That was General Lee's last battle. A court martial later ruled, among other things, that he'd been disrespectful to the commander in chief. Lee and his dogs were sent packing.[40]

Washington rallied retreating troops behind a hedgerow, where they held off the British until the main army marched up to help. Greene was again pressed into service as a field commander, leading the division on Washington's right. "The commander in chief was everywhere," Greene observed, "his presence gave Spirit and Confidence and his command and authority soon brought every thing into Order and Regularity."[41]

With help from a local lieutenant who knew the ground, Greene set cannon atop Comb's Hill. From here he enfiladed the enemy; as the guns blazed hot in the 90-degree day a woman named Mary Ludwig Hayes, the tobacco-chewing wife of a private, lugged water from Wemrock Brook to help the gunners slake their thirst. The soldiers dubbed her "Molly Pitcher."

Private Martin wrote in his memoirs:

One little incident happened, during the heat of the cannonade, which I was eye-witness to, and which I think it would be unpardonable not to mention. A woman whose husband belonged to the Artillery, and who was then attached to a piece in the engagement, attended with her husband at the piece. . . ; while in the act of reaching a cartridge and having one of her feet as far before the other as she could step a cannon shot from the enemy passed directly between her legs without doing any other damage than carrying away all the lower part of her petticoat,—looking at it with apparent unconcern, she observed, that it was lucky it did not pass a little higher, for in that case it might have carried away something else, and ended her and her occupation.[42]

The British pressed their attack for hours; despite the deaths of one hundred men the American battle line—comprised of three forces led by Greene, Lafayette, and Gen. William Alexander—held. Greene's division repelled an attack that Cornwallis personally directed[43] and included the best of the British troops.

Around 5 p.m., Clinton withdrew his troops toward Monmouth Courthouse, leaving his dead for the Americans to bury, traditionally an honor, or a chore, left to the victor.[44] Washington counted 249 English and Hessians buried by American troops—62 dead of heat stroke. About 100 Americans died, 37 of exertion. Horses, too, fell from the heat,[45] including Washington's charger. Alexander Hamilton's horse fell and crushed him nearly to death; the Rhode Island regiments under James Varnum suffered too: Simeon Thayer, a hero of fights at the Delaware River forts, lost an eye, and Capt. Thomas Arnold of East Greenwich lost a leg. Well into the nineteenth century Arnold hobbled on a wooden leg through his hometown, where generations came to know him as Monmouth Tom.[46]

Washington claimed victory at Monmouth, for when the smoke cleared, American troops held the battlefield and buried the British dead. Clinton rolled on to Sandy Hook, which had been his objective all along. From there he moved his troops by transport ships to New York, in preparation for a French invasion. But the French warships drew too much water to pass over the bar at Sandy

Hook, so they could not sail within striking distance of New York. Instead the French sailed north to attack the British occupying Rhode Island.

❧   ❧

When he learned that the French ships might not be able to reach New York, Major-Gen. Nathanael Greene wasted no time in suggesting an attack on the British ensconced in his home state of Rhode Island. "The fleet from Sandy Hook can run into Newport in three days time," Greene wrote Washington in mid-July. And: "General [James] Varnum . . . has very lately returnd from Rhode Island; he says that there are 1500 State troops including the Artillery Regiment. There is the Continental Batallion commanded by Col [Christopher] Greene about 130 strong."[47]

The "Continental Battalion" detached to Rhode Island for the coming battle was Rhode Island's own First Regiment—the only segregated regiment in the army. Plenty of blacks—both slave and free—fought in the revolution. Upon the formation of the First Rhode Island Regiment, about six percent of Washington's troops were black.[48] But Rhode Island was the only state that armed an all-black regiment, promising slaves their freedom for enlisting—much to the consternation of the state's plantation owners in King's County, the southern part of the state.[49]

Not all Rhode Island slaves were keen on the idea, either. Slaveholders could sell them into the service at the price of ten pounds per man, where they'd risk lives and limbs for a country that enslaved them. On Newport, British Lt. Fredrick Mackenzie observed in spring 1778: "Three White-men and five Negroes came off in a small boat last night from South Kingston. Those men intended to come to Newport having fled from their homes to avoid being obliged to serve in the Rebel Army."[50]

As quartermaster general, Nathanael Greene was responsible for putting everything in place for an attack upon his home state. From the main army's camp at White Plains, New York, he wrote to his deputy in Rhode Island:

There is an expedition going on against Newport. The forces that will be collected for this purpose will be considerable. Great exertions, therefore, will be necessary. . . .

A great number of Teams and Boats will be wanted upon the occasion. Pray do not let the expedition suffer from want of any thing in our line.

If tents are likely to be wanted get all that Mr Chace, Mr. Andrews and Mr. Greene have.[51]

The "Mr. Greene" from whom he wanted to buy tents was Greene's own brother, Jacob, a frequent vendor for the army while Greene was quartermaster general. Such blatant nepotism was more acceptable then than now, though it did open Greene to criticism even from contemporaries.

For Greene, the planned attack on Rhode Island was great news; it would finally get the state's eminent citizens off of his back. From the day the British first invaded Newport, on December 7, 1776, Rhode Islanders had badgered Greene to use his influence with Washington to bring the Continental Army home for a battle.

And Rhode Islanders had ample cause to grumble. While their crack troops were off killing and dying in New York, New Jersey, and Philadelphia, their own state capitol was occupied by a large force that occasionally raided nearby towns, sinking boats, burning buildings, and stealing livestock.

"None would wish to have so destructive a cruel war come near there own dwellings where there wives and Children and there all that is worth living for is settled down," Governor Nicholas Cooke wrote to Greene, in one of his many appeals for continental troops.[52]

Greene could empathize. Near his family's homestead at Potowomut, a British warship laid at anchor, and his pregnant wife was living, unhappily, with friends in Boston.

❦   ❧

Nathanael Greene envied John Sullivan, a fellow major-general in George Washington's Army. Washington had given Sullivan the command of troops gathering to attack the British on Rhode Island, a command that Greene was dying to get. Although history has not been kind to Sullivan—he died an addled alcoholic in his native New Hampshire—Greene liked him. In July 1778 Greene wrote Sullivan: "You are the most happy man in the World. What a child of fortune. The expedition going on against Newport I think cannot fail of success. You are the first General that has ever had an opportunity of cooperating with the French forces belonging to the United States," which was true—Sullivan would be fighting at Rhode Island in concert with French marines and the French navy.

"I was an adivsear to this expedition and therefore am deeply interested in the event," Greene wrote Sullivan from the main camp at White Plains, New York. "I wish a little more force had been sent. . . . Every thing depends almost on the success of this expedition. Your friends are anxious, your Enemies are watching. I CHARGE YOU TO BE VICTORIUS."[53]

Greene "whish[ed] most ardently" to join the attack on Rhode Island. "It is going on four years since I have spent an hour at home, save one that I stopt on my march from Boston to New York," he wrote to Henry Marchant, a Rhode Island congressman. "There is no man gone through more fatigue . . . than I have since I belonged to the army."[54]

At first Washington would not let Greene go to Rhode Island; he wanted his quartermaster general to remain with him and the main army of twelve thousand troops at White Plains. By mid-summer Washington relented, writing Congress that he "judged it advisable to send Genl. Greene" to Rhode Island "being fully persuaded his services, as well as in the Quartermaster line as in the field, would be of material importance in the expedition against the Enemy in that Quarter. He is intimately acquainted with the whole of the Country, and besides he has extensive interest and influence upon it."[55]

On July 28, as Greene saddled his horse to ride to Rhode Island from White Plains, a fast-moving fog swept up Rhode Island Sound, putting an end to a fine day by cloaking Newport in a cloud. Late that night, lightning flashed, thunder echoed down the bay, and a hard rain fell, squeezing out the fog.[56] At daybreak the sun shone clear, lighting the furled sails of a fleet that had dropped anchor off Block Island in the fog. The French fleet had arrived for the battle.

All that day the tall ships stood for Newport harbor, their masts crowded with sail. As they drew near the ships projected power: twelve ships of the line, each with three masts, the lead ship flying the French fleur-de-lys; they stood two tiers high, iron anchors dangling from their bows, their gun ports open, brass cannon glinting in the sun.

Col. John Laurens, son of the president of the Continental Congress, observed the "appearance was as sudden as a change of decorations in an opera house."[57]

The arrival of the French fleet caused commotion on the streets of Newport. British troops outside the city withdrew into it, leaving their tents standing in the fields. Oxen drew carts heaped with barrels of food and ammunition, withdrawing them from the piers where they might be taken by the French.[58]

American militiamen gathering across the narrows of the Sakonnet River at Tiverton saw these ships as saviors; what they could not see, below decks, was a beaten, scurvy-wracked crew that had not touched shore in more than three months. The French fleet had set out from Toulon in April, and the sailors had endured a painfully slow crossing. It took eighty-five days for the ships to spy land off the Virginia coast. Provisions of all kinds had run low on these ships, and the tanks were nearly drawn of fresh water.

General Sullivan sailed out to meet the leader of this impressive-looking fleet—Admiral Charles Hector Theodat Count d'Estaing—and to give him an update on when the Americans might be ready to launch the invasion. Sullivan was welcomed aboard with a fifteen-gun salute.

D'Estaing was shocked to learn that Sullivan had gathered only a few thousand troops. "Sullivan's troops are still at home," he complained in a note to a colleague, then to Sullivan he confided: "the position in which I find myself cannot be ended too soon."[59]

Nathanael Greene rode the 170 miles from White Plains to Coventry in two nights and three days. He dismounted at the Coventry iron works on July 30, saddlesore and worn, as darkness settled in around 9 p.m. He had not seen his wife since she'd left Valley Forge in May. Her belly was now swollen and round as she was seven months pregnant. Greene saw for the first time his baby daughter, Martha, over a year old now. She had not been a healthy child, suffering from what his brothers believed to be rickets. His son, George, a talking toddler at two-and-a-half, was a virtual stranger to him.

Greene's time at home was brief, just one day with his pregnant wife and their babies. He wrote a few days later from Providence: "I am here and as busy as a bee in a tar barrel, to speak in the sailors stile." He was writing to Col. Jeremiah Wadsworth, a friend and a commissary in charge of securing goods for the army at White Plains. "Will you want a quantity of Rum? . . . My brothers has some [for sale]; any services you can render them consistent with your trust will be greatly appreciated."[60]

From all over New England men with muskets marched and rode for Rhode Island. From New Haven, the new president of Yale University, Ezra Stiles, observed: "There's an amazing spirit for rushing toward Rhode Island spread 100 miles round. Militia have gone thither from beyond New Haven."[61]

On August 3, 1778 the teenage Marquis d' Lafayette arrived on the outskirts of Providence with two thousand troops peeled off from Washington's main army at White Plains. These were some of Washington's best troops, including the Rhode Islanders under Col. Israel Angell.

From north of Boston came 265 fishermen to ferry the troops across Sakonnet passage under the command of the hero of the Delaware River crossing, the stocky redhead John Glover.

For the entire month of August 1778, Rhode Island was the fulcrum for a new democracy vs. the tyranny of kings. Washington wrote: "If the garrison of that place (consisting of nearly 6,000 Men) had been captured, as there was, in appearance, at least a hundred to one in favor of it, it would have given the finishing blow to British pretensions of sovereignty over this Country; and would, I am persuaded, have hastened the departure of the Troops in New York as fast as their Canvas Wings could convey them."[62]

Trapped in Newport between the French fleet and an army of thousands growing daily at Providence, the British began sinking and burning their own warships so the French could not capture them. On the morning of August 5, the British torched four large frigates, including the *Lark*, which until recently had lain at anchor near Nathanael Greene's homestead. In his daily diary British Lt. Frederick Mackenzie wrote: "The Explosion of some of our Frigates was very great, particularly that of the The Lark, which had 76 barrels of powder in her Magazine. . . . It was a most mortifying sight to us, who were Spectators of this Conflagration, to see so many fine Frigates destroyed."[63]

A most mortifying sight to Mackenzie maybe, but to Greene and other Rhode Islanders who heard the explosions echo along Narragansett Bay, the sights and sounds of British tall ships burning brought feelings of sweet revenge not felt in those parts since the *Gaspee* affair.

❦　❧

Nathanael Greene did double duty during the siege of Rhode Island, serving both as quartermaster general and as a major general commanding half the troops in the field—including the First Rhode Island Regiment, a segregated unit of blacks, Narragansetts, and men of mixed race. The First Rhode Island Regiment wore uniforms of cream-colored pants and jackets, with tall white hats emblazoned with blue anchors and topped with big blue feathers.

Greene marched his troops from Providence to Tiverton on August 4, 1778, followed a day later by nineteen-year-old Marquis de Lafayette and his half of the troops. When they linked up at Tiverton, they had more than 10,000 men that included an all-star cast of officers of the American Revolution: Greene, Lafayette, John Glover of Marblehead, and John Hancock, in command of the Massachusetts militia. Paul Revere wrote home to his girlfriend, "It seems as if half Boston was here."[64]

When the French looked out on the American troops gathered at Tiverton they were none too impressed. Lafayette's aide, Chevalier de Pontigbaud, wrote: "I have never seen a more laughable spectacle; all the tailors and apothecaries in the country must have been called out, I should think;—one could recognize them by their round wigs. They were mounted on bad nags, and looked like a flock of ducks in cross-belts."[65]

Newport's core looked like a quintessential New England town in 1778, with Trinity Episcopal Church's white spire thrusting above the tombstones in the churchyard, the White Horse Tavern serving sailors, clapboard houses with their twelve-over-twelve windows, and the Redwood Library on a hill above town. On August 8, 1778 the black hulls of French warships reflected in the town's harbor; from the waterfront came flames and a great plume of smoke from the twenty houses that the British torched to clear firing lines for their cannon. A large sailing ship, the *Grand Duke Transport*, had been run deliberately aground near the Goat Island wharves to keep the French from seizing it; someone had set it afire, and it too burned, threatening the wharves and storehouses.

In town, British Lt. Frederick Mackenzie wrote:

The burning of the houses and the ship, the sinking of our only remaining Frigates, the sight of the Enemy's fleet within the harbour, the retreat of the Troops within the lines, and the dismay and distress so strongly impressed upon the Countenance of the Inhabitants, who concluded that the Rebels were on the point of landing, and that their lives and property were in the utmost danger formed altogether a very extraordinary Scene.[66]

The noose was tightening around the British garrison on Newport: That day the French dropped 4,000 marines on Jamestown, an island close to Newport's western edge; on the eastern side of Rhode Island, the Americans had gathered 10,122 troops at Tiverton. The combined force planned to attack the next day: The French marines would hit the west side of the island, the Americans would cross the Sakonnet River from Tiverton to strike the east, and the French fleet in Newport Harbor would mercilessly bombard the town.

The British garrison held 6,706 men; the capture of that many soldiers would break England's will to prosecute the war, resulting in victory for the American Revolution.

Attack plans called for an assault on Sunday, August 9, but John Sullivan, the New Hampshire general in charge of the whole expedition, wrote early that morning to the French admiral that he wanted to postpone for one day, to adequately train what he called his "Motley and disarranged Chaos of militia" in the finer points of boat boarding and discipline.[67]

An hour after Sullivan sent his note of postponement to Admiral d'Estaing, word came into his camp that the British had abandoned their fortified posts on hills on the north end of the island. Sullivan immediately launched about two thousand of his troops across the East Passage to secure those abandoned works. Militarily, this was a smart decision; diplomatically it was dumb, for in landing his troops on the island before the French landed theirs, Sullivan had upstaged and insulted his allies.

Col. John Laurens wrote to his father, the president of Congress, that the French "conceived their troops injured by our landing first, and talked like women disputing precedence in a country dance, instead of men pursuing the common interest of two great nations."[68] While the French and Americans quarreled over the delay and the disposition of troops, the British dug in for a fight.

From the British perspective, Shakespeare himself could not have written a more thrilling script: They were surrounded on Rhode Island by marines, a militia, and a fleet of warships, with their own fleet burnt or scuttled to the floor of Narragansett Bay. And then at noon of a Sunday, August 9, 1778, they spied sails on the horizon. For the next ninety minutes more and more sails crested the horizon—ten ships, then a dozen, then twenty.

"At 1 o'clock it became certain that the fleet in sight was that under the Command of [British Admiral] Lord Howe from New York," wrote

Lt. Frederick Mackenzie. . . . "The spirits of the whole Garrison were at this period elevated to the highest pitch."[69]

By 1:30 p.m., sun lit the sails of thirty-five large ships sailing to the garrison's rescue; American spirits dropped in inverse proportion to the rise of the garrison's. D'Estaing withdrew all of his marines from Jamestown. He watched uneasily as Howe's British fleet came on till 5 p.m., when it dropped anchor between Point Judith and Beavertail Light.

Both admirals, Howe and d'Estaing, did not like their positions. Howe was outgunned by the larger French fleet, 846 cannon to 772. He could not afford to force the issue.

D'Estaing knew that another British fleet was due to arrive any day, and if that fleet linked with Howe's his destruction was certain. With summer southwesterly winds blowing up the bay, he felt trapped; he had to get out.

Late that Sunday, d'Estaing sensed a shift in the weather: The wind began to blow northeast, giving his ships a chance to slip their collars and sail dead on for the British fleet. Sullivan practically begged him not to leave, not now with victory so close. Sullivan's written plea reached d'Estaing on the morning of August 10; the only reply was the steady movement of the French fleet away from Newport Harbor.

Lord Howe saw the French fleet sailing straight for him; he gave the order for his ships to slip their cables and they too receded toward the horizon with the French fleet after them, both sides ready to battle in the Atlantic.

Mackenzie wrote: "I believe there never was a Naval engagement on which so much depended, [as] that which is now likely to take place."[70]

❧   ❧

Although the French fleet and its four thousand marines had sailed over the horizon, Gen. John Sullivan decided to press on with the attack on Newport. He finished ferrying all of his ten thousand troops, their cannon, draft horses, and baggage across the East Passage to the island town of Portsmouth and prepared to march on Newport. Barrels of rum came across, too, as the troops were then receiving rations of one gill—four ounces—per man per day, a daily rum consumption of seven hundred gallons.[71]

While a hard wind shook tents in the field on the night of August 11, 1778, Sullivan, himself a fan of the rum, wrote long and floridly:

> [T]*he Commander and Chief on Rhode Island having issued orders for the Army to move on Newport tomorrow morning at 6 o'clock—takes this opportunity to return his cordial thanks to the Brave officers and Soldiers and Volunteers who have with so much alacrity repaired to this place to give their assistance in exterpating the British Tyrant from this Country, the zeal to which they have discovered are to him the most pleasing presages of VICTORY and he is happy to find himself at the head of an Army far superior in number to that of the Enemy, Activated by a sacred regard for the life of their country and fired with just resentment against the Barbarians who have Deluged with Innocent Blood a*[nd] *Spread Desolution on every part of the Continent where they have been suffered to march—. . .*[72]

He went on in this way.

At 6 a.m., when the troops were supposed to be on the march, they were instead hunkered down, trying to survive a tempest. New Englanders called these storms "equinoctials" under the belief that the autumn equinox brought on strong storms. This storm, a month before the equinox, was stronger than most, blowing at least a gale for two days, lashing Rhode Island with cold rain, tearing tents, and laying the cornfields flat.

The troops in the field huddled on the lee side of stone walls. Men died in the fields of exposure, though for the most part they fared better than the horses. One witness wrote: "I saw for the first time that men were more hearty than horses."[73]

On the first day of the blow General Sullivan wrote in his orders:

> *The General sees the Difficulties his brave officers and soldiers are exposed to by the violence of the weather and storm and sincerely wishes that anything in his power could contribute to their relief—he however flatters himself that they will bear with a soldierly patience a misfortune of war which must frequently happen and hopes that in a few days they will be rewarded for all their toyls and hardships and after a compleat conquest of our enemies, to look*

back upon all the toyls and dangers we surmounted might afford us the
greatest satisfaction.

He finished the entry by upping that day's rum rations from a gill to a gill-and-a-half—six ounces, enough to get most men drunk.

The clouds finally lifted after 9 a.m. on Friday, August 14. The next morning the American army marched down Aquidneck Island bound for Newport, some ten thousand strong. Drummers rolled a march while Maj. Gen. Nathanael Greene led the troops, horses, and heavy guns on carriages down West Main Road, while Lafayette led the columns and guns rolling down East Main. The men dressed in uniforms of different styles—Greene's Black Regiment in their uniforms of white topped by blue-feathered plumes; the New Hampshire volunteers in thick green coats with buff white facing; most of the men, being militia, wore shirts of homespun stuff; all carried muskets, canteens, and canvas knapsacks.

They camped on the east side of the island, about two and a half miles away from the British lines outside Newport. Then they began to dig in for a siege of the city.

For days both sides fired cannons at each other mostly without effect, though Mackenzie noted that one ball struck a hut "in which a Soldier . . . was mending his shoes, unfortunately it took off one of his legs."[74]

While they dueled with artillery, both sides kept an anxious eye on the sea, wondering what happened to the naval fleets that had slipped away from Newport to do battle just before the storm. "It is probable that the late Storm drove the fleets far to the Southward, and that we shall not see any part of either for some days," Mackenzie wrote. "The Officers of the Navy differ much in opinion as to the probable fate of the two fleets. However, they all agree that both must have suffered considerably from the effects of the Storm alone."[75]

Whose sails would appear on the horizon?

❧   ☙

Fog shrouded Newport on the morning of August 20, so thick it was difficult to see fifty yards; it wet everything as if it had rained. As the fog burned off around 9 a.m., a frigate and two large sails emerged outside the harbor.

When skies cleared after noon the sails of twelve large ships appeared, standing for Newport; they drew nearer and nearer for about an hour until a look through field glasses resolved the French fleur-de-lys flying from their masts. The black-hulled ships stood on for Newport till about 6 p.m., when they dropped anchor off Brenton's Reef. The ships had been a good deal damaged. Winds had sheared off the three masts of the fleet's flagship, *Languedoc*, and the British had poured a broadside of cannon balls into the crippled ship, leaving ball-sized chunks of blonde wood in its black hull.

Early next morning, Admiral Count d'Estaing sent an aide ashore to tell Sullivan that he would bring his ships no closer; his fleet had been crippled by the gale, and the Count now intended to sail into Boston for repairs. This news made Sullivan apoplectic. He had ten thousand men exposed on an island, and he needed ship support. Sullivan ordered Lafayette and Maj. Gen. Nathanael Greene to sail out to the flagship and beg d'Estaing to reconsider.

The sailing skiff that would carry them down Sakonnet Passage to the flagship was skippered by big John Brown, ringleader of the *Gaspee* affair. As he stepped into the skiff Greene told Lafayette, "If we fail in our negotiation we shall at least get a good dinner."[76]

After being piped aboard the *Languedoc*, a ship of eighty guns, Greene and the young Marquis took their seats at a table of French officers for a council of war. Here was Nathanael Greene, just three years removed from the smoky clothes of an anchorsmith, now wearing a general's epaulettes while negotiating the fate of nations in a stateroom with a French admiral and an aristocrat.

Greene and Lafayette described the scene ashore: more than ten thousand American troops now camped near Newport, where some six thousand British were entrenched behind a line of forts. Greene and Lafayette argued for continued French assistance in pressing an attack on the garrison; but a majority of the French naval officers voted against the attack. After weathering two days of near hurricane conditions at sea their fleet was too fragile to fight; besides, an entirely new British fleet fresh from England had been sighted off Long Island, and if that fleet linked with Admiral Howe's ships then the French would be outgunned and trapped in Narragansett Bay. They unanimously voted to withdraw their fleet from Rhode Island and bring it round to Boston for repairs.

Count d'Estaing gave Greene a chance to appeal. Greene spent the rest of that day, August 21, 1778, aboard ship drafting an argument for why the fleet should stay and do battle. While Brown hovered around him complaining that the "reputations" of the officers at Rhode Island—including Greene's—"depended on the success of the expedition," Greene wrote:

> *The expedition against Rhode Island was undertaken upon no other consid-*
> *eration than that of the French fleet and troops acting in concert with the*
> *American Troops.*
>
> *There has been great expence and much distress brought upon the*
> *country in calling the Militia together at this busy season of the year* [har-
> vest time]. *A force nearly sufficient for the reduction of the place is now*
> *collected and all the necessary apparatus provided for subdueing the*
> *Garrison. If the expedition fails for want of the countenance of the Fleet*
> *and Troops on board, It will produce a great discontent and murmuring*
> *among the people.*
>
> *The Garrison is important, the reduction almost certain. The influence*
> *it would have upon the British Politicks will be very considerable. I think it*
> *highly worth runing some risque to accomplish.*[77]

Greene wrote a couple of pages in this vein, then gave the petition to d'Estaing. The American emissary to the French, John Laurens, found no problem with the tone Greene took, calling the protest a "sensible and spirited remonstrance."[78]

Greene never did get to eat that dinner that he'd been anticipating as he boarded the admiral's flagship. The swing of the ship at anchor as he bent over his petition, quill in hand, made Greene so sick that by dinner he could not even eat. That night a seasick Greene, Lafayette, and Brown sailed back to the army camp outside Newport. General Sullivan was still livid about d'Estaing's plan to sail away, leaving him with ten thousand men exposed on an island.

Sullivan called a council of his highest-ranking officers for the next morning, August 22, 1778. Greene was there, and Lafayette, in his own words, had been "strangely called there," too.[79] To Lafayette's horror the group drafted a strongly written protest to send to d'Estaing. They outlined nine reasons why the fleet should not leave, including this one:

> *5thly Because the honor of the french nation must be injur'd by their fleet*
> *abandoning their allies upon an Island in the midst of an Expedition agreed*

to by the Count himself. This must make Such unfavorable impression on the minds of Americans at Large and create Such Jalousies between them and their hitherto Esteemed Allies *as will in great measure frustrate the good intentions of his Most Christian Majesty* [Louis XVI] *and the american Congress who have mutually Endeavoured to promote the greater harmony and Confidence between the french people and the Americans.*

In closing the American officers called d'Estaing's plan "derogratory [derogatory] to the honor of France" and "highly injurious to the alliance between the two nations."[80]

Nathanael Greene, along with five others, including Generals John Sullivan and John Hancock, signed the petition.

Lafayette refused to sign. He found the petition insulting to the honor of France; reportedly he clapped his hand on the hilt of his sword and swore that France was dearer to him than America could ever be. He was furious.[81]

Before the petition could even be sent that day the French ships lifted their anchors and began to fall away for Boston. "[T]he Devil has got into the fleet," Greene wrote that day to Charles Petit, a friend and the acting quartermaster general. "They are about to desert us, and go round to Boston. . . . I am afraid our expedition is now at an end. . . . Never was I in a more perplexing situation. To evacuate the island is death, to stay may be ruin."[82]

As the French ships began slipping away, ancient prejudices between the Americans—who until recently were Englishmen fighting France in the Seven Years War—and the French began churning, threatening the new alliance. Staring through his good eye (the other having been put out recently at Monmouth), Col. Israel Angell of the 2nd Rhode Island Regiment wrote in his diary "the french . . . left us in a most Rascally manner and what will be the Event God only knows."

One civilian observer of the events at Newport noted: "The Monsieurs have made a most miserable figure and are curs'd by all ranks of people."[83]

In his orders of August 24, General Sullivan inflamed passions by writing "The General cannot help lamenting the sudden & unexpected departure of the French Fleet . . . he yet hopes the Event will prove America able to procure that by our own Arms which his Allies refuse to assist in Obtaining."[84]

This statement—"refuse to assist"—so incensed Lafayette that he nearly quit the American army and returned to France. Sullivan tried to smooth over the affair in his orders of August 26 ("we ought not too suddenly Censure" or "forget the aid and Protection which had been offered by the French" thus far, he wrote, which mollified Lafayette.)

Without support from the French fleet's heavy guns many militiamen wanted no part of the British army's bullets and bayonets. They began drifting away in droves. The day after the fleet left Rhode Island, Greene counted 8,174 men, some 2,000 less than peak strength. Every day saw more men leaving, including John Hancock, who said he was riding back to Boston to lobby Count d'Estaing to return his fleet to Rhode Island. Lafayette wrote the Count that Hancock's return to Boston might have been driven by "little eagerness for British bullets."[85]

By the 28th of August, Greene wrote Washington: "Our strength is now reduced from 9,000 to between 4 and 5,000. . . . The disappointment is vexatious and truly mortifying."[86]

The time had come to end the siege of Newport, but how? Sullivan had to ferry nearly five thousand men across the Sakonnet with an enemy force of six thousand at his back. He and Greene were in a precarious position.

❦   ❧

On August 29, 1778, dawn brought an astonishing sight to the eyes of Frederick Mackenzie, an officer with the Welsh fusiliers. From his fort near the summit of Tonomy Hill, he could see that the American army's tents had disappeared from the fields below.

"[H]ardly a man was to be seen in their Batteries or Trenches," Mackenzie wrote in his diary later that day. "I rode as fast as possible to General Pigot's head-quarters in Newport and informed him of it, and returned to the Camp with orders for the all the troops to get under arms with the utmost expedition."[87]

The British army was going to give chase to the retreating rebels.

Gen. Friedrich Wilhelm von Lossberg took a body of Hessians up the West Road; Gen. Richard Prescott, who was once captured from Newport by a band of Rhode Islanders, took troops to secure the high ground of Honeyman's Hill; and the pudgy Gen. Francis Smith, who had blundered into trouble at Lexington-Concord, led the center column of troops up the East Road.

The shooting began near 7 a.m. A flanking party of about seven hundred light troops ambushed Smith's column at the windmill near Quaker Hill, firing at them from behind stone walls as the militia had at Concord. For Smith, this march must have been awfully reminiscent of his march to Concord on April 19, 1776.[88] "[T]hey were close to the Rebels before they discovered them, and received from them a good deal of heavy fire which did a good deal of execution," Mackenzie wrote.

From his quarters in a Quaker's house, Greene could hear the muskets booming by the windmill while he ate his breakfast. A woman servant, concerned for Greene's safety, said, "The British will have you general."

"I will have my breakfast first," he said. Greene coolly finished eating before riding to assume command of his fifteen hundred men dug in on the island's west side.[89]

On both sides of the island the British drove American troops back toward their entrenched position in Portsmouth. Lossberg's Hessians attacked Greene's command, the American right flank where the Black, or First Rhode Island, Regiment was posted. This was a key posting, for if the British could overrun the flank they could press in on the sides and rear of the American line, cutting off their retreat.

Twice the Hessians charged with their bayonets; twice, in deadly hand-to-hand fighting, the First Rhode Island Regiment drove them back. While the Hessians were pressing the attack three British frigates sailed up the East Passage and began blasting the Black Regiment with twenty-four-pound cannon balls. Nathanael Greene ordered his artillerymen to drag two cannons to the beach to fire back. With those cannon spitting eighteen-pound balls and two cannon in a redoubt on nearby Bristol Point firing twenty-four-pounders, the frigates slipped away to avoid the pounding.

After a lull in the fighting, Lossberg took on reinforcements and again tried to turn the Black Regiment's flank. This time the Hessians succeeded in driving them back. Greene, seeing the threat to his right, ordered the Second Rhode Island Regiment under Col. Israel Angell and another Continental regiment into the fray; he also brought up a group of Massachusetts militia and Sullivan sent over the light troops that had ambushed Captain Smith that morning.

"We soon put the Enemy to rout," Greene crowed to Washington in an after-action report, "and I had the pleasure to see them run in worse disorder than they did at the Battle of Monmouth."[90]

The comparison to Monmouth was apt. Like Monmouth, the Battle of Rhode Island was pretty much a draw: The Americans lost 30 dead, 137 wounded; British losses were 38 dead, 210 wounded. As at Monmouth, both sides could claim victory: For the second time since training at Valley Forge the Americans had stood toe-to-toe with attacking British regulars and had driven them back; yet again the British had kept their objective, in this case maintaining a stranglehold on Rhode Island.

To his wife Greene wrote from his saddle on the day of the battle:

[W]*e have had a considerable action today; we have beat the enemy off the ground where they advanced upon us; the killed and wounded on both sides unknown, but they were considerable for the number of troops we had engaged.*

. . . I write upon my horse and have not slept any for two nights, therefore you'll excuse my writing not very legible as I write upon the field.[91]

❦   ❧

From his perch on Quaker Hill, British Lt. Frederick Mackenzie kept a close eye on the Americans. The day after the Battle of Rhode Island he observed wagonloads of baggage rolling from the American lines on Windmill Hill to Howland's Ferry; a large herd of cattle was driven to the Sakonnet River's edge and ferried over, all signs that the Americans planned to retreat to Tiverton.

The next day, August 31, 1778, Mackenzie wrote in his diary: "Everything quiet last night, 'till about 10 o'Clock," when someone reported noises coming from the river. From a field "we could plainly hear the noise of their Oars, much talking, and many boats in motion. . . . About 12 oClock [midnight] many lights appeared on the Howland's ferry shore" in Tiverton. "At day break it was no longer doubted that the Rebels were gone; not a tent was to be seen on Windmill Hill, and as soon as the Sun rose we were perfectly convinced that the whole of their troops had retreated."

All day on September 1 he could see the American troops dispersing—"some across Mount hope bay, to Kickemuit River; others to Taunton River.

Several marched up the Boston road." A whole fleet of flat-bottomed troop ships came out from Bristol and crossed the bay toward Warwick Neck.

At 2 p.m. a British fleet of near seventy sail, mostly troop transport ships, dropped anchor off Newport. The ships carried some four thousand men sent to reinforce the garrison.[92]

Nathanael Greene noted: "We got off the island in very good season."[93]

From the dispersing army's camp at Tiverton, Rhode Island, Greene made his way to the glum homestead at the Coventry Iron Works that he now wearily shared with brother Jacob and his family. Caty had tried living in the army camp at Tiverton, but, hugely pregnant and not feeling well, she had gone home to Coventry in mid-August.

Neither her health or his was very good as Greene came riding into Coventry in early September 1778. Her pregnancy became a difficult one, and his asthma bothered him throughout the campaign on Rhode Island.

While Greene recuperated at Coventry he found time for reflection in a letter to his friend, John Murray, a former Newport preacher and the founder of the Universalist Church in America. The two men had met in the prewar years at a dinner at James Varnum's house in East Greenwich. In the tradition of Roger Williams all three men were pious nonconformists; at that dinner Murray had scandalized Ezra Stiles, future president of Yale University, by denying Eternal Punishment.[94]

Now in September 1778, Greene wrote Murray:

The Monmouth battle, and the action upon Rhode-Island, were no small triumphs to us who so often had been necessitated to turn our backs. To behold our fellows chasing the British off the field of battle, afforded a pleasure which you can better conceive than I can describe. If, my dear Murray, I had been an unbeliever, I have had sufficient evidence of the intervention of Divine Providence to reclaim me from infidelity: my heart, I do assure you, overflows with gratitude to Him whose arm is mightier than all the Princes of the earth.[95]

In early September, Washington was still fretting about the rift that had developed between the Americans and their French allies. He sent a letter to Greene at Coventry, saying:

I depend much upon your temper and influence to conciliate that animosity, which I plainly perceive by a letter from the Marquis [de Lafayette], *subsists between American Officers and the French in our service. . . . The Marquis speaks kindly of a letter from you to him upon this subject. He will therefore take any advice from you in a friendly light, and if he can be pacified, the other French Gentlemen will of course be satisfied, as they look up to him as their head.*[96]

On September 6 a mob in Boston attacked a group of French officers at a bakery, killing one of them. Even with his wife days away from giving birth at home, Greene felt compelled to ride the eighty-or-so miles to Boston to soothe the still-bruised egos of the French. While there, he spent a lot of time in the elegant Beacon Hill house of John Hancock, entertaining the officers.

He reported to Washington from Boston on September 16:

The Admiral [d'Estaing] *and all the French officers are now upon exceeding good footing with the Gentlemen of the town. General Hancock takes unwearied pains to promote a good understanding with the French officers. His House is full from morning till Night. . . .*

I wish to know your Excellencys pleasure about my returning to Camp [at White Plains, New York]. *I expect Mrs. Greene will put to bed every day. She is very desirous of my stay until that event, and as she has her Heart so much upon it I wish to gratify her for fear of some disagreeable consequence as women sometimes under such circumstances receive great injury by being disappointed.*[97]

Washington gave his permission for Greene to return to Rhode Island from Boston, citing "The particular situation of Mrs Greene."

On the 23rd, as Greene prepared to ride home from Boston, he took time to write Count d'Estaing one last mollifying letter. Besides censuring the Count in his orders book, Sullivan had also sent him an insulting letter. A gale wind beat at the window panes of Hancock's house on Beacon Hill while Greene wrote to the Count:

> *I am Exceedingly hurt at the contents and Stile of General Sullivan's letter and the more I think of it the more I am astonished. . . . I beg your Excellency not to form an opinion of the other American general officers from the complexion of that Letter. I can assure you with great sincerity and truth, that they entertain the highest respect and veneration for your person and character, and give me leave to add that no one feels a warmer regard and greater respect than my self.*[98]

After sealing this letter, Greene mounted his horse and set off in the wind-driven rain down the Post Road for home. As Greene rode through the storm a figure on horseback came toward him, seeking him out. It was a servant sent to tell him Caty Greene was gravely ill.

"She had been in travail two Days," Greene later wrote to John Hancock. "I got Home about nine at night the evening of the Day I left your House. I found Mrs. Greene in bed very ill. The Storm was very severe and I as Wet as if I had been towed the whole distance in Water."[99]

At some time that day, either before or after Greene burst in with wet clothes, Caty Greene delivered their third child, Cornelia Lott Greene, who years later would disappoint her mother by trying to steal the best of her slaves.[100]

❦   ❧

Gen. John Sullivan tried to do Nathanael Greene a favor. In mid-September 1778 he wrote to George Washington, asking whether Greene could stay on in Rhode Island, where Sullivan still commanded 3,500 troops; "Greene's absence would be most sensibly felt by me."

The idea of spending a winter home in Coventry where his wife had just delivered their third child must have had appeal to Greene. But as hard as camp life was, Greene loved the army.

In his last letter from Coventry, Greene told Washington:

> *I shall set out for camp to morrow or next Day* [October 6 or 7] *at furthest. . . . I was told yesterday that General Sullivan had wrote to your*

Excellency to have me stationd here this Winter. However agreeable it is to be near my family, and among my Friends, I cannot wish it to take place, as it would be very unfriendly to the business of my department [the quarter-master general's post]. *I wrote yesterday to General Sullivan for leave to join the grand Army, and expect his answer to Day.*[101]

Sullivan's answer came by courier: "I feel myself too soon deprived of the Sharer of my Confidences, The assistant of my Councils and partner in supporting the Burthens of the war." But Sullivan assented; Greene could go.[102]

The main body of Washington's army was then in Fredericksburg, New York, north of White Plains, where Greene had an especially good horse named McCully awaiting him. He brought with him a new hat—at a time when the depreciation of Continental currency had driven the price of a hat to $400—and a bolt of blue cloth for a new uniform.

From White Plains, Greene got called to Philadelphia to meet with Congress and he didn't like it. Caty was now with him, having just arrived in the camp at Middlebrook with George, their son, almost three. Their daughters, Martha, age one, and three-month-old Cornelia, were left in Coventry with Jacob. Caty and George had endured a hard journey, riding in a rickety coach from Rhode Island to camp. "Her health was somewhat impaird in coming, but George stood it out finely. He is a fine hardy fellow, full of play and merriment," Greene wrote to Griffin.[103]

En route to Philadelphia the trio stopped at Trenton, where Caty and George would stay in the stately brick home of John Cox while Greene did his business in Philadelphia. Cox was one of Greene's two assistants in the quarter-masters department; he was sickly that winter, but his wife and many daughters—he eventually had six—kept Caty comfortable.

Before Nathanael set out from Cox's a blizzard struck, leaving him snowbound with his wife and child. Instead of sinking into domestic tranquility, while the fire crackled and snow swirled past the tall windows, Greene fretted about how well horses at camp had weathered the storm.[104]

The Delaware River finally froze thick enough for Greene to cross it on December 31, and he spent that New Year's Eve, 1778, alone in Philadelphia, where he groused: "There is nothing new in the City. Political feuds are very prevalent and luxury and extravagance beyound description. The City is crowded with people and all kinds of diversions are going on."[105]

Greene expected to be in Philadelphia for a couple of days; he wound up spending more than a month. Washington had also been called on to meet with Congress so he was stuck there as well. Washington had stopped holding councils of war, but he asked Greene's opinion on what the army's strategy should be for the campaign of 1779.

By candlelight in the pre-dawn darkness of January 5, Greene responded:

There is three principal objects to be attended to in the plan of the next Campaign. To take a position favorable for subsisting the army with ease and at the least Expence, To scourge the Indians at the proper season, and route [rout] the Enemy from N York should the state of the Garrison there render it practicable. . . .

To scourge the Indians properly there should be considerable bodies of men march into their Country by different routes and at a season when their Corn is about half grown. The month of June will be the most proper time.[106]

Greene proposed wiping out the primary food source for the Native Americans in New York's Finger Lakes Region. In the French and Indian Wars most of those tribes had settled with the British, and they maintained that allegiance in this war. For most of 1779, Washington followed Greene's advice to the letter, keeping the army in a defensive position in New Jersey while sending an expedition into upstate New York to fight the Iroquois Six Nations Confederacy. Five of the six tribes of the Confederacy had aligned themselves with Tory militiamen for raids as far south as Pennsylvania's Wyoming Valley, where they routed an American militia group of 360 men, taking 227 scalps.

Gen. Horatio Gates, who won fame at the Battle of Saratoga, had an aversion to Indian warfare; he'd backed out on an earlier scheme to fight the Iroquois and passed on this one as well, so Washington sent Gates to Rhode Island to relieve Gen. John Sullivan.[107] Washington planned to send Sullivan and 2,500 men to annihilate the Seneca and other tribal villages of log cabins and fieldstone houses set amidst cultivated orchards and fields.

While Washington was considering the expedition to the north, Greene wrote to his cousin Griffin: "It may not be amiss for you to lodge some good liquors at Albany in the course of the Winter; this is a secret hint." Greene held a business partnership with Griffin, and he figured the price of liquor would rapidly increase when the army came through.[108]

Sullivan did not reach Seneca territory in time to destroy their corn when half grown, but destroy he did. Between mid-August and late September 1779, Sullivan's troops ruined 160,000 bushels of corn and torched forty towns, mostly Indian settlements.[109] The only real battle came at the Indian settlement of Newtown, where Sullivan's troops squared off with Tory Rangers, some British regulars, and four hundred Indians. It ended in a rout. Sullivan had dragged artillery through the footpaths of Iroquois country, and his firepower over-matched anything else on the frontier.

After the battle, Lt. William Barton of New Jersey—not to be mistaken for the William Barton who'd captured a general at Newport—sent a scouting party to count the Indians killed.

"Towards noon they found them," Barton wrote, "and skinned two of them from their hips down for boot legs, one pair for the major, the other for myself."[110]

Burning villages and skinning the dead did not serve to end the joint Indian–Tory raids on the American border settlements. On the contrary, starving, angry tribes were forced into the British camp at Niagara for sustenance, and became even more enmeshed with the King's cause.

❦   ❧

Most of Nathanael Greene's time in 1779 was consumed with supplying Sullivan's expedition up the Susquehanna against the Seneca tribe. Feeding and transporting an army through what was then wilderness was exactly the kind of painstaking "druggery" that had almost scared him away from accepting the quar-termaster's post. His papers from this time show request after request for money, pack saddles, forage, tools. Greene and his two primary assistants made lots of money that year, some 2,400 pounds sterling apiece, more than almost anyone else in North America and enough to excite jealousy that he felt compelled to address.[111] In a letter to James Duane, head of the Treasury Board, Greene wrote:

> *It has been hinted to me, that some members of Congress think I have been to griping in my demands, and am making a fortune too rapidly. As this is an insinuation of a personal nature, and implies a charge of taking in generous advantage of the public necessity, I feel myself not a little hurt at it.*
>
> *There is not a man in the army that has been a greater slave to public business from the infancy of this war than I have. . . . I have been in every action that has taken place with the Grand Army since the commencement of the War, except those upon Long Island and at the White Plains; and although I have never deriv'd any great Military merit, yet no one has been more expos'd, or more intent upon doing his duty.*[112]

As generous as they were, Greene's commissions were paid in rapidly depreciating continental dollars. Congress had no power to levy taxes so it just kept issuing more money to finance the war; the more money it printed the less that money was worth, so that by 1781 none would take it, giving birth to the phrase "not worth a continental."

There were no banks to pay interest on savings, no stock market in which to invest, and with continental currency plummeting to eventual worthlessness, hanging onto stacks of cash would have been stupid. So Greene invested, in ships, in land, and in business enterprises such as the Batsto iron furnace in New Jersey, which won a contract to supply the army with shot and shells. (Like his forge in Coventry it burned to the ground, and, though rebuilt, it never did turn him a profit.)

Besides his partnership with Griffin in Jacob Greene & Co., Greene chartered a business with Barnabas Dean and Col. Jeremiah Wadsworth; Wadsworth was one of Greene's closest friends and, after Greene's death, one of Caty Greene's married lovers.[113] The three men referred to the partnership through a code name: the "2030 Company." Greene kept the company's identity secret because he didn't want his brothers in Rhode Island to know that he'd invested heavily without them.[114]

Through his businesses Greene held part interest in twenty ships outfitted for privateering—essentially licensed piracy. The government would grant a ship's owners license to capture and keep the cargo of any ship supplying the British. America could not afford much of a navy, and privateers formed a substitute; Washington also invested in them.

The British, too, employed privateers to harass American suppliers. Greene groused in 1779 that British-flagged ships were "as thick upon the coast as grasshoppers."[115]

Privateering was risky business: A successful capture could yield a fortune, but losses were high; ships did not give up without a fight, rival privateers were a threat, and the British Navy was constantly on the prowl for privateers. Although Greene's investments in privateers started well, they ended, as did virtually all of his wartime investments, in complete busts.

Despite the copious criticism Greene received for being well compensated, he performed near miracles with the quartermaster's department. Accounting for inflation, the department spent less money in his tenure than it spent before he took over; and thanks to efficiencies in transportation, goods were getting to the places that needed them—soldiers weren't nearly naked and starving.

Indeed, in March 1779, Washington could boast to Lafayette: "The American troops are again in huts [in Middlebrook, New Jersey], but in a more agreeable and fertile country than they were in last winter at Valley Forge, and they are better clad and more healthy than they have ever been since the formation of the army."

Martha Washington had come to Middlebrook headquarters, much to Greene's relief, for he had once noted that Washington became grouchy without her.[116] Caty Greene was there, too, and with the troops living in relative comfort there was time for dinners and balls. She was just twenty-four years old, a dozen years younger than her husband.

"We had a little dance at my quarters a few Evenings past," Greene wrote in mid-March from Middlebrook. "His Excellency and Mrs. Greene danced upwards of three hours without once sitting down. Upon the whole we had a pretty little frisk."[117]

❦   ❧

The waning days of 1779 brought two big events, one good, one bad.

The bad news, from Greene's perspective, came from Savannah, where Count d'Estaing again tried to work with American troops in taking a

British-controlled city, as he had at Newport. This time he failed utterly, losing eight hundred men.

The good news hailed from Rhode Island; on October 26, 1779, Col. Ephraim Bowen sent a message via the express chain of horses that linked the Ocean State to Greene at headquarters, now on the Hudson River:

> *I have the Pleasure to Acquaint you of the Evacuation of this Island by the British Army on Monday night last.* . . . *The Enemy have Left about Fourteen hundred Tons of Excellent Hay, Sixty of* [or] *Seventy Tons of Straw,* [and] *upwards of three hundred Cords of Wood* [merely a week's supply of firewood for the garrison]. . . . *I shall get you a pair of English blankets.*[118]

Bowen made good on that promise to send blankets; Greene doubtlessly appreciated them as that winter of 1779–80 was one of the coldest of the entire eighteenth century. It came early and it came on hard.

Nathanael Greene wrote in early November 1779: "The weather begins to get cold and puts us in mind of Winter quarters. . . . It therefore becomes necessary to look out for a proper place to hut the Army in."[119]

As quartermaster general, Greene was responsible for setting up a winter quarters for twelve thousand men, a good-sized village replete with housing, latrines, supply routes, and streets. The camp had to be on easily defensible ground, and this year Washington demanded that it be located fairly far from New York; the British had consolidated almost all of their northern forces in New York, about eighteen thousand men, and Washington was concerned that they planned a winter attack.

"With this table of difficulties before me, I have been perplexed not a little to find out where to fix the Army," Greene wrote to John Cox, an aide and a partner in the Batsto Furnace. "I have rode hot and cold, wet and dry, night and day, in traversing the country, in search of the most proper place for quartering the troops. In the whole of my research I have found only two places, that I can recommend as tolerable."[120]

Greene's final recommendation was a camp near Morristown in a grove called Jockey's Hollow. Washington approved of the choice on November 30, 1779, and the cold was already upon them.

"Set the whole world in motion," Greene wrote to an aide as soon as he got word of Washington's approval. "I beg of you not to lose a moment's time in forwarding Stores of all kinds as soon as may be."[121]

Caty—seven months along in her fourth pregnancy—came to camp from Coventry before it was even laid out. She took quarters in Morristown at Jacob Arnold's tavern on the village green. Much to Arnold's dismay, Greene moved in with her and took over the tavern as a cramped winter quarters for him and Caty, their toddler George, and their soon-to-be-born baby.

FIVE

Treason of the Blackest Dye

T he first regiments marched from the West Point Citadel into Morristown on December 2, 1779, arriving in a "severe storm of hail & snow."[1] They pitched their floorless tents in crusty snow and set to work building log huts, a thousand cabins that cleared six hundred acres of trees.

On December 5 a second, heavier snow fell, setting a pattern for that winter of heavy snows followed by bitter cold. In that weather snow did not melt; it just kept piling up. A blizzard struck in the first days of January; snow lay four feet deep with drifts three times that high. Teams could not draw sleds, let alone wagons, in snow that deep. Food that Greene had been able to store in magazines outside Morristown could not be hauled in, and, as at Valley Forge, abject hunger stole into camp. If the commissary and quartermaster general's departments had been as broken as they'd been the year before, mass starvation would have hit Morristown in that extreme winter.

Greene wrote to his deputy quartermaster for New Jersey in early January 1780: "Our army is without Meat or Bread; and have been for two or three days past. Poor Fellows! they exhibit a picture truly distressing. More than half naked, and above two thirds starved."[2]

Greene wrote to his friend, Jeremiah Wadsworth, that the camp was snowbound and

> *it is well we are, for if it was good traveling, I believe the Soliders would take up their packs and march, they having been without provision two or three days. The distress of the Army is very great, and not less on account of clothing. The hour is coming, and is now come, that we have been preaching about.* . . .
>
> *A few Cattle arrivd this morning or else the Army must have been disbanded or let loose upon the Inhabitants; the latter would have been the case; but you know how cautious the Genl* [Washington] *is of taking desperate measures.*[3]

General Washington was loathe to take "desperate measures," but to save his army he would. On January 7 soldiers took matters into their own hands, wading through waist-deep snow to plunder Morristown's houses and farms, conduct that in other times would have brought down a lashing. On January 8, Washington issued a circular to the a dozen county magistrates, apologizing for his men's behavior and appealing for help from the residents of New Jersey: "For a Fortnight past the Troops both Officers and Men, have been almost perishing," he wrote. He called upon the "virtuous Inhabitants" of the state to send in cattle and grain. Washington's plea for sustenance was really a velvet fist. He couched it as a request but backed it with the threat of force: "But at the same time I think it my duty to inform you, that should we be disappointed in our hopes, the extremity of the case will compel us to have recourse to a different mode, which will be disagreeable to me."[4]

In a letter to the local militia commander, Greene asked for a battalion of militia to turn out their ox teams and "break" or plow the roads between camp and Hackettstown, where he had stored some provisions. "The Roads must be kept open by the Inhabitants or the Army cannot be subsisted," Greene wrote the commander. "And unless the good people immediately lend their assistance to foreward supplies the Army must disband."[5]

The people did respond; whether from fear, patriotism, or simple humanity for fellow men in distress, the people of New Jersey sent teams to break roads, wheat flour to bake bread, and cattle for fresh beef. On January 27, 1780, Washington wrote Congress that the Army was now "comfortable and easy on the score of provisions." The magistrates and people of New Jersey had paid "the earliest and most chearful attention" to his plea.

In so doing, the people of New Jersey saved the American Army.

❧   ❧

From his cramped quarters in Jacob Arnold's tavern, Nathanael Greene wrote to a friend:

> *I am happy to inform you that Mrs. Greene is in bed with a fine boy not unlike George* [George Washington Greene, his first son.] *She was put to bed under as promising circumstances as heart could wish, but her delicate constitution, and her former ill treatment under the hands of the old women that attended her* [in Rhode Island], *I fear will not permit a very speedy recovery. She has been very ill, but is on the mending hand. This is the ninth day since she was put to bed.*[6]

The boy, Nathanael Ray Greene, was born in an army camp on January 31, 1780.

Greene's friend, Col. Charles Petit, heard news of the birth announced at an "assembly," or dance, in Philadelphia. Officers in the camp at Morristown also held a couple of assemblies of their own: "I have many things to say to you, but was at the Assembly last Night and feel not a little fatigued and clouded," Greene wrote in early March to his friend, Col. Jeremiah Wadsworth.

> *We are merry at Camp but have little to eat either for man* [or] *beast. . . .*
> *We are now so poor in Camp, that I have not money to pay the expences of the Express riders to carry the public dispaches. Our provisions is out, and*

forage gone. The Roads are impassable and no communication to be had across the Delaware. Thus we are shet up in Morris[town] without the bare hope of deliverance.[7]

The next day the camp's wagon drivers quit because there was no cash to pay them and no forage for their horses.

Hard times notwithstanding, there were opportunities for fun in camp. Caty Greene liked to tell this story, though the telling of it brought her trouble:

After the officers and their wives ate dinner at Col. Clement Biddle's quarters in Morristown, the women retired from the table to another room while the men drank. George Olney, a Rhode Islander serving as a civilian auditor for the quartermasters department, bluntly refused to drink and joined his tea-totaling wife, known only as Mrs. Olney, in the women's parlor.

This would not do. As Washington's aide, Tench Tilghman, recalled the affair: "It was proposed that a party should be sent to demand [Olney], and if the Ladies refused to give him up, that he should be brought by force. This party His Excellency offered to head."

With mock formality, Washington led his officers into the room and demanded Olney—"which the Ladies refused," Tilghman wrote. So in jest, they began to take him by force.

The way Caty Greene told the story, as the men tried to wrench Olney away to drink with them, Mrs. Olney brought the frolic to a halt by screeching at Washington, "If you do not let go my hand, I will tear the hair from your head. Though you are a general, you are but a man."

Caty, who liked Washington, then flashed a bit of what she called "unbecoming temper" of her own at Mrs. Olney. Nathanael Greene intervened by taking the Olneys into another room.

Caty told the story to Ephraim Bowen's wife in Rhode Island, and in the retelling it was embellished so that Mrs. Olney threatened not only to tear out Washington's hair but his eyes as well.

As the story circulated through polite society, an embarrassed Mrs. Olney wrote a letter to Caty accusing her of ruining her reputation by telling a completely false story.

Caty stood her ground, writing back:

[A]s to your tearing out the Genls Eyes I heard, nor said, nothing off but you did say you would tear out his hear [hair]. . . . if it is false why did I show you such unbecoming temper, or why did Genl Greene as a friend to you boath, take you into a room to talk to you very ceriously upon it. . . . It is very evident Genl Greene did not think it a jest.

Mrs. Olney conceded only that after the incident Greene had taken her and her husband aside, but he did not lecture them, he "very calmly, and with great moderation advised Mr. Olney to adopt a less positive and blunt way of refusing to drink."[8]

The arrival of spring brought no improvements to the Morristown camp. Greene wrote Wadsworth in May: "The Army is ready to disband this moment for want of proper provision. The Soldiery are neither fed or paid; and are getting sour amazingly fast. Such a temper never appeard in our Army before. God knows how it will end."[9]

It ended in mutiny.

On May 25, 1780, a regiment of the Connecticut troops in Morristown formed a line, beat their drums, and began a mutinous march out of camp. Food supplies were again inconsistent—some days musty bread, some days a little meat, and then nothing. They were sick of starving.

Private Joseph Plumb Martin, who marched with the mutineers, wrote of his fellow soldiers:

The men were now exasperated beyond endurance; they could not stand it any longer; they saw no alternative but to starve to death, or break up the army, give all up and go home. This was a hard matter for the soldiers to think upon; they were truly patriotic; they loved their country, and had already suffered every thing short of death in its cause; and now, after such extreme hardships to give up all, was too much; but to starve to death was too much also.[10]

As they shouldered their muskets to march, officers surrounded them with armed Pennsylvania troops, sending the Connecticut men grumbling back to their camps.

"We dispersed to our huts, and laid by our arms of our own accord," Martin recalled, "but the worm of hunger kept knawing so keen kept us from being entirely quiet."

Tory spies carried word of the mutiny to the British in New York, then under the command of Hessian Gen. Baron Wilhelm von Knyphausen, the general who had made Greene "mad, vext, sick, and sorry" by storming Fort Washington in 1776. The baron figured that with troops mutinying, Washington must be vulnerable. This would be a good time to roll into New Jersey for an attack.

Caty Greene, son George, and months-old Nathanael left New Jersey in early June 1780, just after the shooting started. She rode with her two young sons in a carriage that Nathanael Greene bought from a Tory woman named Mrs. Kennedy, probably the wife of Archibald Kennedy, who became an English earl. Washington had considered buying the carriage for himself, but was told it was "too old-fashioned and uncouth" for a man of his stature.

The Kennedy family's coat of arms was blazoned on the doors of Caty's carriage, which mortified her husband. After she reached Rhode Island, Greene wrote Caty: "I wish you to get your Carriage painted anew with the [Greene] family Arms upon it. I should not chuse you should ride in it with the present Arms upon it; especially as they are tory Arms."[11]

In that same letter Greene asked Caty for

[A] *black and white feather to wear; the General officers being directed to wear them by way of distinction. If you have any or any can be got handy* [I] *beg youl send me a couple.*

I believe I have mentioned in all my letter the shattered condition of my shirts, they are going to ruin a pace, beg youl forward my new ones. . . . Mr. Olney is as particular as ever.

While Caty was riding north in her uncouth carriage, the Baron von Knyphausen was marching six thousand troops over a bridge of boats connected by planks spanning Staten Island Sound. He came into New Jersey on June 6,

1780, buoyed with the news of a big British victory in Charleston, South Carolina, and with the belief that Washington's troops were ready to mutiny. Knyphausen hoped to rouse the local Loyalists and win support from Washington's mutinous troops. He would be sorely disappointed on both counts.

Baron von Knyphausen's troops torched the first village they marched through, Connecticut Farms; they also shot dead Hannah Caldwell, the wife of a local minister. Instead of friendly Loyalists, Knyphausen encountered angry New Jersey militia who drove his men from Springfield, New Jersey, clear back to the pontoon bridge beyond Elizabethtown.

The two sides held their positions for a couple of weeks, each puzzled by the actions of the other. Washington grew tired of waiting. He could see no logic behind Knyphausen's attack; he assumed it must be a feint to draw attention, with a major assault to follow on the American fortress at West Point. Washington put most of his men in motion toward West Point, keeping only one thousand regulars plus militia in Springfield, all under the command of Maj. Gen. Nathanael Greene.

On June 9, 1780, Greene wrote to his wife from outside Elizabethtown: "What their further intentions are we know not; and therefore have to wait their motions."[12]

*   *

The sun rises early in mid-June, and on this day, June 23, 1780, it had been up for about an hour near 6 a.m., when alarm guns boomed over Greene's camp. Drummers beat "to arms," a snappy riff announcing the approach of an enemy force.

Greene was then encamped in Springfield, New Jersey, a nice village with a town common and a white church steeple thrusting up between the foothills of the Watchung Mountains and the clear Rahway River. From his post Greene saw "about five thousand infantry with a large body of Cavalry and fifteen or twenty pieces of Artillery" marching his way. He reported to Washington: "Their march was rapid and compact."[13]

Greene, grossly outnumbered with only one thousand regulars and perhaps fifteen hundred militiamen, posted his troops on the high ground behind the town. He assigned Col. Israel Angell's 2nd Rhode Island Regiment with one cannon to harass the British as they crossed the bridge across the Rahway River. As at Red Bank in 1777, a Hessian commander once again confronted Rhode Island regulars.

Dr. James Thacher, a Continental surgeon with Greene's troops, wrote in his diary that day:

> *Colonel Angell's regiment of Rhode Island with several small parties, were posted at a bridge over which the enemy were to pass, and their whole force of five or six thousand men was actually held in check by those brave soldiers for more than forty minutes, amidst the severest firing of cannon and musketry. The enemy, however, with their superior force advanced into the village and wantonly set fire to the buildings.*[14]

Thacher reported, "We had the mortification of seeing the church and twenty or thirty" houses and stores crackling with fire.

A courier relayed to Washington that Greene was retreating in the face of a much larger enemy; Washington reluctantly turned his troops around to help, but they had only marched five miles when word came from Greene that he'd need no help. After burning Springfield, Knyphausen's troops had retreated back into New York.

Greene reported losses of fourteen killed and seventy-four wounded, while observing, "The inhabitants of Elizabeth Town inform us, that they counted eighteen wagon load of dead and wounded" British and Hessian troops staggering back toward New York.

Greene wrote Washington from Springfield: "I lament that our force was too small to save the town from ruin. I wish every American could have been a Spectator, they would have felt for the sufferers and joined to revenge the injury."[15]

This was the last battle of any size fought in the North.

❦ ❧

Operations in the North had ground to a stalemate, with neither side claiming a clear victory since the fall of 1777. So King George III had dictated a new strategy to bring the Rebels to heel: Subdue the Southern colonies and the rebellious North would fall for lack of supplies.

As early as March 1778, Lord George Germain conveyed the new Southern strategy to Sir Henry Clinton, then commander in chief: "the conquest of these provinces is considered by the King as an object of great importance.

"Should the success we may reasonably hope for attend these enterprises, it may not be too much to expect that all America . . . south of the Susquehanna would return to their allegiance."[16]

A key to the British strategy was the assumption that in the South, Loyalists outnumbered rebels. Colonial governors of the Southern states had convinced the British ministry that the Carolinas were loaded with Loyalists who would practically strew the army's path with flowers. In Germain's summation: "it is not doubted that large numbers of the inhabitants would flock to the King's standard."[17]

Loyalists were more numerous in the South, but the Southern social structure had so many factions and fissures that it was quickly crumbling toward a cruel civil war, pitting neighbor against neighbor in deadly fighting that often had little to do with who would rule the nation.[18] But the king's plan was working: His troops now occupied Savannah, and on June 15, 1780, a letter arrived in Congress announcing the loss of an entire army in Charleston—the single biggest American defeat of the war.

Charleston was the New York City of the South—thanks to extensive rice plantations farmed by some 70,000 slaves, it held more wealth than any other city in America.[19] England had sent a squadron of warships and 8,500 men to capture that key city, and on May 12, 1780, they'd succeeded: After a long siege, beaten American troops led by Gen. Benjamin Lincoln—a short, narcoleptic 225-pound man who suffered a leg wound at Saratoga that left him bow-legged[20]—marched out of the garrison to lay down their arms in surrender.

For weeks conflicting reports came from Charleston, some telling of a great American victory, others telling of disaster. On May 30, a copy of the Loyalist newspaper *Rivington's Royal Gazette* reached Greene at Morristown, with an accurate, believable account of the British victory.[21] The loss in terms of men and materiel exceeded even Greene's loss at Fort Washington. At Charleston the Americans lost 2,571 regular officers and men, plus 800 militiamen. British returns also showed the capture of 5,315 muskets, 15 stands of regimental colors, 33,000 musket balls, and 376 barrels of powder at a time when arms and provisions were so scarce that even prosperous Virginia could not find muskets for its new, 2,500-man militia.[22]

With Lincoln's capture, Congress needed to name a new general for the Southern army. Greene wanted the post, but he was then on bad terms with Congress.

❦   ❧

In mid-July 1780, Congress enacted an overhaul of the quartermaster's department that Nathanael Greene found to be a personal affront. Greene felt the new plan, which reduced the number of his deputies and cut the pay of those who remained, was a conspiracy "calculated" to make him fail or quit. So he quit. In a letter that used scathing language for its time—comparing Congress to the "administration" of England for example—Greene submitted his resignation. That letter, and a subsequent report from a Congressional committee that reported Greene's demand that the act be repealed, so angered Congress that some members threatened to remove Greene from the army. With Washington's intervention the whole contretemps blew over; Greene agreed to stay on as quartermaster until his replacement could be found (Timothy Pickering took over in late September), and Congress agreed to keep Greene as a commissioned line general.[23]

In that summer of 1780, Washington remained determined to attack the large, heavily fortified British garrison in New York. Greene thought Washington was tilting at windmills. Greene wrote to Wadsworth:

> *Has not the project something* Don Quixotal *in its appearance, to think of reducing a Garrison of ten or twelve thousand regular Troops, and six or Eight irregular, at a time when there is not one quarter part force sufficient to give protection to the Country, and when we have not money enough to forward the public despaches necessary to direct the prepertions? I confess it has this appearance to me, what ever may be the event of the measure.*[24]

Nonetheless Greene worked hard at his quartermaster duties, gathering boats and food and forage for Washington's planned attack. With the department in shambles, Greene found it impossible to obtain the supplies he needed for Washington's adventure. Finally in August 1780, Washington ordered Greene to take from New York and New Jersey farmers whatever he needed: hay, grain, cattle, good horses. Soldiers sent on foraging missions used the order as an excuse to plunder. Their behavior so angered Greene that he decided to kill one of his own soldiers to set an example. Greene once wrote that he adhered to the maxim: "pay well and hang well."[25] He could not pay, but he could and would hang. From Three Pigeons, New Jersey, Greene wrote Washington on August 26:

> *The instances of plunder and violence is equal to any thing committed by the Hessians. Two soldiers were taken that were out upon the business both of which fired on the Inhabitants to prevent their coming to give intelligence. I think it would have a good effect to hang one of these fellows in the face of the troops without form of a tryal. . . . if your Excellency will give permission I will have one hung up this afternoon where the Army is to march by.*[26]

Washington agreed, and the next day Greene reported to Henry "Light-Horse Harry" Lee: "I directed one fellow belonging to the 10th Pennsylvania Regiment, to be hung without judge or jury as an example to the rest."[27]

Lee had already set a ghoulish standard for staging executions as an example. He once ordered the beheading of a deserter and had propped the severed head up on the camp gallows as a desertion deterrent. Although Washington had been scandalized by this, Lee reported back to him that the beheading "had a very immediate effect for the better" on troop morale.[28]

❧　❧

When Congress needed a new general for the Southern command it reached back three years into the glory days of the American Revolution and chose Gen. Horatio Gates, whose reputation was still riding high from his army's 1777 victories at Bennington and Saratoga.

In mid-July, while Greene was feuding with Congress, Gates rode into camp on North Carolina's Deep River. Though Gates commanded some veteran troops of the Maryland Delaware Division, most of his men were raw militia sent into that theater after the Charleston campaign. After just two days in camp, Gates ordered this army into motion: He wanted to march on Camden, South Carolina, a prosperous town at a junction of trade routes 180 miles away.

After a hard march of eighteen days, Gates rested his troops within ten miles of Camden. Then he ordered a nighttime march. His officers could not believe it: Most of Gates's troops were militia who had little training in maneuvering in columns and lines, and Gates was sending them on a nighttime march on unfamiliar ground held by a strong enemy.

Gates told his officers he had seven thousand men; Maryland Col. Otho Williams doubted it. Williams sent an adjutant around to count the troops and learned they had 3,052 men, two-thirds of them militia. Gates told Williams: "These are enough for our purposes."

At the same time his troops were marching through a humid August night for Camden, Gen. Lord Cornwallis was moving his army north through the night along the Great Road toward Gates. Cornwallis led more than two thousand troops, half of them the best British regulars and the rest battle-tested Tories. Though the British were outnumbered, they were better-equipped, better trained, and were clearly the superior force.

At daybreak the American militia felt the percussion of British cannon fire in the pits of their empty stomachs. Through the forest's morning mist they saw men in red striding toward them with fixed bayonets, shouting, "Huzzah! Huzzah!" The American militia on the left side of the line dropped their muskets and ran. Gates tried to stop them but got swept up in the tide. The veteran regular troops held their ground on the American right, but they were soon surrounded. America lost more than six hundred men killed, wounded, or captured.

Gates, astride the son of Fearnought, a famous racehorse, beat it back to Charlotte—and beyond. In three days Gates covered the 180 miles his army had marched in nineteen, retreating all the way back to Hillsborough.[29]

Naturally much sport was made of Gates's galloping retreat. Nathanael Greene read Gates's letter announcing the defeat on September 5, five days before Congress publicly announced the defeat. Greene could not resist one sarcastic shot at Gates, a central figure of the old Conway Cabal: "His retreat is equal to that of Xenophon"—a Greek soldier who led a months-long retreat from Persia of fifteen hundred miles—"but only a little more rapid."[30]

❧ ❧

While the British had taken the war to the South, Washington was still doggedly pursuing his quixotic plan to capture New York. A fleet of French warships dropped anchor off Newport, which Washington would use as a staging area for the planned invasion of New York.

In Newport, the young Marquis de Lafayette kept badgering the French Army's commander to attack British-occupied New York City; he told the commander that the attack was also Washington's wish. The commander—Jean Baptiste Donatien de Vimeur Comte de Rochambeau—did not believe it. Like Greene, Rochambeau felt it folly to attack New York; he suspected this impetuous young officer was employing Washington's name to support his own ambitions. Rochambeau and the admiral in charge of the French fleet at Newport decided that they had to speak with Washington in person to discuss their future operations.[31]

Washington commanded his army from the field in northern New Jersey; he agreed to meet Rochambeau halfway, at the home of Jeremiah Wadsworth in Hartford, Connecticut.

Washington wrote Greene in mid-September: "Tomorrow I set out for Hartford, on an interview with the French General and Admiral. In my absence the command of the army devolves upon you. I have so intire confidence in your prudence and abilities, that I leave the conduct of it to your discretion."[32]

Greene felt flattered by having command of the American Army, joking to Caty: "This makes a great man of me for a few days."[33]

The first few days of Greene's command passed easily enough; he wrote Washington an update: "The army is without rum." Food was scarce, but an impressments party turned up two hundred head of cattle, and "There has been some firing on the East side of the North [Hudson] river at the shipping that lay near Tallard's [Teller's] Point; but I have no count of what effect it has more than to make the shipping move a little further from Shore."[34]

The firing that Greene heard had forced the British sloop *Vulture* to slip back down the Hudson River without picking up a spy that it had dropped on the western shore. The spy, a British adjutant general named John André, had spent that night on the banks of the Hudson River clandestinely negotiating the surrender of the American citadel at West Point with the fort's commander— Gen. Benedict Arnold. The two had talked until sunup, making it dangerous for André, in his scarlet red coat, to be rowed back to the ship. He agreed to spend that day with Arnold at a house on the bluff. As the two men ate breakfast there they heard the same firing that Greene had heard from his camp: An enterprising American major had trained some cannon on the *Vulture*, forcing it to slip away. When the *Vulture* went, it took André's ride.

The next day, Friday, September 22, André set out for New York on horseback, wearing a borrowed coat and a beaverskin cap. A party of American militiamen camped outside Tarrytown stopped and searched him, stealing his watch. When they yanked off André's high boots they found the plans for West Point, the fort's troop strength, and the disposition of its cannon, everything an opponent would want to know.

A mounted courier was sent to tell Gen. Benedict Arnold that a spy had been taken. The papers taken from André were forwarded to General Washington, who was then riding back toward Greene's camp from his meeting with Rochambeau. The courier sent to find Washington missed him.

On Monday morning, September 25, Washington sent word to Arnold that he'd be passing through West Point on his way back to the main Army camp in New Jersey, and he expected to breakfast at Arnold's house that day. Arnold sat down to breakfast with the aides Washington had sent forward, including Col. Alexander Hamilton. As they ate the courier rode up and gave Arnold a message: A spy, John Anderson (André's pseudonym), had been caught.

Arnold excused himself from the table. He went upstairs and told his young wife, according to the version that Nathanael Greene heard: "I have this moment received two letters which oblige me to leave you and my country forever."[35]

Arnold told his guests he had some business to tend to at West Point; he'd be back to meet his Excellency in an hour. He then rode hard for the river, where the *Vulture* was again plying the waters a dozen miles downstream.

Not a half-hour later Washington arrived at Arnold's house; he took his breakfast, then went on to West Point to see Arnold and inspect the works. He was shocked at the fort's condition. Without actually sabotaging the works, Arnold had let them go to ruin.

Washington returned to Arnold's house on the river's east bank to mull things over; then Hamilton handed him a packet that had just come in by courier: the West Point plans taken from André. Washington was uncharacteristically emotional, some said near tears, as he told Hamilton and Lafayette: "Arnold has betrayed us! Whom can we trust now?"[36]

Hamilton and another officer mounted horses and thundered off after Arnold, but he had made good his escape to the *Vulture*, leaving his teenage wife, Peggy, and their baby.

❦   ❦

On September 25, 1780, hours after General Greene had given the order to douse fires and candles and go to bed, a courier came galloping into his camp bearing a letter from Col. Alexander Hamilton. The messenger had ridden hard from West Point, almost fifty miles north of Greene's camp in Orangetown. By candlelight Greene read: "There has unfolded at this place a scene of the blackest tr[e]ason. Arnold has fled to the Enemy. André the British Adjt Genl is in our possession as a spy. His capture unraveled the mystery. West Point was to have been the sacrafice."[37]

Greene was still in charge of the American Army, pending Washington's return. He feared that with Arnold now exposed as a spy, the British would quickly attempt to storm West Point, a critical Hudson River fortification. Despite the darkness of the hour, 11 p.m., Greene ordered a drummer to beat to arms. He ordered the assembled Pennsylvania brigades to march immediately, without baggage, for West Point. He commanded the rest of the troops to be ready to march on "the shortest notice."

Early the next morning, Greene told his officers to stand in front of their men and read his written orders:

Treason of the Blackest dye was yesterday discoverd. General Arnold who commanded at West Point, lost to every sentiment of Honor, of private of publick obligation, was about to deliver up that important post into the hands of the enemy. Such an event must have given the American cause a deadly wound if not a fatal stab. Happyly the Treason has been timely discovered to prevent the fatal misfortune. The

Providential train of circumstances which led to it affords the most convincing proff that the Liberties of America is the object of divine Protection. . . .

Arnold has made his escape to the Enemy, but Mr. André (the adjt General to the British Army who came out to negociate the Business) is our prisoner.[38]

❧　❧

In Nathanael Greene's words, Benedict Arnold had been "the idol of America" before he turned traitor, and he'd earned that idolization. When shooting broke out on the Lexington Green, Arnold was a Connecticut militia captain and a merchant of wealth with a shock of black hair, gray eyes, and a strong, stocky body. His company arrived for the siege of Boston, and with a cantankerous Ethan Allen he helped lead the raid that captured the cannons of Fort Ticonderoga, which Henry Knox used to drive the British from Boston.

Arnold was a smart and fearless commander. Twice he'd been wounded in the war—once in a blizzard outside of Quebec on an epic, unsuccessful attempt to take that city, and once at Saratoga, where he'd stormed British entrenchments, exposed their flank, and played a key role in capturing an army of five thousand men.

At the time his treason was discovered, Arnold was a thirty-eight-year-old man married to a beautiful, gray-eyed blonde not half his age. Arnold, the military commander in Philadelphia, married the eighteen-year-old Peggy Shippen in April 1779; she was a woman of Loyalist sympathies who liked living the high life, and he enjoyed providing her with it.[39]

A month after his marriage Arnold began selling his services to the British. His liaison to the British commander in chief was a major, John André. London-born of Swiss parents, André was at the time of his capture a twenty-eight-year-old who possessed a great wit.

Arnold had been on the British payroll for a year when he began badgering Washington for the command of West Point. Washington, wanting to do well by a popular hero who had twice been wounded while serving heroically, gave him the command.[40]

Arnold repaid the favor by offering to surrender West Point to the British for twenty thousand pounds. This was the deal that he was discussing with André when the sun rose on September 25, 1780.

After he fled on horseback to the *Vulture*, Arnold sent Washington a message saying his wife "is as good and innocent as an angel and is incapable of wrongdoing." This, too, was a lie.

Peggy Shippen Arnold lay abed the rest of that day and most of the next in a clingy, gauzy robe. She appeared to be hysterical, accusing everyone in sight of wanting to murder her baby. When Washington came in to see her, she said, "No, that is not General Washington. That is the man who was a-going to assist Col. Varick in killing my baby."

The sight of this poor, teenage mother in her thin, form-fitting robe touched all of the American officers. Hamilton wrote to his wife. "Her sufferings were so eloquent that I wished myself her brother to have a right to become her defender."

"Two days she was raving distracted," Greene wrote to Caty.

Even Washington was touched: He gave her a pass to travel. She stopped at the home of a British colonel where she told a friend the story of how she'd scammed Washington and his officers into letting her go. She had not only known about the scheme to give up West Point; she had encouraged her husband to do it.

✤   ✤

From his camp in Orangetown, New York, Greene wrote to his wife: "I expect it will fall to my lot to sit as president of the court which will decide upon the crimes of . . . André. It will be a disagreeable business, but it must be done."[41]

True to Greene's expectations, Washington assigned him to preside over André's military tribunal. On September 29, 1780, Greene and thirteen other general officers solemnly heard the case inside the old Dutch Church in Tappan, New York.

André told the court his story of sneaking ashore from the war sloop *Vulture* to meet with Arnold on the western banks of the Hudson.

"Did you consider yourself under the protection of the flag?" the tribunal asked. This was the key question: Had André come ashore with a flag of truce to meet Arnold on an officer-to-officer basis? Or had he snuck ashore as a common spy?

"Certainly not," André answered; "if I had, I might have returned under" the protection of that flag. Instead he'd donned a disguise and ridden through the country under a false name.[42]

The tribunal was unanimous: André had come ashore as a common spy and "agreeable to the law and usage of nations" he must "suffer death." According to Greene's grandson, as he signed the death warrant, tears fell from Greene's eyes.

Execution was set for October 1, but the British commander in chief, Sir Henry Clinton, won a one-day reprieve. Clinton sent a Lt.-General Robertson to speak with Washington; Washington sent Greene as his emissary to meet Robertson at Dobbs Ferry on the wet clay banks of the Hudson. According to Robertson's report, Greene said, "If we give up André we shall expect you to give up Arnold."

Robertson answered only with silence and "a look of indignant reproof."

After the meeting Greene sent Robertson a message: He had "communicated to General Washington the substance of your conversation. . . . It made no alteration in his opinion or determination."[43]

André was to be hung from a gibbet on a hill in Tappan at noon, October 2, 1780.

Even Greene felt for André. He wrote to Caty: "Mr. André is a very accomplished character, and while we abhor the act we cannot help pitying the man."[44] André possessed true talent. He was an artist, spoke five languages, and during the British occupation of Philadelphia he'd used his wit to write comedic sketches that kept his troops laughing.

In a letter written on the morning of André's execution, Greene told Caty's uncle, Rhode Island Gov. William Greene:

> *The gallows is erected in full view of the place where I am writing. . . . Since the fall of Lucifer, nothing has equaled the fall of Arnold. His Military reputation in Europe and America was flattering to the vanity of the first Generals of the Age. He will now sink as low as he has been high before; and as the devil made war upon heaven after his fall, so I expect Arnold will upon America.*[45]

After writing that morning, Greene rode up to where the gallows stood. The coffin that would hold André lay on the bed of a wagon that pulled up beneath the hangman's noose. André, dressed in his uniform of scarlet jacket and white pants, climbed into the back of the wagon; he stepped onto his coffin and, hands on his hips, walked the length of it.

Dr. James Thacher, diarist and Greene's regimental surgeon, heard André say, "It will be but a momentary pain."[46]

The executioner, his face smeared in black grease, stepped forward to slip the noose over André's neck; André held him off and himself put the noose over his own collar, drawing the knot snugly by his right ear. He took a handkerchief from his scarlet coat and tied it over his eyes; an officer commanding the execution said his hands must be tied. Arnold slipped off his blindfold, pulled out another handkerchief, then slipped his blindfold back into place; his arms were bound behind his back with his own kerchief.

Then, an artificer who was present wrote: "The wagon was suddenly drawn from under the gallows which, together with the length of the rope, gave him a most tremendous swing back and forth, but in a few moments he hung entirely still."[47]

With Benedict Arnold gone, West Point needed a commander; Nathanael Greene asked Washington for the job: "I take my liberty just to intimate my inclination for the appointment," he wrote Washington on October 5, 1780. "I hope there is nothing indelicate or improper in the application."[48]

While applying for this post, Greene was also lobbying a friend in Congress for a bigger prize: Command of the Southern Department.

The difference between the two commands—West Point and the Southern Department—was radical. The commander at West Point would live in relative comfort and safety, with a house and a citadel to protect him and his family; the commander of the Southern Department would have what was then the most demanding, dangerous job in the army.

Greene was aware that since the fall of Savannah in 1778 the South had become a graveyard for generals, not by taking their lives but by killing their careers and reputations. He called the South "a Serbonion Bog," a reference to a bog in ancient Egypt that was believed to have swallowed whole divisions.

Naturally, Caty hoped that he would not obtain the Southern command. "She is much Alarmed for fear you Should go to the Southward," his brother Jacob wrote from Coventry. "You will Do well to Satisfy her of this Matter if you are not Agoing which I wish you may not as Nothing but Disgrace and Disappointment had Attended Every Commander on that Station."[49]

Jacob Greene was right, "Disgrace and Disappointment" had befallen all three generals who'd had the misfortune to command in the South— Robert Howe at Savannah; Benjamin Lincoln in the siege of Charleston; and most recently Horatio Gates, a general Greene never did like, outside of Camden.

Gates's defeat came more than five years after the first shots fired at Lexington-Concord. Now even the Revolution's early supporters were thoroughly sick of the war. The disastrous loss of Charleston, Gates's defeat at Camden, and the demoralizing revelation that the great Benedict Arnold was in fact a traitor all signaled that after five long years the American Revolution was finally being snuffed out.

❦   ❧

Washington did not keep Greene waiting. One day after Greene asked for the West Point command, Washington wrote to say yes, he could have it, but not to get too comfortable there:

> There is no disposition that can be made of the Army at this time under our pres[ent] uncertainties that may not be subjected to material change. . . . If under this information you should incline to take the immediate Command of the Detachmt which is about to March for West Point . . . it will be quite agreeable to me that you should do so.[50]

Greene wrote to his wife about the promotion but warned her: "This is only a temporary disposition for the fall. It is yet uncertain what disposition will be made for the winter. Perhaps I may spend the winter there and perhaps not"—a hint that he may still move south. He told Caty:

> *The situation* [at West Point] *is not much to my liking, there being little prospect of glory or comfort; and therefore I am almost afraid to give you an invitation to come and see me. However if you think you can be happy in this dreary situation with me, I shall be happy to receive you to my Arms, as soon as you can render it convenient to come.*[51]

On receiving Greene's letter, Caty drove her carriage into Providence to have the Greene coat of arms painted over the Kennedy family's Tory coat of arms; this would allow her a safer passage through Patriot-friendly country to West Point.

She was staying in James Varnum's Providence house when she received word from Greene at West Point:

> *My dear Angel*
>
> *What I have been dreading has come to pass. His Excellency General Washington by order of Congress has appointed me to the command of the Southern Army: Gen Gates being recalled to under*[go] *an examination into his conduct. This is so foreign from my wishes that I am distressed exceedingly: especially as I have just receivd your letter of the second of the month where you describe your distress and suffering in such a feeling manner as melts my soul into the deepest distress.*
>
> *I had been pleasing myself with the agreeable prospect of spending the winter here with you.* . . . *How unfriendly is war to domestic happiness.*[52]

Actually, Greene was telling a white lie when he wrote that he'd been "dreading" an appointment to the Southern command; he'd been lobbying for it since April 1779, when Washington had told him: "I shall not hesitate in preferring you to this command" over other generals, but the choice then belonged to Congress.[53]

Now after losing three armies under their hand-picked generals, Congress decided that it would let Washington choose the next Southern commander.

From headquarters in New Jersey, Washington wrote Greene: "As Congress have been pleased to leave the Officer to command on this occasion to my choice, it is my choice to appoint you."[54]

Washington followed this up with another letter telling Greene:

> *You will therefore proceed without delay to the southern Army, now in North Carolina, and take the command accordingly. Uninformed as I am of the enemy's force in that quarter, of our own, or of the resources which it will be in our power to command for carrying on the War, I can give you no particular instructions but must leave you to govern yourself intirely according to your own prudence and judgment and the circumstances in which you find yourself.*[55]

BOOK II

The Southern Campaigns

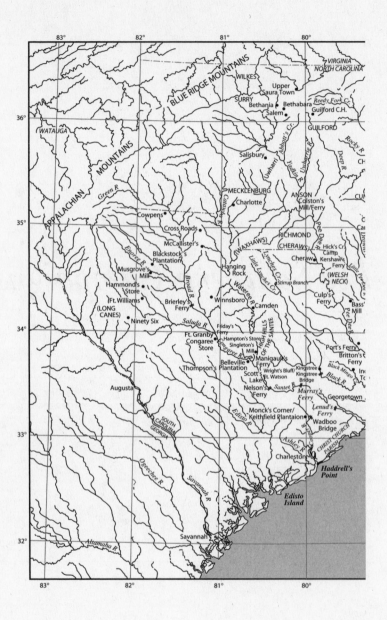

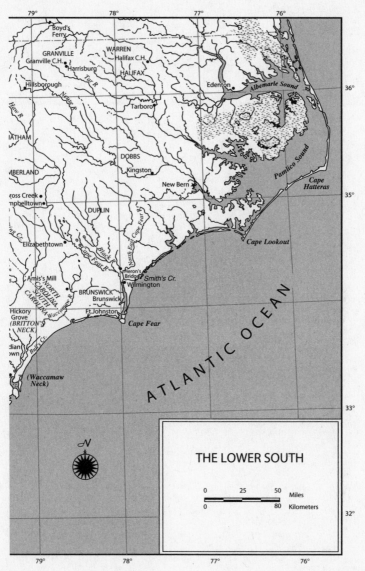

Map of the lower south showing key sites in North Carolina, South Carolina, and Georgia at the time of Greene's Southern Campaign. From THE PAPERS OF GENERAL NATHANAEL GREENE, VOL. VIII: 30 MARCH–10 JULY 1781, edited by Dennis M. Conrad. Copyright © 1995 by the University of North Carolina Press. Used by permission of the publisher.

SIX

The Cowpens

On October 21, 1780, Maj. Gen. Nathanael Greene pulled out of West Point bound for the South with four wagons pulled by sixteen good horses, such cash as he could borrow from the quartermaster, and a heart full of doubt.[1] He wrote home to Rhode Island Gov. William Greene, his wife's uncle and foster father:

> *I leave the Northern World with a heavy heart, as it will be such a great remove from my nearest and dearest connections. Mrs. Greene [Caty] will be made very miserable upon the occasion; and what will serve to make it more still grievous is, its duration is altogether uncertain; and the distance is so great; and my fortune so small, that I shall have but little opportunity to see any part of my family until my return.[2]*

Greene's "fortune" was indeed small; he owned a lot of land, but real estate in a war-ravaged country was not worth much. To his wife, Greene wrote what was essentially a will: His assets were a poorly producing farm in Westerly, Rhode Island, and another one in Newark, New Jersey; half-ownership of three thousand acres on the West Bank of the Hudson River; fifteen hundred pounds invested in his secret partnership with Jeremiah Wadsworth and Barnabas Dean, fifteen hundred pounds invested with Col. Charles Petit, and a thousand pounds invested in the Batsto furnace. The money he'd invested with his brother Jacob and cousin Griffin he figured correctly was a loss.[3]

Greene's wagons rolled from West Point into the main army camp at Preakness, New Jersey, where he picked up the Baron von Steuben as his inspector general and traveling friend. From there the trip south had its pleasant moments and its tedious chores, including nearly two weeks of talking with Congressional committees in Philadelphia.

During his Philadelphia layover, Greene received rare, good news from the South, in the form of a letter from his good friend, Brig. Gen. George Weedon. Washington had been a regular at Weedon's tavern in Fredericksburg, Virginia, before the war, and Weedon had fought under Greene in heroic efforts at Brandywine and Germantown. Now in mid-October 1780, he wrote Greene from Fredericksburg: "[Y]ou know good News is scarce and we ought to make the most of it. Here goes." He went on to report the news of a great victory by American militiamen over a strong party of Tory militia camped atop King's Mountain in South Carolina.

The British officer assigned to lead the Tory militia in the Carolina backcountry was Maj. Patrick Ferguson, a Scotsman and a marksman of great mechanical genius with a reputation as an aggressive hothead. The new British Commander in the South, Lord Charles Cornwallis, felt that Ferguson was too aggressive to be entrusted in a leadership role, but he had inherited Ferguson from the previous commander and agreed to let him head a force of a thousand Loyalist militiamen on a mission to quell the backcountry.

Ferguson immediately blundered: He sent a message across the Blue Ridge Mountains telling the "Over Mountain Men" that they'd better submit peacefully to his army or he would march his men over the mountains, "hang their leaders, and lay their country waste with fire and sword."[4] The Over Mountain Men were Appalachian pioneers, men who had ignored England's command against settling on Cherokee land in and over the Blue Ridge Mountains. These men, mostly of Scots-Irish ancestry, had grown rugged while fighting the Cherokee and living on the frontier in mountainous territory that is now Tennessee and the western parts of North Carolina and Virginia. The Over Mountain Men took Ferguson at his word. And rather than wait for him to come into their country, they grouped up, crossed the mountains, and went looking for him.

The Over Mountain Men rendezvoused with some back country militia from the eastern slope of the mountains, and tracked Ferguson and his band to a camp on the summit of King's Mountain, a sublime mountain that rises above a series of ridges near the border of South and North Carolina. About 1,800 men responded to Ferguson's challenge, but only about half of them had the horses necessary to push on with enough speed to catch him.

On October 7, 1780, about 440 Over Mountain Men, dressed in coarse, homespun hunting shirts of linsey-woolsey and caps of tallow-greased leather and bearskin, gathered at the base of King's Mountain. With an equal number of back country militia, between 900 and a thousand men in all, they had ridden since dawn through a steady rain. Now after noon they tied up their horses, formed a ring around the bottom of King's Mountain, then climbed steadily up it, drawing a tighter and tighter noose around Ferguson and his men. The clouds cleared and the day turned dry, a blessing, for it allowed them to keep their gunpowder dry. Near the summit they opened fire with their long American rifles. A Virginia colonel assigned to watch the horses picketed at King's Mountain's base observed: "The mountain was cloaked with fire and smoke, and seemed to thunder."[5] Three times Ferguson's men tried to break through, and each time they were driven back into the confines of their camp. Ferguson, wearing a distinctive hunting shirt of blue-and-white checks, spurred his horse for one last dash through the lines. He was immediately shot off his horse. They counted a half-dozen different balls in his body, testament to the accuracy of the Over Mountain Men's fire. He died on the spot and was wrapped in a raw beef hide and buried beneath rocks piled into a Scottish cairn that still marks his grave.[6] All of his army of 1,018 men were killed, captured, our wounded that day, stultifying efforts to recruit Loyalist militia and forcing Cornwallis to pull out of North Carolina.

Although most of the fighters on both sides were militiamen, the Battle of King's Mountain had a profound effect on the history of two warring nations, Great Britain and the United States. Nathanael Greene was still en route to the South, but by weakening the Tory militia's grip on the backcountry, the Over Mountain Men gave him a footing on which to launch a successful Southern campaign. Sir Henry Clinton, then commander in chief of British forces in

America, accurately summed up King's Mountain as "the first link in a chain of evils that followed each other in regular succession until they at last ended in the total loss of America."[7]

Upon hearing of the victory at King's Mountain, Greene wrote in understated fashion: "It is great, and will have good Consequences."[8]

❧   ❧

Greene's business with Congress held him in Philadelphia until November 3, when he, Steuben, and their little wagon train got rolling again. They stopped to visit Martha Washington at Mount Vernon, a place that Steuben felt was more ostentatious than comfortable, then rolled into Richmond hoping to cajole Gov. Thomas Jefferson and a slumbering legislature to send wagons and supplies southward.

"My dear," Greene wrote to his wife on November 18, 1780: "I am now in the capital of Virginia; and should feel myself tolerably easy notwithstanding the difficulties which I forsee I have to contend with, was it not for the distress and anxiety which you are in; the very contemplation of which hangs heavy upon my spirits; and renders my journey melancholy and dull."[9]

To Washington, Greene wrote from Richmond the next day:

> *Matters here are in the greatest state of confusion imaginable; and the business of government at a stand for want of money and public credit. Our prospects with supplies are very discouraging. The Gouvernour* [Jefferson] *says their situation as to cloathing is desperate. Nor is the business of transportation in a much more eligible condition.*[10]

Greene left Steuben—who'd been filling Greene's head with military strategy he'd heard directly from Frederick the Great[11]—to command troops in Virginia; then he pressed from Richmond, crossing the Roanoke River into North Carolina's Piedmont Region. As he crossed into North Carolina, the country in which Greene now moved was as strange to this Rhode Island Yankee as any foreign country. He hungered to know this ground that, against long odds, he hoped to conquer.

On Greene's first day in North Carolina, December 1, 1780, he wrote militia Gen. Edward Stevens:

> *I want you to appoint a good and intelligent officer with 3 privates to go up the Yadkin* [River] *as high as Hughes Creek to explore carefully the River, the Depth of the Water, the Current and the Rocks, and every other Obstruction that will impeded the Business of Transportation. All which I wish him to report to me. Let the Officer be very intelligible, and have a charge to be particular in his Observations. It is immaterial of what rank he is. . . .*
>
> *When the officer gets up to Hughes Creek, I wish him to take a Horse and ride across the Country from that place thro' the Town of Bethania to the upper Saura Town, and report the Distance and Condition of the Roads.*[12]

A colonel who worked in the commissary department under Greene's predecessor, Gen. Horatio Gates, observed that after one night's study of the landscape and supply routes Greene "better understood them than Gates had done in the whole period of his command."[13]

Besides plumbing the depths of the Yadkin River, Greene also sent a party to scout the Dan River and its tributaries. The Carolinas acted as a huge drainage basin for the Blue Ridge and Great Smoky Mountains, and Greene was determined to use the country's network of rivers to his advantage. He remembered how well the big, shallow-drafted Durham boats had served the Continental Army in crossing the Delaware, as he wrote Stevens: "It is my intention to construct Boats of a peculiar kind . . . that will carry Forty or Fifty barrels and yet draw little more Water than a common canoe half loaded."[14]

After reading the lay of the land, Greene's next order of business was to find his army. It had been two months since he'd last heard from Gates. The Southern army had then been camped in Hillsborough; Greene expected to find them there, but they had moved on.

Greene found what was left of his army in Charlotte, North Carolina, on December 2, 1780. Charlotte was then a village of just two streets, twenty houses, and a courthouse.[15] From there he wrote to his wife that his army consisted of "nothing but a few half starved Soldiers who are remarkable for nothing but poverty and distress."[16]

Their commander, Horatio Gates, appeared no better off. He had come to the South five months before as the Hero of Saratoga. Now, at fifty-two years old and terribly myopic with a squinting gaze, he looked like a thoroughly beaten man.[17] When Greene found him encamped at Charlotte, Gates had just heard news of the death of his only son. That death, Greene reported, "has almost broken his heart: it has effectually his spirits."[18]

Upon seeing Gates and what was left of the army in Charlotte, Nathanael Greene felt a change of heart toward his old nemesis. Under these circumstances the meeting of two men who never had liked each other could have been awkward, but each was magnanimous to the other. In his last orders as Southern commander, Gates changed the next day's password to "Springfield"—the site of Greene's triumph in New Jersey; for a countersign Gates chose "Greene."[19]

And on Greene's first morning as Southern commander, December 5, 1780, he returned "thanks to the honorable General Gates, for the polite manner in which he introduced him to his command."[20]

Greene then got down to business, ordering a return of the numbers of troops in camp, their enlistment terms, their condition. The results were not good: He had 2,307 men on the rolls, but just 1,482 were present and fit; of these, he wrote, "the whole force fit for duty that are properly clothed and equipt does not amount to 800 men."[21]

Greene found these men living in winter quarters with no tents and a few crude huts; most of them slept outside on damp ground. For food they ate only what they could forage every day.

General "Light-Horse Harry" Lee, who joined Greene's southern troops in January 1781, wrote of Greene:

This illustrious man had now reached his thirty-eighth year. In person, he was rather corpulent and above the common size. His complexion was fair and florid; his countenance serene and mild, indicating a goodness which seemed to shade and soften the fire and greatness of its expression. His health was delicate, but preserved by temperance and exercise.[22]

In a sense Greene, the stiff-kneed asthmatic son of a Quaker preacher, a man with no formal training for war, had just taken over a chess game from a player who had played miserably and lost most of his pieces—real, breathing pawns and horses, clerics and kings.

Sketch of Nathanael Greene. This is a fanciful drawing by an unknown artist, probably drawn in the mid-1800s and published in a biography of Greene written by his grandson. From George Washington Greene, *The Life of Nathanael Greene*. Vol. 1. New York: Hurd and Houghton; Cambridge: Riverside Press, 1871.

The man dominating the board on the other side of the table—Lord Charles Cornwallis, now forty-two—was a grandmaster, to the military manner born. Cornwallis's own, well-connected father called him a "very military" boy. At seventeen, after being nearly blinded in one eye from a field hockey stick on the playing fields of Eton, he was commissioned an ensign in the First Foot guards. Thirsting for more knowledge of war, he enrolled in a military school in Turin, where he learned ballroom dancing along with mathematics, fortifications, and military sciences. By twenty-three he was a battle-tested captain, having fought the French in Europe in the Seven Years War.[23]

As a member of the House of Lords, Cornwallis had consistently opposed the king's belligerent attitude toward the American colonies; yet when open rebellion broke out he'd volunteered to fight, arriving for the siege of Boston in 1776.

In his camp at Winnsboro, South Carolina, sixty miles from Greene, Cornwallis commanded a field army of about four thousand men with the best of training and equipment. By that measure, Greene's eight hundred men with the proper equipage were outnumbered in the field by five to one. Besides his field army, Cornwallis had troops garrisoned in Savannah, Charleston, and in a whole chain of outposts that described an arc through the Carolina backcountry. By the end of that month Cornwallis's troop strength in the Southern theater totaled some nine thousand men. By this measure, when Nathanael Greene took over America's Southern army in December 1780, he and his eight hundred ready, regular troops were outnumbered in that theatre by more than ten to one.

❧   ❧

On December 7, 1780, Nathanael Greene wrote to Baron von Steuben from Charlotte, North Carolina: "I arrived at this place the 2d Inst. And found the army under General Gates in a most deplorable situation, entirely without tents and almost starved with hunger and cold. The Virginia troops are literally naked and undisciplined. The troops are supplied with provision by daily collections, and that in a country ravaged by the enemy."[24]

Greene knew he could not keep his army here where Horatio Gates had put them, scattered on wet ground around an old brick courthouse, foraging daily in a war-wrecked country. Greene planned to split his little army in two, a decision characterized by one historian as "the most audacious and ingenious piece of military strategy of the war."[25]

At the outbreak of the Revolution, the sum of Nathanael Greene's military knowledge had been confined to what he could glean from books. In dividing his already small force in the face of a superior army, Greene threw the books out the window. Intuitively it would be easier for Cornwallis's field army of four thousand men to attack and beat two smaller armies, one at a time, than it would be to engage a larger one. Conventional theory still held that you don't risk your army to defeat in detail by splitting it. Napoleon Bonaparte, who later coined the maxim that Greene was practicing—"divide to live, unite to conquer"—was then just eleven years old.[26]

Greene's decision was not the lucky mistake of a novice; he did it deliberately.

"It makes the most of my inferior force," Greene wrote to an unknown correspondent, "for it compels my adversary to divide his, and holds him in doubt as to his own line of conduct."[27]

Greene put most of his men on the march for a new camp where he could drill and provision them. But first he needed to find good ground for the camp. True to his nature, Greene was very picky about the ground, writing in his orders to his engineer, Col. Thaddeus Kosciuszko:

> You will go with Major Polke and examine the Country from the Mouth of Little River twenty or thirty Miles down the Peedee [River] and search for a good position for the army. You will report the make of the Country, the nature of the soil, the quality of the water, the quantity of Produce, number of mills, and the water transportation that may be had up and down the River. You will also enquire respecting the creeks in the Rear the fords and the difficulty of passing them, all which you will report as soon as possible.[28]

Kosciuszko poled down the Pee Dee River, and just over the state line in South Carolina he found a fertile area that could support the bulk of Greene's army.

Before marching for the new camp, Greene placed the cream of his troops under the command of another general, Daniel Morgan. Greene gave Morgan about 600 men—half of them Continental infantrymen, plus Col. William Washington's Light Dragoons, and 180 battle-tested Virginia militiamen. "I give this," Greene proudly wrote to Lafayette, "the name of a flying Army."

Daniel Morgan, the commander of Greene's "Flying Army," was a heroic figure: large for his time at six feet tall and strong. Morgan was an up-from-the-bootstraps brawler who ended many an argument with a punch in the mouth. He fought with his father and left the family farm in New Jersey at seventeen; at nineteen he served as a teamster or wagoner in the French and Indian Wars.

Wagoners were a notorious bunch of hard-drinking, hard-driving guys, and Morgan's time among them gave him the sobriquet of the "Old Wagoner." While hauling goods for the British in the French and Indian Wars, a British officer peeved about something struck him with the flat of his sword. He struck the wrong man: Morgan punched the officer, earning him a sentence of five hundred lashes across his bare back. For the rest of Morgan's life his back bore scars from that lashing, but he got a good story out of it: The drum major charged with applying the lashes miscounted and gave him 499. "I counted them myself," Morgan liked to say, "and am sure that I am right; nay, I convinced the drum major of his mistake . . . so I am still their creditor to the amount of one lash."[29]

The thick zebra stripes across his back weren't Morgan's only scars. In an ambush during the French and Indian Wars a musket ball passed through the back of his neck, shattered his lower left teeth, and passed through the upper left lip, leaving a livid scar. Greene knew Morgan and his corps of riflemen from the siege of Boston and from Valley Forge. He knew a good leader when he saw one.

On December 16, 1780, Greene ordered Morgan to march the Flying Army from Charlotte more than one hundred miles west, deep into the back-country beyond the Catawba River. "The object of this detachment," Greene wrote Morgan in his orders, "is to give protection to that part of the country and spirit up the people, [and] to annoy the enemy in that quarter. . . ."[30]

That day Greene ordered the remainder of his army, some 1,100 men that included hard-core survivors of Gates's ill-advised Camden campaign, to be ready to march for the new camp when the weather cleared. It rained for four days.

Finally on December 20 they got underway, trudging through muddy roads toward "a camp of repose" where Hick's Creek met the wide Pee Dee River. On December 26, 1780, Nathanael Greene's army arrived at their winter camp after what he called "a very tedious and disagreeable" march over bad roads with weak draft horses plodding through the mud. The seventy-five-mile trek took six days.

Hicks Creek entered the Pee Dee River in the sandy hills of the Piedmont, just above the fall line of the rivers that flowed down into a marshy area known as the Tidewater. One Hessian officer described the Carolina low country below the falls as "a habitat of snakes and crocodiles [actually alligators], strewn with bodies of stagnant water and covered with impenetrable woods." Another noted: "at every step in the woods one is likely to meet with a rattlesnake or some other venomous creature," which wasn't mere hyperbole. Carolina rattlesnakes grew six feet long and six inches thick; water moccasins thrived in the swamps; bull snakes added their hollow, thundering call to the cacophony of frogs, 'gators, red wolves, and bugs. In the low country moss bearded the live oaks and cypress trees. Hessian Capt. Johann Hinrichs found it "a peculiar spectacle to see cattle in the woods, eating hay from the trees."[31]

Greene, a life-long Rhode Islander before the war, was shocked at the wanton cruelty that he found down South. In the North he'd known of rape and plunder and the indiscriminate burning of houses, but down here passions ran higher; in the South the war was personal.

The North still had civil government meeting in state capitals, making and enforcing laws. Georgia now had no government, and North Carolina's was but a "shadow," meeting rarely and in secret.[32] Here a civil war raged, pitting neighbor against neighbor, frequently fighting for the right to plunder each other's property while settling grudges. After a month in-country Greene wrote Caty:

> You can have no idea of the distress and misery that prevails in this quarter. Hundreds of families that formerly livd in great opulence are now reducd to beggary and want. . . . Human misery has become a subject for sport and ridicule. With us the difference between Whig and Tory is little more than a division of sentiment; but here they prosecute each other with little less than savage fury. . . .
>
> A Captain who is now with me and who has just got his family from near the Lines of the Enemy had his Sister murderd a few days since, and seven of her children wounded, the oldest not twelve years of age. The sufferings and distress of the Inhabitants beggars all description.[33]

Warm weather in December also surprised this Rhode Island Yankee. From Hicks Creek Camp he wrote to his wife: "I am posted in the Wilderness on a great river, endeavoring to reform the army and improve its discipline. The weather is mild and the climate moderate, so much so, that we all live in Markees" or marques, large canvas tents for the officers, though even Greene had to share his with a colonel, Otho Williams.[34]

Greene's methods to "improve" discipline included publicly shooting a three-time deserter, Thomas Chapman of the Maryland line. Greene signed the order to have "the said Thomas Chapman shott to Death" on January 4, 1781, adding "in the Fifth Year of the Independance of the United States."[35]

§   §

From his tent in the wilderness on a bend in the Pee Dee River, Greene worried about Daniel Morgan's detachment, camped somewhere in the South Carolina backcountry. Morgan had with him more than a third of Greene's Southern army, and all of its best men. Greene sounded like a fretting father as he wrote Morgan in early January 1781: "I am not a little impatient to hear from you, not knowing where, or in what condition you are. It is of importance I should be informed as minutely as possible, of your strength, situation, state of provisions, and means of transportation, all which I beg you to give me an account of as early as you can."[36]

Greene had good reason to worry: Gen. Alexander Leslie had just sailed up the Santee River with 1,530 reinforcements for Gen. Lord Charles Cornwallis; the British now had nine thousand soldiers in outposts, garrisons, and in the fields from North Carolina to Georgia; to face them, Greene now had a paper army of less than two thousand.

Morgan's first letter was already en route to camp when Greene chastised him for not writing; it took several days for a colonel to carry it through swamps and across the wide Catawba and Pee Dee Rivers, swollen from days of rain. Greene ripped it open on January 7, 1781; it was a good news/bad news kind of letter.

The good: Morgan had sent a troop of light horse under Col. William Washington, a cousin of the general's, to chase a Tory force of 250 mounted militiamen; Washington caught up with them forty miles from Morgan's camp at a place called Hammond's Store, a crossroads with a house, a barn, and a store. There, Washington's mounted men killed, captured, or wounded all but sixty before pressing on to Fort Williams, a plantation behind stockade fencing. The Loyalist militia stationed there fled, and Washington captured the outpost.

The bad news: Morgan's men and their horses were famished. "This Country has been so exhausted that the supplies for my Detachment have been precarious and scant ever since my Arival." He had to move, Morgan said, and "I should wish to move into Georgia. To me it appears an Adviseable Scheme."[37]

Consistent with his management style, Greene really thought over Morgan's "scheme" for one night, considering all the pros and cons. Henry Lee said of Greene: "He was patient in hearing every thing offered, never interrupting or slighting what was said; and having possessed himself of the subject fully, he would enter into a critical comparison of the opposite arguments, convincing his hearers, as he proceeded, of the propriety of the decision he was about to pronounce."[38]

And after considering Morgan's argument Greene said no. Moving into Georgia would take Morgan's troops even farther away from the main army at Hick's Creek, South Carolina, and with Leslie's reinforcements mucking through the swamps toward a rendezvous with Cornwallis in Winnsboro, Greene didn't dare break up his army any more than he already had.[39]

This turned out to be a smart decision: Three days after he made it, Greene got word that British troops were marching westward from Winnsboro, making a beeline toward Morgan. The intelligence was good: Cornwallis, alarmed by William Washington's capture of Fort Williams, had ordered the British Legion under Banastre "Ban" Tarleton to rid the countryside of Morgan and his troops.

"Col. Tarlton is said to be on his way to pay you a visit," Greene wrote Morgan. "I doubt not but he will have a decent reception and a proper dismission."[40]

❦   ❧

Ban Tarleton once bragged that he had "ravished," or raped, more women than any man in America. He'd earned a measure of fame in 1776 when, at age twenty-two, he'd captured Gen. Charles Lee in the widow White's tavern. More recently, he had earned infamy in the eyes of Americans due to his actions in a remote region of South Carolina called the Waxhaws. Here in May 1780, after the fall of Charleston, Tarleton pushed his troops of the British Legion 105 miles in 54 hours in order to catch 350 Virginia Continentals retreating from outside of Charleston. The Virginians were led by Col. Abraham Buford, who blundered: As Tarleton's horsemen charged his line, Buford told his men to hold their fire until they came close. That kind of coolness in the face of a charge works well when fighting infantry, but with horses coming on fast, his men fired just one volley before they were hacked to pieces.

Buford quickly raised the white flag, but the green-jacketed American Loyalists in the Legion refused his plea for quarters. Buford's battlefield surgeon Robert Brownfield observed years after the battle: "[F]or fifteen minutes after every man was prostrate they went over the ground plunging their bayonets into every one that exhibited any signs of life, and in some instances, where several had fallen over the other, these monsters were seen to throw off on the point of the bayonet the uppermost, to come at those beneath."[41]

All but 14 of Buford's 350 men were killed or wounded, and many who lived were maimed, such as Capt. John Stokes, who "received twenty-three wounds, and as he never for a moment lost his recollection, he often reported to me the manner and order in which they were inflicted," reported Dr. Brownfield. A blow from a dragoon's sword "cut off his right hand through the metacarpal bones," followed by an amputated finger on the left, and eight or ten hacks to the wrist and shoulder. "His head was then laid open almost the whole length of the crown to the eyebrows."[42]

From his actions this day, later historians tagged Tarleton with the sobriquet "Bloody" Ban Tarleton.

Cornwallis sent Tarleton's troops after Morgan, writing on January 2, 1781: "If Morgan is . . . anywhere within your reach, I should wish you to push him to the utmost."[43] About a week later Tarleton was ready to make his push; he'd gathered 1,200 men and four days' worth of food at Brooke's Bush River Plantation.

From his camp at Grindal Shoals on the wide Pacolet River, Morgan got word that Tarleton was moving rapidly north, toward him. For Greene, the stakes were high: If Tarleton wiped out Morgan and his Flying Army, the war in the South was effectively over. Cornwallis would roll up the rest of Greene's split army, and Greene would become a historical footnote as yet another American general who lost an army in the South. Morgan began a retreat farther north, toward the Broad River; swollen now with days of rain, it would be a hard river to retreat across.

On January 15, Morgan explained in a letter to Greene why he chose to retreat: "The enemy's great superiority of numbers and our distance from the main army, will enable Lord Cornwallis to detach so superior a force against me, as to render it essential to our safety to avoid coming to action; nor will this always be in my power."[44]

When Morgan began his retreat, Tarleton was just thirty miles away and gaining. Complicating matters for Morgan, the local militia general, Thomas Sumter, utterly refused to send him men or provisions, even going so far as to tell his officers not to cooperate with the Continental troops.[45] Morgan reported Sumter's refusal to Greene, who dealt with it in an ingenious way: Rather than taking an imperious tone by commanding Sumter to participate with federal troops, he wrote Sumter a flattering letter praising his "weight and influence among your Country men."[46] Then Greene wrote Morgan to ignore Sumter's insubordination "as it is better to conciliate than aggravate matters" with an influential partisan leader.[47]

At sunset on January 15, Tarleton pitched a camp, but it was just a ruse; his men marched through that night, moving within six miles of Morgan's camp on Thicketty Creek. When Morgan's scouts gave him that news he cancelled breakfast, leaving half-cooked food simmering over fires while his troops made a hasty retreat.

About five miles from the flooded ford at Broad River, Morgan came to a place called the Cowpens, an open pasture of good springs and a few undulating hills. Here he had to make a choice: He could push on and try to cross the river, a good move if he got away with it but disastrous should Tarleton catch him mid-river; or he could turn and fight. Fighting here was risky; he believed he was outnumbered; the open ground favored the linear tactics at which the British excelled; and the river blocked any chance for retreat. If the American troops fought here there would be no turning back.

Morgan's first choice had been to cross the Broad River and fight on the other side.[48] Now with Tarleton pushing close on his heels he decided that a river crossing was too hazardous. He would make his stand at the Cowpens.

On the afternoon of January 16, 1781, the day that he had left his breakfast simmering over the fire, Morgan rode ahead of his Flying Army to reconnoiter the ground at Cowpens. Capt. Dennis Trammel, who lived near the Cowpens and helped in the reconnaissance, recalled Morgan declaring: "Captain, here is Morgan's grave or victory."[49]

❦   ❧

In the early evening darkness of January 23, 1781, an American major rode into Nathanael Greene's camp on the wilderness of the Pee Dee River. The major, Edward Giles, carried an important letter from General Morgan to General Greene. By candlelight in his marquee, Greene read:

> *Dear Sir*
>
> *The Troops I had the Honor to command have been so fortunate as to obtain a compleat Victory over a Detachment from the British Army commanded by Lt. Colonel Tarlton. The Action happened on the 17th Instant about Sunrise at the Cowpens.*[50]

Morgan's letter, written a day after the Battle of Cowpens, provided a detailed account of the fighting. Greene and Giles edited Morgan's writing in order to dress it up for official presentation to Congress.

"An hour before daylight one of my Scouts returned and informed me that Lt Colonel Tarlton had advanced within five miles of our Camp," Morgan wrote Greene. When Morgan's scouts informed him that Tarleton was closing in he shook his troops awake, yelling: "Boys, get up! Benny is coming." Morgan's troops woke well-fed with fresh beef that had been driven into the Cowpens pasture the night before. They formed the battle lines.

"I hastened to form as good a Disposition as Circumstances would admit," he wrote Greene, "and from the alacrity of the Troops we were soon prepared to receive them."

In lining up his troops to receive Tarleton, Morgan followed an inspired battle plan that he had dreamed up while walking the undulating pastures of the Cowpens the night before. He formed his men in three lines, with militiamen standing at the bottom of the pasture as the front line. These were veterans of several militia fights, and many had fought at King's Mountain. In their ranks were sharp-shooting riflemen. Morgan told them that they did not need to square off in a bayonet fight with the British regulars; all he expected of them was three good volleys, then they could run from the field.

"Just hold up your heads, boys, three fires and you are free," Morgan told his militia, "and then when you return to your homes, how the old folks will bless you, and the girls will kiss you, for your gallant conduct."[51]

His second line was again comprised of militia, South Carolinians under the command of the taciturn colonel, soon to be general, Andrew Pickens. Most had seen some service.

A third line, comprised of veteran Continentals and long-service Virginia militiamen, held the high ground of the gently sloping field. He told the Continentals and Virginians: When you see the militiamen fleeing, do not panic; this was part of the plan.

Morgan told Greene that he'd had eight hundred men to do battle at Cowpens. In fact, Morgan probably had two thousand men at Cowpens that day.[52] Tarleton could not see all of Morgan's troops stationed in tiers atop the gently rolling hills of Cowpens; but even if he could have he would have liked his odds. His 1,076 men were most likely outnumbered by nearly two to one, but superior numbers did not guarantee victory over better-trained troops.

As Tarleton approached the edge of the Cowpens, he liked what he saw: The ground was "certainly as proper a place for action as Colonel Tarleton could desire," he wrote in his memoirs. "America does not produce many [places] more suitable to the nature of the troops of his command."[53] And the troops at his command were among the world's best.

Soon after daybreak, Tarleton formed a line of more than five hundred infantrymen who, with drums beating, began a steady advance up the pasture. Thomas Young, a sixteen-year-old militiaman riding with William Washington's cavalry observed from his horse:

"About sunrise, the British line advanced at a sort of trot with a loud halloo. It was the most beautiful line I ever saw"—527 men with fixed bayonets, resplendent in their red jackets standing a yard apart, with fifty horsemen on each flank. The British troops came on shouting; Morgan yelled to his troops: "They give us the British halloo, boys—give THEM the Indian halloo, by God!"[54]

Most of the militia fired one volley, except for South Carolina's Union County men, who popped off two before falling back before the British bayonets. By the time the British hit the line of seasoned Continentals stationed at the top of the hills, their lines had been thinned; still they had enough men to begin flanking the right side of the American line.

Lt. Col. John Eager Howard ("as good an officer as the world affords" in Nathanael Greene's opinion), ordered the American right to wheel to the right and close off that flank. Men in the center saw troops wheeling away from the action and believed that the order had been given to retreat. As the British came on, the American line began an orderly, organized retreat. Morgan was perplexed. He "quickly rode up to me and expressed apprehensions," Howard recalled, "but I soon removed his fears by pointing to the line, and observing that men were not beaten who retreated in that order."

Morgan agreed; he rode to the top of the next hill. When his troops filed up to it Morgan yelled: "Face about, boys! Give them one good fire, and the victory is ours!"

British troops trotting up the hill at quickstep mistook the retreat for a rout; they "set up a great shout" and came running.

"The enemy pressed upon us in rather disorder," Howard recalled, "expecting the fate of the day was decided. They were by this time within 30 yards of us with two field pieces; my men with uncommon coolness gave them an unexpected and deadly fire."[55]

After firing a volley at close range it was the Americans' turn to give chase at the point of the bayonet. After a cavalry clash in which Tarleton and Lt. William Washington literally crossed swords in a desultory duel on horseback, the British fled the field leaving 100 dead upon it. Morgan captured more than 800 men, 229 of them wounded; he also took 800 muskets, 100 good dragoon horses, 70 black men used as slaves, 35 wagons, the colors of the 7th Regiment, 2 field pieces, a forge, and, he wrote Greene, "all their Music."[56]

In one hour, Gen. Lord Charles Cornwallis had lost 86 percent of his light infantry, while Greene's Flying Army lived to fight again.

On finishing Morgan's letter announcing the news of Cowpens, Greene ordered the cannon in his camp to fire a "feu de joye" while officers and men toasted Morgan's Flying Army with a stiff drink called cherry bounce.[57]

When Dan Morgan bested the British troops at Cowpens on January 17, 1781, it was as if he'd torn a hornet's nest. Now the hornets were angrily spilling out.

Lord Charles Cornwallis was not pleased to learn the day after the battle that he'd just lost one thousand men. But the next day he received 1,500 more: Gen. Alexander Leslie's troops had finally marched into camp after days of mucking through swamps to reach Winnsboro.

If Leslie's men believed they'd find a little rest at Winnsboro, they were sorely disappointed. As soon as they arrived, Cornwallis put his field army of more than 2,500 men on the march to catch Morgan and then, ultimately, to fight and defeat the main block of the Southern army under Maj. Gen. Nathanael Greene.

Morgan wanted no part of Cornwallis's combined force; he began a retreat toward Salisbury, closer to the American Army's main camp 150 miles away on Hick's Creek, where General Greene commanded.

"I receive intelligance every half hour of the enemies rapid approach," Morgan wrote Greene, at mid-day of January 25. "In consequence of which, I am sending of [off] my waggons" to speed up the march. "I intend to move toward Salisbury in order to get Near the main army. I know they intend to bring me to action, which I intend carefully to avoid."[58]

On January 29, Morgan wrote Greene with some strange, alarming news: Cornwallis had burned all of his own wagons, his tents, even his barrels of rum in order to lighten his load. This bonfire of goods was unheard of, stunning even his own troops; yet as they watched their rum drain into the soils of North Carolina, the officers and men bore it with "the most general and chearfull acquiescence," Cornwallis wrote.

After the bonfire British Brig. Gen. Charles O'Hara wrote to a duke:

In this situation, without Baggage, necessaries, or Provisions of any sort for Officer or Soldier, in the most barren inhospitable unhealthy part of North America, opposed to the most savage, inveterate perfidious cruel Enemy, with zeal and with Bayonets only, it was resolved to follow Green's Army to the end of the World.[59]

SEVEN

Rise, and Fight Again

O n January 28, 1781, a curious contingent of six horsemen splashed through the watery wilderness of central North Carolina. Among them, in a blue coat with buff facing and gold epaulets, rode the "slightly corpulent" figure of Maj. Gen. Nathanael Greene.

In a strange, some have said reckless, maneuver, Greene left the protection of his main army; he wanted to confer in person with Dan Morgan and some of his other generals about what they should do next. Around this time Greene wrote to his wife, Caty: "The birds are singing and the frogs are peeping in the same manner they are in April to the Northward; and vegirtation is as in great forwardness as in the beginning of May."[1] The country he rode through was as dangerous as it was lush. At least half of the people in it opposed the revolution, and a cruel civil war ravaged the backcountry with neighbor murdering neighbor.

Greene rode protected only by three dragoons, an aide, and a guide. They covered more than a hundred miles in two nights, riding into Morgan's camp on the Catawba River on the third day, doubtlessly tired and splattered with mud. Morgan, the Old Wagoner, was in bad shape, suffering from hemorrhoids and stiff with rheumatism.

Greene's main army of about eight hundred regulars and a few hundred militiamen were left under the command of Gen. Isaac Huger, a reliable if unspectacular officer. Huger was the only general at the siege of Charleston canny enough to avoid capture.

With Cornwallis aggressively pushing an attack, the time had come for Greene to link up his two armies in hopes of giving Cornwallis a good fight. For the rendezvous Greene picked the hamlet of Salisbury, North Carolina. From Morgan's camp on the Catawba River this was a march of about thirty miles; for Huger's troops down at Hick's Creek Camp it was more like seventy. Greene sent a messenger splashing back across the rivers to tell Huger: "I beg you to hasten your march [with the main army] towards Salisbury as fast as possible."[2]

For a man being aggressively chased by a powerful nation's large army, Greene showed remarkable coolness. The more he thought about Cornwallis's decision to burn his baggage, the more Greene liked it, for he sensed that the grandmaster had committed a blunder.

Greene wrote to Huger from Morgan's camp: "It is necessary we should take every possible precaution to guard against a misfortune. But I am not without hopes of ruining Lord Cornwallis if he persists in his mad scheme of pushing through the Country . . . Here is a fine field and great glory ahead."[3]

※   ※

On February 1, 1780, the young cavalry commander Ban Tarleton dismounted at a North Carolina crossroads called Torrence's Tavern, and began rifling through the blood-blotched clothes of one of the dozen or so American militiamen his legion had just killed. In a pocket he found a recruiting poster that had been written by Nathanael Greene:

Let me conjure you, my countrymen, to fly to arms and repair to Head Quarters without loss of time and bring with you ten days provision. You have every thing that is dear and valuable at stake; if you will not face the approaching danger your Country is inevitably lost. On the contrary if you repair to arms and confine yourselves to the duties of the field Lord Cornwallis must certainly be ruined. The Continental Army is marching with all possible dispatch from Peedee to this place. But without your aid their arrival will be of no consequence.[4]

The militiaman who had responded to this flyer by mustering at Torrence's Tavern was dead, as were many of his friends. Now with Cornwallis's troops rolling steadily through the North Carolina countryside, few more would turn out to help Greene's little army.

Greene's recruitment flyer told prospective militiamen to meet him at David Carr's house, sixteen miles east of the Catawba River on the road to Salisbury. Unaware of the slaughter at Torrence's Tavern he rode alone to that house, having ordered Morgan's troops to march for Salisbury and the planned rendezvous with the main army. Greene waited there until after midnight "and not one man came to our assistance," he plaintively wrote to Baron von Steuben.[5]

Greene rode through the night toward Salisbury, where he stopped for breakfast at a place called Steele's Tavern. An army surgeon, Dr. William Reed, saw him there, cold and wet from his nighttime ride.

"What, alone, general?" Reed said.

"Yes," said Greene, "tired, hungry, alone, and penniless."

The tavern owner, Mrs. Steele, stole away then crept back into the room, quietly closing the door behind her. She extended her hands to Greene, each holding a little bag of hard coin.

"Take these," she said, "for you need them, and I can do without them."

A portrait of King George III still hung over her fireplace from the prewar years; Greene turned the portrait toward the wall and scrawled on the back: "Hide thy face, George, and blush."[6]

On February 5, Greene wrote Huger to forget about the Salisbury rendezvous, and to push on farther north to a hamlet called Guilford Courthouse. "No Militia have joined us, nor can I learn with any certainty whether any are collecting in our rear," he complained to Huger. "I intend to try to collect the Militi[a] about Guilford if possible; and if we can find a good position, prepare to receive the enemies attack. It is not improbable from Lord Cornwallises pushing disposition, and the contempt he has for our Army, we may precipitate him into some capital misfortune."[7]

When Nathanael Greene first took over the Southern command he boasted to Alexander Hamilton: "I call no councils of war; and I communicate my intentions to very few."[8] Now after two months at the helm, Greene called for a war council to sound out his two brigadier generals and a colonel on the imminent threat they faced. The four men—Greene, Huger, Morgan, and Col. Otho

Williams—met at Guilford Courthouse, where Morgan's light troops finally hooked up with Huger and the main army. All of the soldiers were worn out from weeks of marching, marching, marching through muddy roads in steady retreat from Cornwallis's army. The troops under Huger had worn through their shoes, marching more than one hundred miles from their camp on the Pee Dee River. A colonel on that march, Benjamin Ford, noted: "[F]rom Peedee to Gilford the Army might have been tracked by the Blood from the feet of the men who were all barefooted."[9]

Morgan's troops had come farther than that, riding 130 miles across three wide, winter-cold rivers since their battle at Cowpens.

On February 9, Greene laid it out for his Council of War: At Guilford Courthouse he had 1,426 infantry "many of whom are badly armed and distressed for the Want of Clothing," plus 600 militia "badly armed."[10]

Cornwallis, now less than twenty miles away, had nearly three thousand men, mostly regulars, all of them clothed, shod, and armed with the best musketry.

"The Question being put," read the minutes of the meeting, "whether we ought to risque an Action with the enemy or not; it was determined unanimously that we ought to avoid a general Action at all Events, and the Army ought to retreat immediately over the Roanoke River."[11]

If Greene could put the wide Dan River between his troops and Cornwallis's, then he could buy time to recruit men and supplies from Virginia, one of the richer and more powerful states. But retreating was nearly as risky as fighting. Greene's goal, the wide Roanoke or Dan River, flowed through Virginia some seventy miles to the north; that was a long march for weary, barefoot men slowed, Greene wrote, by "Heavy rains, deep creeks, bad roads, poor horses and broken harnesses."[12]

In deciding to race for the Dan, Greene deliberately put his troops in a vise with a wide river in their front and a determined, superior enemy pushing them from behind. If they got caught before crossing the river, "we stand ten chances to one of getting defeated," Greene wrote to the militia general Thomas Sumter, "& if defeated all the Southern states must fail. . . . Our force is so small & in such distress that I have little to hope & everything to fear."[13]

Cornwallis knew that Greene's troops were fatigued and that militia recruiting was not going well; he concluded that in his weakened condition, Greene "would do everything in his power to avoid an action on the South side of the Dan. It being my business to force him to fight," he vowed to make "great expedition to get between Greene and the fords of the Dan."[14] He assumed Greene would march for the shallow fords on the upper part of the Dan River, where his troops could wade across without boats. Cornwallis marched his troops at a punishing pace, hoping to beat Greene to Dix's Ford.

The race to the Dan was on.

When Greene broke camp at Guilford Courthouse for the seventy-mile push to the Dan, he and Cornwallis were about equidistant to the shallow ford at Dix's Ferry. Greene was closer to fords lower down the river at Boyd's Ferry, but this was a deepwater crossing. Cornwallis didn't know it, but Nathanael Greene had access to boats. His quartermaster, Edward Carrington, had collected all the boats between Dix's and the deepwater ford at Boyd's Ferry, six boats in all.

Greene hoped to buy time by keeping his elite light troops near Cornwallis on a path toward Dix's Ferry, while the main body of troops stole away toward the lower ford at Boyd's, where they could ferry across deep water before Cornwallis caught on.

From Guilford Courthouse, Greene did not have much of a head start on Cornwallis and his baggage-free troops.

"I expect [Cornwallis] will be at this place by to morrow noon at the farthest," Greene wrote on February 9, "nor do I know whether it will be in our power to avoid an action, the enemy moves with such rapidity."[15]

❧   ❧

Nathanael Greene's first move in the race for the Dan was to detach seven hundred of his best men and march them closer to Cornwallis to protect his own flanks. Gen. Daniel Morgan, the hero of Cowpens, would have led them, but he was so sore from his rheumatism and hemorrhoids that he could not even mount a horse; Greene gave Morgan permission to go home to Virginia and put Col. Otho Williams, a veteran of Gates's Camden campaign, in charge of the light troops.

On Sunday, February 11 Williams wrote Greene about a close call:

Accident informed the Enemy were within six or Eight miles of my quarters.
I detached Col ["Light-Horse" Harry] Lee with a Troop of Dragoons

[mounted infantry] *& put the rest of the Light Troops in Motion to Cross the Haw River at a Bridge. Col Lee met the Enemy's advance, stood a Charge and Captured 3 or 4 Men whom I send to you. They say Ld Cornwallis & the whole British Army preceeded by Col Tarlton's Legion is close in our rear.*[16]

With Cornwallis pressing them so hard, Lee's legion dared not sleep without sentinels guarding against surprise: "each man, during the retreat, was entitled to but six hours' repose in forty-eight," Lee wrote.[17] They slept fitfully without tents, sharing one blanket for every four men, "the heat of the fires was the only protection from rain and sometimes snow."

Every night the light troops marched at 3 a.m. "to gain such a distance in front as would secure breakfast . . . [the] only meal during this rapid and hazardous retreat." The meal was "always scanty, though good in quality and very nutritious being bacon and corn meal."[18]

With their breakfast of bacon and meal, the light troops fared better than the main army; Col. Benjamin Ford, who rode with Greene on the retreat, said that the main army ate only "what we collected from the Inhabitants which was but a very bad supply[;] many Days elapsed without our getting anything."[19]

Greene summed it up to Washington: "The miserable situation of the troops for want of clothing has rendered the march the most painfull imaginable, several hundreds of the Soldiers tracking the ground with their bloody feet."[20]

Colonel Williams, commanding the light troops in Greene's rear, kept the general abreast of Cornwallis's rapid advance. On the third day of the race to the Dan, as he, too, now angled away from Dix's Ferry to the lower ford at Boyd's, Williams wrote:

7 oClock PM

> *Tuesday 13th Feby 1781*

> *My Dear General at Sun Down the Enemy were only 22 miles from you and may be in motion now or will* [be] *most probably by 3 oClock in the morning. Their intelligence is good. They . . . mov'd with great rapidity. . . .*

> *Rely on it, my Dr Sir it is possible for you to be overtaken before you can cross the Dan even if you had 20 Boats. . . . I shall use every precaution but cannot help being uneasy.*[21]

About the time Williams was scratching out this letter, his troops spied campfires in front of them, fires lit by Greene's main army on the wrong side of the Dan River. As they rode toward the fires with Cornwallis close behind, Williams and his officers felt sick; it looked like they'd have to turn their troops towards Cornwallis for a suicidal fight in what would likely be a vain attempt to protect the ragged, barefoot, poorly equipped men of the main army.

When they rode into the camp, Williams and Lee saw that the fires were unattended: Greene's army had already pushed on for Boyd's Ferry, fourteen miles north. Lee wrote: "[T]he fires were instantly kindled; the cold and wet, the cares and toils of the day, were soon forgotten in the enjoyment of repose."[22]

The repose did not last long: At midnight Williams's light troops marched again, over roads deep and broken and sharpened with frost. As light crept into the eastern sky on February 14, a mounted messenger gave Williams a letter from Greene written at 4 a.m. Greene said he had not slept four hours total since he'd last seen Williams at Guilford Courthouse four days previously. Now Greene was preparing "for the worst."[23]

Later that afternoon of Valentine's Day, 1781, Williams received a brighter letter from Greene: "The greater part of our wagons are over, and the troops are crossing."[24]

The crossing was slow with six smallish boats to ferry more than a thousand men across a wide, rain-swollen river.[25] And Cornwallis's vanguard was still pressing down.

Around sunset, Williams reached the river, where he received a third letter, written by Greene at "1/2 past 5 o'clock: All our troops are over, and the stage is clear." Williams and his light troops had covered forty miles in twenty hours. Now, Greene was ready to give them a "hearty welcome."[26]

On Thursday morning, February 15, 1781, the foot-sore, red-coated troops of Lord Cornwallis marched up to the banks of the Dan River, where they saw the campfires of the American Army burning brightly on the other side. Nathanael Greene's army had taken every boat in the Roanoke Valley across the river with them, and there was nothing Cornwallis could do but stare.

"In the camp of Greene, joy beamed in every face," wrote Gen. Henry Lee.[27]

Greene's aide, Ichabod Burnet, wrote that America's Southern army was now "safe over the river and . . . laughing at the enemy who are on the opposite bank."[28]

   ❧   ⚘

Nathanael Greene deliberately kept his men near the Dan River in hopes of goading Cornwallis to attempt a crossing: "Our Army is . . . encamped at Halifax Courthouse in Virginia, in order to tempt the Enemy to cross the [Dan]River, as the most pleasing prospect presents itself of a strong reinforcement from the Militia of this State."[29]

But Cornwallis was smart; he did not take the bait. He wrote: "My force being ill-suited to enter . . . so powerful a province as Virginia, and North Carolina being in the utmost confusion, after giving the troops a halt of one day I proceeded by easy marches to Hillsboro."[30]

Here in northern North Carolina, without tents or baggage and 240 miles from his supply lines at Camden, Cornwallis was forced to kill some of his own draft horses for meat.

At Halifax Courthouse in Virginia, Greene and his troops were living relatively well. Virginia *was* a powerful province with a stable if poorly managed government and a strong economy. Here Greene's men bathed their bloody feet and slept warmly next to blazing fires. Henry Lee recalled in his memoirs that the army finally enjoyed "wholesome and abundant supplies of food in the rich and friendly county of Halifax."[31]

The respite did not last; now that he'd lured Cornwallis into the wilds of North Carolina, Greene was determined to raise enough troops in Virginia to press an attack. After just two days of rest, Greene sent Henry Lee's horsemen back into North Carolina to harass the British troops as they retreated toward Hillsborough, North Carolina, to refresh; two nights after that Greene himself, protected only by a small "escort" of William Washington's cavalry, joined Lee's legion in their secret camp.[32] This was the equivalent of a modern-day general joining his special forces in the field.

On February 21, just a week after beating Cornwallis across the Dan, Greene wrote: "The Army will cross the river in the Morning, with a considerable reinforcement of Militia. If we can get up with the Enemy, I have no doubt of giving a good account of them."[33]

But the militia drifted in and out of camp on their terms, driving Greene crazy. He complained in a letter to General Washington: "Our Militia had been upon such a loose and uncertain footing ever since we crossed the Dan [River], that I could attempt nothing within confidence tho' we kept within ten or twelve miles of the Enemy for several Days."[34]

❧   ❧

Nathanael Greene and Lord Charles Cornwallis played a nerve-wracking game in the wilds of northern North Carolina. Like boxers circling in search of an opening they continuously camped near each other looking for the right conditions to press an attack. Through the entire month of February 1781 and well into March, Nathanael Greene never took off his clothes, not even to sleep or bathe; he did not even change his shirt. He was too busy, too aware that as he dogged Cornwallis's troops, they might attack him at any moment. He got very little sleep during this time, a time in which he received, he liked to say, "the greatest compliment" ever paid him.

The praise came from a Col. John Green of Virginia, no relation. One night Greene heard the colonel snoring in his tent; Greene poked him and said, "Good heavens, colonel, how can you sleep with the enemy so near, and this the very hour for a surprise?"

Colonel Green drowsily puzzled a response for a moment, then said: "Why, general, I knew you were awake."[35]

Fatigue pole-axed Greene in early March; the chronic ache in his eyes flared up and nearly blinded him for a few days. From camp Greene wrote:

I am rendered incapable of business my self by a violent inflammation in my eyes. I have been bleeding and physicking for several days to correct it, and in part have succeeded; but the inflammation is still troublesome and my eyes weak and painful.

In this state of difficulty and distress, I am not a little embarrassed for want of more perfect information respecting the enemies movements and intentions, as well as what is going on in their Camp.[36]

Despite his pain Greene stayed on the move, pushing his army into a different camp almost nightly to keep Cornwallis guessing. On March 9 at a camp on the

Haw River, Greene overhauled his army, transforming it from a force designed to defend against attack to an army ready to strike: "The light infantry is dissolvd, and the Army will take upon itself an entire new formation," Greene told Henry Lee. "I propose in lieu of the light infantry two parties of observation."[37]

By moving from light troops—designed to skirmish with the enemy—to infantry, Greene was signaling an intention to tackle Cornwallis head on. The reason for this refooting was reinforcements—Virginia had sent seven battalions of militia and two Continental regiments, and North Carolina had drummed up eight battalions of militia. Greene now had twice as many troops as Cornwallis; he figured that while he had the militia in camp he'd press an attack before they could leave. This offensive footing represented a sea change in Greene's thinking; barely a week before he'd written Baron von Steuben: "To risque a general action may perhaps be impolitic as one half of the Army are too unexperienced & too uninformed to withstand the storm of a bloody Battle."[38]

Now such a storm was in the wind.

❧   ❧

After breaking camp on the Haw River, Nathanael Greene marched his troops up the aptly named Troublesome Creek on the road to Guilford Courthouse, a hamlet of a hundred people in northern North Carolina. Greene knew this land well. This was the place where he'd joined the two wings of his army to begin the race to the Dan. Then he'd been trying to avoid an attack; now he was trying to precipitate one.

Lord Cornwallis camped but twelve miles away, also looking for a fight.

As Greene later wrote Washington: "When both parties are agreed in a matter, all obstacles are soon removed."[39]

Greene reached Guilford Courthouse on March 14, quickly setting up a camp there on a clear, cold night. Around 2 a.m., Greene received a message in his headquarters: A large body of horsemen was approaching and was now about six miles away.

A messenger brought updates every half-hour: The enemy continued, though slowly, to approach; an intelligence officer sent to spy on the British column moving toward Greene heard the rumbling of wheels, a sure sign that Cornwallis was advancing with his artillery.

At 4 a.m. on March 15, 1781, Greene ordered Henry Lee's legion to mount up and meet the enemy. In Lee's memoirs he recalled: "The sun had just risen above the trees, and shining bright, the refulgence from the British muskets, as the soldiers presented, frightened [my] horse," which tossed him. He remounted another horse and ordered a retreat to Greene's camp.[40] A sharp exchange of musket fire between Lee's infantry and the British announced the Battle of Guilford Courthouse.

The British came on slowly, marching along the Great Salisbury Road toward Guilford Courthouse. The dirt road passed through dense woods until it hit a rivulet called Little Horsepen Creek; across the creek were some plowed, muddy fields, about four hundred yards square, and beyond them more woods with dense underbrush. The road rose across the fields, through the woods, up to Guilford Courthouse in a series of undulating hills.

Greene took time to methodically deploy his troops on either side of the Salisbury Road. On this day Greene commanded more men than Cornwallis: about 4,400 to 1,900, which is why he decided to fight. In deploying his men, Greene took some of the advice offered by the Old Wagoner Daniel Morgan, who had written from his sickbed: "You'l have from what I see, a great number of militia—if they fight you'l beat Cornwallis[,] if not, he will beat you and perhaps cut your regulars to pieces, which will be losing all our hopes."[41]

As Morgan suggested, Greene hid sharp-shooting riflemen in the woods on both sides of the road. And as Morgan had done at Cowpens, Greene formed his troops in three lines: At the bottom of the hill stood the first line, comprised of a thousand North Carolina militia; they stood behind a split rail fence.

A few hundred yards behind them was another line of veteran militia from Virginia. Many of them were men who had run at Camden, and now felt that they had something to prove. Brig. Gen. Edward Stevens put forty riflemen behind his regiment of Virginians to shoot down any of his own men who might try to flee this fight the way his men had at Camden.[42]

Near the top of the hill at Guilford Courthouse stood a line of more than 1,400 Continentals, the best of Greene's troops.

Around noon, Greene rode down to give a pep talk to the North Carolina militia behind the split rail fence. As a strategist Greene demonstrated true genius; as a motivator of men, he was no Morgan. Greene removed his hat and mopped his brow in the noonday sun. He spoke of liberty and honor. Then

Greene rode back through the woods to the top of the hill, and the militia were left alone to stare across the plowed fields in anticipation of seeing crack British and Hessian troops emerge from the woods.

Around 1 p.m., militia Maj. Richard Harrison wrote to his pregnant wife on her predicted delivery day:

> *It is scarcely possible to paint the agitations of my mind . . . struggling with two of the greatest events that are in nature at the same time: the fate of my Nancy and my country. Oh, my God, I trust them with thee; do with them for the best!*
>
> *. . . Our general is a great and good man, his army numerous and apparently confident of victory. . . . This is the very day that I hope will be given me a creature capable of enjoying what its father hopes to deserve and earn—the sweets of Liberty and Grace.*[43]

Soon the sound of marching music filtered through the woods: squealing fifes, wailing pipes of the Scottish Highlanders, the snappy beat of snare drums. The sound grew louder, and then the first British and Hessian troops stepped from the woods into the field, which was wet and muddy from recent rains. Two brigades filed off left and right, forming a wide line. And then they charged.

A British sergeant, Robert Lamb, recalled:

> *Instantly the movement was made, in excellent order, in a smart run, with arms charged: when arrived within forty yards of the enemy's line, it was perceived that their whole force had their arms presented, and resting on a rail fence. . . . They were taking aim with the nicest precision.*
>
> *At this awful period, a general pause took place; both parties surveyed each other for the moment with the most anxious suspense.*[44]

British Col. James Webster rode forward. He called: "Come on my brave fusiliers."

"This operated like an inspiring voice, they rushed forward amidst the enemy's fire," Lamb wrote of the charge. American muskets thundered, firing flame and lead; acrid gun smoke hovered. "[D]readful was the havoc on both sides," Lamb recalled. "At last the Americans gave way and the brigade advanced to the attack of their second line."

Even though the second line expected the militia to retreat, the sight of one thousand panicked men "throwing away arms, knapsacks, even canteens" as they dashed past must have been frightening.[45]

The second wave of fighting happened in the woods; trees broke the smooth progress of the British line so the redcoats fought clustered in groups. These were good soldiers, outnumbered by two to one but still carrying the day. They pushed the Virginians back, unevenly; a large British force emerged from the woods on the left of their own line and plunged into a bowl-shaped clearing smack in front of Greene's 1st Maryland and Delaware Continentals. These were some of America's best men. The Maryland leader, Lt. Col. John Eager Howard, ordered an effective blast of musket fire into England's elite 2nd Guards.

Cornwallis ordered his artillery's six-pounders[46] to fire grapeshot—dense spheres of lead a little larger than golf balls—into the mass of men fighting; the shot would kill as many British as Americans. A wounded general lying near the cannon begged Cornwallis not to do it; his commander hesitated.

And Cornwallis repeated the order.

Cannon thundered, blowing bloody holes through men on both sides. For Cornwallis, the grapeshot had the desired effect—everyone scattered, saving the 2nd Guard from complete destruction.

As British troops continued to emerge unevenly from the woods, pushing toward Guilford Courthouse, Greene withdrew his troops. He left his four artillery pieces because all the horses used to draw them were dead on the field.

Greene wrote to Samuel Huntington, the president of Congress: "We retreated in good order to the Reedy Fork River, and crossed at the ford about 3 Miles from the field of Action, and there halted and drew up the Troops until we collected most of our Stragglers."[47]

From there, Greene put his men on a ten-mile, nighttime march to camp at Speedwell's Iron Works up on Troublesome Creek. Cornwallis was in no condition to pursue.

By the rules of warfare, the British won the Battle of Guilford Courthouse, for at the end of the day they held the ground. But it was a Pyrrhic victory.

Cornwallis began that day with 1,900 men; he ended it with less than 1,400. He had 93 killed and 50 wounded who died on the field that night; another 400 were wounded, including Bloody Ban Tarleton, who lost the index and middle fingers of his right hand.

Greene wrote to Baron von Steuben: "The Enemy got the ground the other Day, but we the victory. They had the splendor, we the advantage."[48]

❧   ❧

After the battle, the British troops camped at Guilford Courthouse. They had not eaten in more than a day, and they spent that night hungry, in a hard rain, haunted by the dead and dying. Light-Horse Harry Lee lurked in the nearby woods, spying on the British camp. In his memoirs, Lee recalled: "The night succeeding this day of blood was rainy, dark, and cold; the dead unburied, the wounded unsheltered, the groans of the dying and the shrieks of the living, cast a deeper shade over the gloom of nature."[49]

While Cornwallis's troops camped famished and wet amid the dying at Guilford Courthouse, Greene and his men slogged through the nighttime rain into camp along Troublesome Creek; they arrived at dawn of a gray day, fatigued, footsore—and ready to fight again. In his orders that morning of March 16, 1781, Greene told his officers "to secure their Arms & Ammunition & make every preparation for another field Day."

That night Greene was so worn down, he fainted.

In reporting the Battle of Guilford Courthouse to Congress, Greene wrote: "They have met with a defeat in victory." Describing it to Joseph Reed, president of the Pennsylvania Council, Greene wrote on March 18, 1781:

> The battle was long, obstinate, and bloody. We were obligd to give up the ground, and lost our Artillery. But the enemy have been so soundly beatn, that they dare not move towards us since the action; notwithstanding we lay within ten Miles of them for two days. Except the ground and the Artillery they have gained not Advantage, on the contrary they are little short of being ruined.[50]

Which was true; Cornwallis's army was almost ruined.

In the ten weeks since Cornwallis had left Winnsboro in his "mad scheme" to pursue Morgan and Greene, he had lost half of his troops; he'd begun with at least 2,500 men, though probably more like 3,200; he now had less than 1,400 hungry, tattered troops trying to survive in the rain at Guilford Courthouse. Through skirmishes, disease, desertion, and the battles of Cowpens and Guilford Courthouse, Cornwallis had lost the majority of his army. The Lord Cornwallis, born to be a military man, had been beaten by Nathanael Greene, the bookish, gimpy, asthmatic son of a Quaker preacher.

After camping two haunted nights on the battlefield, the British troops moved on for Wilmington, North Carolina, a coastal port two hundred miles away. Cornwallis wrote: "With a third of my army sick and wounded . . . the remainder without shoes and worn down with fatigue, I thought it was time to look for some place of rest and refitment."[51]

Greene rested and refit at Speedwells Iron Works for a week, plotting his next move. For the first time in six weeks he felt relaxed, writing again to Reed:

> *We have little to eat, less to drink, and lodge in the woods in the midst of smoke. Indeed our fatigue is excessive. I was so much overcome night before last that I fainted.*
>
> *Our army is in good spirits; but the Militia are leaving us in great numbers, to return home to kiss their wives and sweet hearts.*
>
> *I have never felt easy* [in the six weeks] *since the enemy crossed the Catawba until since the defeat of the 15th; but now I am perfectly easy being perswaded it is out of the enemies power to do us any great injury.*[52]

On March 24, 1781, Nathanael Greene broke his camp on Troublesome Creek and marched out to strike Cornwallis a fatal blow. He wrote to Light-Horse Harry Lee: "It is my intention to attack the enemy the moment we can get up with them. I am agreed in opinion with you that Lord Cornwallis dont wish to fight us, but you may depend upon it, he will not refuse to fight if we push him."[53]

Rain and muddy roads slowed Greene's chase of Cornwallis, as did shortages of bullets and food. He laid up on South Buffalo Creek for a couple of days while his men stuffed paper cartridges with gunpowder and lead for ammunition.

Cornwallis had a seven-day head start on his march to Wilmington, but he, too, was bogged down by bad roads and by his dying wounded. Greene's army almost caught him at Ramsey's Mill, arriving there a day after Cornwallis fled, leaving his dead unburied. Here at Ramsey's Mill, North Carolina, Greene decided to break off the chase.

"I wish it was in my power to pursue them farther," he wrote to Abner Nash, North Carolina's nominal governor, "but the want of provisions and a considerable part of the Virginia Militias time of service being expird, will prevent our farther pursuit."[54]

Now with a small and dwindling army, deep in the North Carolina wilderness, with no supply lines, "I am at a loss what is best to be done," Greene wrote Washington. And then Greene laid out a plan that was as unorthodox and as ingenious as his decisions to split his army and to retreat across the Dan.

"I am determined to carry the War immediately into South Carolina," he wrote in that same letter to Washington, a plan that meant slogging over all that same swampy territory he and his army had crossed on the race to the Dan.[55] Once again Greene was defying conventional military wisdom by turning his back on Cornwallis, exposing his flank by leaving an arguably stronger force to his rear. By moving down into South Carolina, Greene presented Cornwallis with two unpalatable choices: He could follow Greene into South Carolina, thus giving up North Carolina, or remain where he was and risk losing his chain of outposts arcing across the South Carolina backcountry.

To Washington, Greene explained:

All things considered I think the movement is warranted by the soundest reasons both political and military. The Manoeuvre will be critical and dangerous and the troops exposed to every hardship. But as I share it with them I hope they will bear up under it with that magnanimity which has already supported them, and for which they deserve every thing of their Country.

❦   ❧

Nathanael Greene wanted rum, some strong riding horses that "go easy," maybe some plump turkeys, and a half-cask of some port or claret wine.

Greene dreamed of food, drink, and good horses as he marched south through the thick, boggy woods of North Carolina. He had none of those things. He wrote his wish list to Abner Nash, governor of North Carolina, who had promised to send him bacon, cattle, English cheese, "and a wagonload of turkeys, chickens, fresh butter, turnips, etc."

"I thank your Excellency for your good intentions respecting the Poultry," Greene wrote Nash on April 13, 1781, "but I had not the good fortune to receive any."[56]

Indeed Greene and his men never received any of the goods promised, nor those on his wish list, except some rum, as they trudged the 140 miles toward Camden, South Carolina. Greene's army marched without the protection of Henry Lee's dragoons and light infantry—Greene had sent them down the Pee Dee River to hook up with militia Gen. Francis Marion. He sent his militia into South Carolina in three lightening-like prongs with Marion and Lee in the east, Sumter operating near Greene in the center, and Andrew Pickens patrolling the west. The militia generals had orders to capture whatever British outposts they could take. Camden housed one of the larger British outposts, and Greene planned to attack that one himself.

A rough-hewn, stockade fence with five cannon ensconced in redoubts formed a protective square around much of the town of Camden. Within its wooden walls were a store, a jail, a split-log stables, and one nice house, the home of merchant Joseph Kershaw, who had been driven into exile from Camden to Bermuda. While there, Kershaw had outfitted a ship full of goods to sell in America but the British intercepted it, a loss that ruined him financially, and his sons had to sell the house after his death. Nine hundred British troops lived within the confines of this swampy stockade town near the banks of the Wateree River, a key water route for supplying the backcountry.

Greene churned on for Camden through country he called "extremely difficult to operate in, being much cut to pieces by Deep Creeks, and impassible Morasses; and many parts are covered with such heavy timber and thick under brush as exposes an Army" to surprise attack.

It took twelve days of steady marching through the swamps and heavy timber before Greene's troops pulled up at the walls of Camden on April 22. He reported to Congress:

> We have run every hazard and been exposed to every danger not only of being beaten, but of totally ruined. I have been anxiously awaiting for succor, but the prospect appears to me to be remote . . .
>
> At our arrival at Camden we took a post . . . about half a mile in front of their Works, which upon reconnoitering were found to be much stronger than represented, and the garrison much larger.[57]

Greene determined that the stockade town was too strong to attack, so he formed another plan. He withdrew his army to Hobkirk's Hill, a high sandy ridge less than two miles north of Camden. Here he would wait, hoping to induce the enemy to sally from the fort to attack him, as they had done at Newport. Camping so close to the enemy, he ordered roll call taken "at least three times a day" and warned "every part of the army" must be ready "to stand to Arms at a Moments warning."[58]

He camped in battlefield formation that night, with every man sleeping where he would be stationed in the event of a battle on that ground. It was a good thing he did.

The nine hundred men behind the stockade fence of Camden fell under the command of Lord Francis Rawdon, who'd been saddled, so the *Encyclopedia of the American Revolution* tells us, with "a curious reputation as the ugliest man in England." He once made the observation that American women wouldn't submit to rape "with the proper resignation."[59]

Rawdon was twenty-six, tall, strong, and, like Cornwallis, aristocratic. He was an ensign and an Oxford student at sixteen, and stormed to the top of Breed's Hill at Boston at eighteen. Rawdon was also like Cornwallis in his aggressiveness; when he saw Greene encamped outside his gates with 1,500 men, he decided that rather than be attacked he'd be the attacker.

On the morning of April 25, 1781, Greene buoyed his men's spirits by writing in his orders that every man would receive two days' worth of food and "a gill of spirits . . . as soon as the spirits arrive."[60]

Around 10 a.m., before the rum wagon came up, Greene heard the thunder of musketry at the base of the hill not three hundred yards away, the sound of Rawdon's troops meeting Greene's sentinels.

The British pushed up Hobkirk's Hill in a line; Greene ordered his men to form a wider line across the face of the hill to flank them.

When Rawdon saw Greene's line spreading wide across Hobkirk's Hill to flank his, he smartly brought up his reserve infantry to form an even wider line to outflank Greene.

For months, Greene had been complaining about the lack of officers in his Southern army, a shortage that was now about to hurt him.[61] Officers were as crucial to eighteenth-century armies as quarterbacks are to football teams; Greene called them "the Soul of an Army." On the battlefield they read the ever-evolving situation, barked the orders that men were to move to, and made necessary changes.

As the British marched steadily up Hobkirk's Hill, Greene ordered his men not to fire but to charge with the bayonet.

The British stopped and fired. A shot cut down Capt. William Beatty of the Maryland line, described by Greene as "a most excellent Officer and an ornament to his profession."[62] With Beatty down much of the Maryland line stood far from their next nearest officer, Col. John Gunby, now trying to control his understaffed Maryland regiments. Gunby saw the center of his line charging before the men at either end of the line even heard the charge order, causing his men to form the shape of a bow. Gunby shouted, "Halt!"

He meant for the men in the center to wait, but those who heard the command became confused by it: First Greene had told them not to shoot, which generally meant that they'd go on the offensive, pressing a bayonet attack. Then Gunby told them to halt before a charging British force. The orders made no sense and the men broke ranks and ran.

Greene rode along the ridge trying to restore order; Col. William Davie recalled: "General Greene exposed himself greatly in this action . . . ; so much so, that one of the officers observed to me, that his conduct during the action resembled more that of a captain of grenadiers, than that of a major-general."[63]

Colonel Washington's cavalry, hoping to cut off the British from retreating into Camden, had attacked Rawdon's troops from behind, where they became bogged down by capturing stragglers and trying to process prisoners. Without cavalry, Greene could not stop the Maryland men's panicked flight. He ordered the rest of his men to retreat, stopping to camp in the same sandy, shadowy Pine Barrens where Horatio Gates had lost an army.

"Camden seems to have some evil genius about it," Greene wrote. "What ever is attempted near that place is unfortunate."[64]

Before the retreat the battle had been bloody; Greene's artillery blew the British off the Great Road with much carnage. The British lost 258 killed, wounded, and missing—more than one-fourth of Rawdon's force. Greene's initial report showed 270 casualties, but nearly half of those were men missing who had not understood the order to rally at Saunders Creek. About a third of them eventually returned.[65]

Losing the Battle of Hobkirk's Hill really galled Greene. "Had we defeated the enemy not a man of the party could have got back into town," he groused in a letter to Light-Horse Harry Lee. Rawdon's "sally was what every body wished for, but the event was unfortunate. The loss on either side is not greatly different one from the other. I think the enemy's must have been the greatest. The disgrace is more vexatious than anything else."[66]

Greene took out his frustrations on Colonel Gunby, ordering a court of inquiry to study Gunby's actions that day, then castigating Gunby in his written orders: "Col. Gunby's Spirit and activity . . . were unexceptional. But his order for the Regt. to retire, which broke the line, was extremely improper and unmilitary; and in all probability the only cause why we did not obtain a Complete Victory."[67]

Gunby, who had led the First Maryland with distinction at Guilford, naturally took umbrage; he blamed the defeat on Greene, circulating the story that Greene was lax in letting Rawdon's troops approach so closely before detecting them, leaving his men vulnerable to surprise. Gunby's story of surprised troops "cooking and washing about the camp" when Rawdon opened fire has been widely circulated as the reason Greene lost the Battle of Hobkirk's Hill. But if Gunby's men really were taken by surprise after Greene issued explicit orders to camp on their arms and be ready to fight on a moment's notice, then he probably deserved his censure. The most likely cause of the defeat that day was too few officers and a lucky shot that took down another one, Beatty, early in the battle.[68] Col. William Washington's decision to tie up his dragoons in processing prisoners while Rawdon's second line moved to flank the American right also contributed to the day's defeat.

As he licked his wounds in the Pine Barrens, Greene made plans to attack Rawdon again. The day after the battle his password and countersign were "Persevere" and "Fortitude."

Catching up on some correspondence, he wrote to the French minister to the United States, Chevalier de La Luzerne: "We fight get beat rise and fight again. The whole Country is one continued scene of blood and slaughter."[69]

And to Lafayette on May 1, 1781, Greene wrote: "We fight[,] get beat, rise and fight again. We have a bloody field; but little glory."[70]

EIGHT

Eutaw Springs

O n a spring night in 1781, on the banks of a creek in South Carolina, Nathanael Greene summoned one of his colonels earlier than he customarily did. The colonel, William Davie, recalled that Greene was more depressed that night than he'd ever seen him. The recent defeat at Hobkirk's Hill had cost Greene perhaps one-fifth of his force of 950 men. The British force of the same size had lost more men but their field commander, Lord Francis Rawdon, had received reinforcements of another five hundred.

Inside his tent, Greene spread a crude map on the table and said, "Rawdon has now a decided superiority of force. He has pushed us to a sufficient distance to leave him free to act on any object within his reach." Greene explained how Rawdon could defeat him by driving him back into the Appalachian Mountains, severing him from Lee and Marion's partisan forces, which he could then mop up with troops from his chain of outposts.

"We must always calculate on the maxim that your enemy will do what he ought to do," Greene told Davie. "We will dispute every inch of ground in the best manner we can—but Rawdon will push me back to the mountains, Lord Cornwallis will establish a chain of posts along the James River [in Virginia] and the Southern States, thus cut off, will die like the Tail of a Snake."[1]

Not all of the news coming into Greene's constantly shifting camps had been bad. Right after the Battle of Hobkirk's Hill he'd heard that Francis Marion and Light-Horse Harry Lee had previously teamed up to capture Fort Watson, a small fort that stood atop an Indian mound with a commanding view of the Santee River. The Santee was the supply route for British-occupied Camden, and the Americans now controlled it.

If Greene was depressed while talking with Davie on the evening of May 9, 1781, his mood had certainly changed by the morning of May 11. With the sun barely up on that spring morning, another colonel, Guilford Dudley, rode up to an abandoned house near "a large creek of still deep water" in the heart of South Carolina.

The house was serving as Greene's headquarters and Colonel Dudley had been invited to breakfast with the general. As he swung from his saddle to dismount outside the gated fence, Dudley spied Greene's broad frame standing in the front door.

When Dudley strolled through the front gate on that morning he found the general in a jovial mood. Greene usually greeted his officers with a firm handshake, but this morning his grip was perfunctory and quick.

"Have you heard the news?" Greene said.

"No, sir, what news?"

"Rawdon evacuated Camden yesterday afternoon."

With his river supply line cut off and Greene's still-formidable presence lurking in the region, Rawdon had abandoned Camden. Yet another British outpost had fallen: first Fort Watson, now Camden. With Pickens, Marion, and Lee leading raids, the British outposts began falling like dominoes: Orangeburg, Fort Motte on the Santee River, Fort Granby on the Congaree. Without firing a shot British troops abandoned the post at Nelson's Ferry on the Santee and even left their stronghold in the port of Georgetown, so that by June all of the British outposts in the north and central sections of South Carolina were gone. When Greene had turned south and left Cornwallis in North Carolina, he had predicted that if Cornwallis did not follow, the Americans would roll up the South Carolina outposts. Cornwallis had not followed, choosing instead to link up with the British forces, then led by Benedict Arnold, invading Virginia.

And so far Nathanael Greene's plan was working.

❦   ❧

After Camden fell, Nathanael Greene put his army on the march toward the biggest British outpost in South Carolina, a frontier town called Ninety-Six. The source of its name is a mystery; the best guess is that Charleston traders believed the town was ninety-six miles from the Cherokee village of Keowee, a trading post in the foothills of the Blue Ridge Mountains.[2] Three roads criss-crossed at Ninety-Six, sandy roads so heavily traveled that more than two centuries later you can see them still, trenches cut into the earth by churning wagon wheels. The country around Nintey-Six was a Loyalist hotbed that had witnessed much murder and cruelty as neighbors turned on each other in a brutal civil war. In his memoirs Maj. Gen. William Moultrie wrote: "It was genrally said, and believed, that in the district of Ninety-Six alone, fourteen hundred unhappy widows and orphans were left to bemoan the fate of their unfortunate fathers, husbands and brothers, killed and murdered."[3]

The whole town was surrounded by a stockade fence built to withstand Cherokee raids. Since the Revolution began the British had significantly strengthened the works; the town now fell under the protection of "the Star Fort," a system of pointed parapets built atop a twenty-five-foot earthen bank covered with abatis—sharpened tree trunks. Riflemen firing from the sixteen points of the Star Fort could create a devastating cross-fire. Two block houses protected the other end of town, creating a formidable fortress.

On May 22, 1781, after a march of twelve days through early summer heat, Greene's army pulled up before the walls of Ninety-Six and found the place better fortified than expected. Inside the stockade garrison were 550 veteran Loyalist soldiers. With fewer than 900 men, Greene could not just storm the palisades of a garrison reinforced by 550; the cannon of the Star Fort would cut his men to pieces as they approached over open ground. So he decided to lay siege to the place, blocking supplies from reaching the fort while digging a long, zig-zag trench to cover his men for a close-up assault on the fort's walls. This was classic, European siege warfare, and the only knowledge Greene had of that had been gleaned from books. For advice he turned to his Polish aide, Thaddeus Kosciuszko, who had studied at a French school of artillery and military engineering.

Kosciuszko, described as quiet and urbane, had borrowed heavily to come to America and fight in the Revolution. And his career had been great: He'd picked the ground for the Saratoga battlefield, and he helped build and plan West Point. But at Ninety-Six, Kosciuszko blundered: He decided to attack the garrison's strongest point, the Star Fort, and he started digging his trenches eighty yards from the fort—far too close. On the first morning of the siege a party of Loyalists burst out of the fort, bayoneted Greene's trench-diggers, or "sappers," and stole their entrenching tools.

Greene then began his works at what Lee called "a more respectful distance" of some three hundred yards. The ground around Ninety-Six was hard-baked clay, "like digging soft stone," Kosciuszko said.[4] Troops and slaves, impressed from the local farmers, wore out their backs swinging picks and digging in hard-baked clay in early June, when the Southern sun burned hot overhead. Mosquitoes hummed and bit sweaty skin; water, hauled in heavy buckets, was far away and hard to come by. Most nights Loyalist troops sallied forth from the Star Fort and there was deadly hand-to-hand fighting in the trenches. For four hellish weeks they dug and dug and dug.

❦   ❧

On the fifteenth day of the siege of Ninety-Six, a messenger rode into Greene's camp to tell him that Fort Cornwallis, the last of the Georgia outposts, had fallen. Its commander, Thomas "Burnt Foot" Brown had been captured, along with three hundred British and Tory soldiers, and, Greene wrote in his after orders "about two hundred Negro's."

The capture of the slaves represented a windfall for American militia; at the urging of Thomas Sumter, Greene had reluctantly approved a plan that paid militiamen who agreed to serve for ten months with captured slaves in lieu of cash. Payment varied by rank from "one grown negro" for a private to "three grown negroes and one small negro" for a regimental commander.[5] The form of payment in people encouraged the militia to fracture African families by stealing slaves whenever they found them, from Loyalist and Whig alike. In summarily approving what became known as "Sumter's Law," Greene wrote: "If we can gain our Country by this means the purchase will be small altho at a high rate upon the common calculation for military service."[6]

Burnt Foot Brown was a key capture, too; before the war he'd owned five thousand acres by the Broad and Savannah Rivers, which he farmed with indentured servants instead of slaves. From the outset he'd spoken against revolution, which had so angered the local Sons of Liberty that they'd scalped him, tarred his legs, and held his feet over a fire, burning off two toes. In so doing they created a smart and determined enemy who raised a band of Loyalists that committed its own atrocities.[7] Brown was so hated in Georgia that Greene feared he would be murdered in captivity; he granted Brown parole and let him go to Savannah with an armed escort of his regular troops, whom Greene also paroled on promise that they would quit the fight.

Retaliatory murders were rampant in Georgia and around Ninety-Six. Greene complained to Pickens that one party of American militia riding along the Saluda River "plunders without mercy and murders the defenceless people just on private peak [pique]." Greene implored Elijah Clarke, a popular militia colonel, "to use your influence to restrain two very capital evils which rage in this Country and which if not prevented must soon depopulate it. I mean private murders and plundering."[8]

On the day that he wrote that letter to Clarke, June 7, 1781, Greene read a letter from a Quaker leader, Abel Thomas, who'd been dogging Greene's steps since he'd left Camden. Thomas wrote that he had tried to pass through Greene's camp near Camden but had been turned back; he had started north toward his Pennsylvania home but thought better of it. Now he wanted a permit to "Pass among Thy men. . . . I feel Love in my hart To thee and to all men kind."[9]

Greene, whose father had been a Quaker preacher, replied: "I am sensible your principles and professions are opposed to war, but I know you are fond of both political and religeous liberty. This is what we are contending for, and by the blessing of god we hope to establish them upon such a broad basis as to put it out of the power of enemies to shake its foundation."[10]

From the outskirts of Ninety-Six, Greene got word via a Charleston newspaper that a large British fleet from Ireland carrying thousands of troops had arrived at Charleston. "Doubtless the Enemy will attempt to raise the Siege of this place," Greene wrote Lafayette, and he was right. Lord Rawdon was already en route to Ninety-Six with a force of two thousand men.

On day twenty-six of the siege, in the evening, a local man came riding into camp, chatting with the soldiers as he passed. No one took much notice; as Henry Lee wrote: "our friends in the country were in the habit of visiting camp, and were permitted to go wherever their curiosity led them."[11] The countryman suddenly spurred his horse toward the garrison's closed door. High above his head he held a flapping piece of paper, a letter for the fort's commander, Col. John Cruger. American muskets thundered; the fort's door swung open; and the messenger rode through, unhurt.

Minutes later, the men on Greene's line heard cheers rising from the garrison, and Greene knew: Lord Rawdon and his two thousand men were near. Even with Henry Lee's Legion back in camp from Georgia, Greene did not have enough men to fight the 550 men in the fort plus Rawdon's reinforcements. He faced a decision: run away; try to fight Rawdon's two thousand reinforcements somewhere far from Ninety-Six; or try a bloody, full-scale assault of the fort in hopes of taking it before the arrival of Rawdon's troops.

Light-Horse Harry Lee figured Greene "probably would have decided on the safe course"—retreating—"had not his soldiers, with one voice, entreated to be led against the fort."[12] After a month of digging, Greene's troops were tantalizingly close to the walls of the Star Fort. He decided to give them a chance to storm it.

❦   ❧

June 18, 1781: In the shadowless glare of high noon the cannon roared, signaling Nathanael Greene's army to storm the garrison of Ninety-Six.

Greene's "forlorn hope"—the men assigned to rushing the high parapets of the Star Fort—plunged into the trenches carrying muskets with fixed bayonets, axes, and pikes. The bayonets were for killing, the axes to chop up the sharpened tree trunks on the fort's sloping walls, and the pikes to pull down sandbags from the parapets to make the walls easier to scale.

From inside the fort, Colonel Cruger could hear Greene's men chopping his abatis and pulling down his sandbags. He sent his own men into the dry moat at the base of his fort; they, too, were pushing bayonets. The two groups met in the ditch. Here in the glare and hellish heat of mid-afternoon men yelled, grunted, and gasped as they thrust steel into flesh, killing and dying in a bloody pit.

Lee wrote: "Here ensued a desperate conflict."

After an hour, Greene called off the attack, pulling his forlorn hope's survivors from the trenches. Henry Lee's Legion had succeeded in taking a part of the garrison, but Tories, too firmly entrenched to dislodge, still held the Star Fort.

With four hundred yards of trench and a tunnel-like mine dug to the base of the fort, Nathanael Greene had been so close to blowing the fort wide open. Now he was out of time. Rawdon was too close to continue the siege. "It is mortifying," Greene wrote, "to be obliged to leave a Garrison so near reduced."[13]

Lee's assessment was: "Three days more and Ninety-six must have fallen."[14]

Even with Rawdon's two thousand troops steadily advancing, Greene did not move that night; he encamped outside the walls of Ninety-Six. Thirty-one of his men lay dead in the ditch and on the spiky walls of the Star Fort. Greene sent a man bearing a flag of truce into the fort, asking Cruger for permission to approach the fort and retrieve American dead. Cruger replied the next day: He would send out the American dead for burial.

June 19 was a day of digging dozens of graves in the hard, sun-baked earth of the fields round Ninety-Six. Only when their own were buried did Greene's men retreat up the cooling waters of the Saluda River.

Forty-eight hours later, Rawdon's reinforcements marched into the garrison.

❧   ☙

The fifth anniversary of American Independence, July 4, 1781, found Nathanael Greene riding away from his main army to join Henry Lee's Legion of light horse skirting the edge of danger. To plot his next move, Greene wanted good intelligence of British movements in the garrison of Ninety-Six; he figured the best way to get it was to ride closer and see for himself. Once again he left his main army under the care of Gen. Isaac Huger while he rode under protection of his special forces to skulk around the outskirts of Ninety-Six, peering at the works through his pocket spyglass.

On July 10 an American spy actually spoke with the fort's commander, Col. John Cruger, and confirmed it: The British were abandoning the post the next day. Any Loyalist living in the Ninety-Six district had to move with them below the Tory stronghold of Orangeburg, in the low country toward the coastal city of Charleston; those who remained in the Ninety-Six District would forfeit any protection.

Once again Nathanael Greene had won by losing; Guilford Court House, Camden, and now Ninety-Six had fallen from British control. When Greene took command of the Southern army on December 2, 1780, the British firmly held South Carolina and Georgia; they controlled those states from the sea to the mountains through a chain of backcountry outposts arcing from Augusta, Georgia, to Georgetown, South Carolina. Both sides could have laid a tenuous claim to North Carolina: Cornwallis fielded an army of 4,000 in nearby Winnsboro, when Greene took charge of his paper army of 2,307 in Charlotte. Now scarcely more than seven months later, Greene had run Cornwallis clear out of North Carolina into Virginia, and had then captured every one of his backcountry outposts all the way down to Georgia. It was a brilliant, unorthodox campaign orchestrated by a thirty-eight-year-old man then at the height of his powers.

Greene now wanted to attack the long column of British soldiers escorting eight hundred Loyalist militiamen and other refugees from Ninety-Six along the Ridge Road on a sad, 110-mile trek to Orangeburg and below. The mid-summer march was brutal; some fifty British soldiers dropped dead from the heat.

For a few hungry days Greene's troops camped outside Orangeburg, hoping to draw British troops entrenched there into a fight; but they did not come out. Here the American Army ran out of meat and bread. Lowland rice served as a substitute for bread. For meat, Lee wrote, "Frogs abounded in some neighboring ponds, and on them chiefly did the light troops subsist. . . . Even the alligator was used by a few."[15]

There was some skirmishing—an American advance party captured three wagons from sutlers selling spirits to the British Army, but were disappointed to find only two hogsheads of rum, a small cask of wine, and some "shrub," a concoction of rum and fresh citrus.

Now in mid-July, a brutal time of heat, humidity, and clouds of malarial mosquitoes, Greene decided to give his army a rest. He pointed them to a place poetically named the High Hills of the Santee. These hills rose like huge sand dunes from the banks of the Santee River. They humped up about two hundred feet above the river, not much but enough to lift men and horses above the snakes, alligators, and mosquitoes of low country swamps into drier, breezier air. The chain of hills ran twenty-four miles long and five miles across at its widest; cool springs and rivulets drained into the Santee. Much of the High Hills had been cultivated with corn and grain, creating an undulating quilt of greens and tans, providing food and forage for men and horses.

On July 16, 1781, Greene's army plunked down in a place called James' Old Field in the High Hills. From camp he wrote to North Carolina Gov. Thomas Burke: "The Army has sufferd incredible hardships; and requires a little relaxation."

Capt. Robert Kirkwood of the Delaware line carefully figured that in the one hundred days since they'd turned their backs on Cornwallis to plunge into South Carolina, the light troops had marched 771 sweaty miles through the enervating heat of a Southern summer.[16]

While the troops relaxed, Greene did not. In camp he had more men than muskets, no clothes for his troops, and no money to pay them. "When I tell you I am in distress," he wrote Robert Morris, the nation's superintendent of finance, "don't imagine I mean little difficulties but suppose my situation to be like a Ships crew in a Storm where the Vessel is ready to sink and the water gains ground in the hold with every exertion to prevent it. . . . I foresee more difficulties than I readily see how to conquer."[17]

The underlying cause of supply problems, Greene wrote Morris, was Congress's failure to tax the states and centralize power. He was a strong Federalist years before Alexander Hamilton, James Monroe, and John Jay wrote the *Federalist Papers*. If Congressmen continued to surrender "so much of their just and necessary prerogative into the hands of the different States," Greene wrote Morris, then internecine "broils and feuds will frequently convulse the empire for want of a sufficient respect and dependence of the States upon Congress."

From camp in the High Hills of the Santee, Nathanael Greene's thoughts turned home to Rhode Island. He was sick of the war, the heartbreak and desolation of it. He wrote his wife:

> I suppose you are at Westerly. I wish I was there with you, free from the bus-
> tle of the World and the miseries of war. My nature recoils at the horrid scenes

*which this Country affords, and longs for a peaceful retirement where love
and, softer pleasures are to be found. Here turn which way you will, you hear
nothing but the mournful widow, and the plaints of fatherless Child; and
behold nothing but houses desolated, and plantations laid waste. Ruin is in
every form, misery in every shape. . . .*

    The heart you sent me is in my Watch, and your picture in my bosom [in
a locket].[18]

Almost as soon as Greene pitched his camp he received a letter penned six
weeks before by the Marquis de Lafayette, whom Greene had put in charge of
the Southern army's troops in Virginia.

"Propositions of Peace have been made," Lafayette wrote, "and A Mediation
offered." By now the American Revolution had drawn in most of Europe's major
powers—Spain and Denmark had joined France in declaring war on England,
which hired soldiers from Germany; the Empress Catharine of Russia had
offered to mediate between the warring nations, and Great Britain had accepted
that offer.

"The Ennemy's plan," guessed Lafayette, "Must Be to Secure the Southern
States. They will persuade [argue] that over Running [a state] is possessing" it—
a keen insight by the young marquis.[19] The proposed truce would be based on
the concept of *uti possidetis*, the principle of combatants retaining all ground that
they possessed at war's end.

When Greene took over the Southern army, the British could have laid some
claim to possession of everything south of Virginia; now they had no force in
North Carolina, and America had always kept a functioning civil government
there. Both sides could still lay a tenuous claim on South Carolina and Georgia—
Greene held most of the ground, but the British held key cities, Charleston and
Savannah, in both states, and no civil government operated in either state.

At this point in his career, Greene's vision was preternaturally clear.
Though he would not have favored any agreement short of full independence
for all of the thirteen states,[20] Greene had anticipated the possibility of a peace
based on *uti possidetis*; indeed that possibility formed the foundation for his
strategy—reclaiming as much land as quickly as he could while badgering the
former leaders of Georgia and South Carolina to get their governments up and
running.

Throughout the spring and summer of 1781 he tried his best to study developments north of him—Lafayette's Virginia campaign against Cornwallis, Washington's movements around New York City, and the French Army's situation in Newport.

That summer Washington twice visited Rochambeau for consultation on the best way to combine the French and American forces. They met once at Newport—where cannons of the French forts welcomed him with a salute that shook the ground—and once in Weathersfield, Connecticut; the two men agreed that the French Army should march from Rhode Island to join forces with Washington's troops over by West Point on the Hudson River. There they'd monitor the movements of the French Navy's fleet and try to link their troops with it for a joint attack on some port city held by the British.

While retreating toward the High Hills of the Santee in June, Greene had written James Varnum, his former company commander in the Kentish Guards:

> *I think the greatest stroke may be struck in Virginia. If the* [French] *fleet was to run immediately into Chessapeak Bay and land a force sufficient to cut off Lord Cornwallis's retreat and possess the Shipping and Garrison. . . . All this might be effected in a short time and would pave the way to still greater success.*[21]

This, of course, is exactly what happened nearly four months later at Yorktown.

In that summer of 1781, Nathanael Greene did not give all his troops a cooling rest in the High Hills of the Santee. He detached Light-Horse Harry Lee's legion and most of his other cavalry to work with 1,100 militiamen under the command of the partisan Gen. Thomas Sumter. Their mission—later tabbed the "Dog Days Expedition" by nineteenth-century novelist William G. Simms[22]—was to run the last of the Loyalists out of the Piedmont, forcing them to retreat "into the lower country" below Orangeburg to the gates of Charleston.

Though he publicly praised Sumter's conduct in the campaign, Greene felt that he could have done a better job of deploying his troops; but the Dog Days expedition did succeed in capturing a couple of small British posts, more than

141 men, nearly 200 horses, and a few wagons—one loaded with ammunition and another holding bags of coins that Greene split among the troops.

The most important accomplishment of the Dog Days expedition was proving to the locals—Tory and Whig alike—that the American Army was strong enough to bring the war right up to the gates of Charleston. Besides the garrison at Charleston, the British still had an army in the field between Orangeburg and Charleston on the Congaree River, about sixteen miles from Greene's camp. From his canvas marquee pitched in James's Old Fields, Greene turned his attention to that army; if he could capture it, the British would have no force in the field outside of Virginia.

Greene's aide, William Pierce, wrote home to Virginia: "We are gathering a respectable force together, and perhaps before many weeks shall pass away, we shall again be struggling in some bloody conflict. Mischief is a-brewing by the general, who keeps us in constant hot water, and never fails to make us fight."[23]

Pierce was right; on August 23, Greene broke down his "camp of repose" in the High Hills and ordered his refreshed army to march.

❦   ❧

Lord Francis Rawdon, Greene's adversary at Hobkirk's Hill and in the final days of the siege of Ninety-Six, fell sick in the Southern sun; he set sail for England, relinquishing his command of the field forces in the South to a lieutenant colonel named Alexander Stewart.

At age forty, Stewart was just a year older than Greene; but like the other two commanders Greene had vanquished, Cornwallis and Rawdon, he had many more years of military experience than Greene, having joined the army as an ensign at age fourteen. Stewart took direct command of about 1,500 troops that had retreated from Ninety-Six to Orangeburg, about seventy miles northeast of Charleston. Stewart could not find provisions for his troops there, so he moved them farther north up the Congaree River—just sixteen straight-line miles from Nathanael Greene's camp in the High Hills. This caught Greene's attention; he wanted to attack, but what he called "great Rains" fell, filling the swamps between his camp and Stewart's so they were impassable ("the Water being up to a Horses Belly for Miles together in the low grounds.")

If the terrain had been a clock's face, Greene would have been camped at three o'clock, and Stewart sixteen miles away at six o'clock. With the swamps between them, the only way Greene could get at Stewart was to first march north, then west, in a counterclockwise motion, then cross the Wateree at Camden Ferry. He wanted to march during the cool hours of day, so at 5 a.m. on August 23 Greene's troops struck out for Camden, looking for a fight. They marched for fourteen days and ninety miles before finally finding Stewart's camp at McCord's Ferry on the Congaree River. And it was empty. The British had fallen back forty miles to a place called Eutaw Springs.

❦   ❧

The British troops were hungry; so in the early morning hours of September 8, 1781, their commander sent a few hundred of them out from camp at Eutaw Springs to forage in the fields for sweet potatoes. Eutaw Springs was a nice, rural place in a forest of oak and cypress trees. An underground river burst forth here in two springs; the springs drained into Eutaw Creek, which flowed through a crevice into the Santee River. Where the clear springs bubbled there stood a three-story, brick mansion with a big, walled garden; the mansion overlooked eight acres cleared for crops in a heavily wooded area. British tents now stood in neat rows in the clearing, home to between 1,800 and 2,000 veteran troops.

While the foraging party was rooting for sweet potatoes, Nathanael Greene's army was marching slowly, inexorably, down the River Road toward them. Greene's troops had camped the previous night at a plantation just seven miles from Eutaw Springs. That morning of September 8, 1781, he'd woken his men early, putting them on the march at 4 a.m.

The troops moved in fits and starts, covering about three miles in three hours. At around 7 a.m. Greene halted so his men could swig a fortifying belt of rum. Col. Otho Williams, Greene's friend and tentmate, recalled:

> We . . . moved in order of battle about three miles, when we halted, and took a little of that Liquid which is not unnecessary to exhillarate the Chimiral Spirits upon such occasions. Again we advanced, and soon afterwards our light troops met the van of the enemy, who were marching out to meet us.
>
> Very serious, very important reflections began to obtrude.[24]

Sporadic musket fire boomed through the park-like forest of oak and cypress. The American light troops had not, as Williams believed, met the van, or forward part, of the main British Army; they had surprised the sweet potato party, most of whom were captured unarmed.

Around 9 a.m. on a clear, hot day, the Americans did come up against the British advance parties about three miles from Eutaw Springs: "The Enemies advanced parties were soon driven in," Greene reported, "and a most tremendous firing began."[25]

A most tremendous firing indeed: The woods around Eutaw Springs literally shook from the blasts of cannon balls. As he had at Guilford Court House, Greene built his first line of militia; unlike Guilford Courthouse, they fought like battle-tested troops, firing seventeen rounds per man before the British drove them back into the woods.

Greene's second line, comprised of North Carolina Continentals under Col. Jethro Sumner, drove the British back to the edge of their camp. Greene had kept his best men, the Maryland veterans of Guilford Court House, along with some Virginia Continentals, in reserve. Now they came on with level bayonets. In his memoirs, Henry Lee wrote that men died on the field "mutually transfixed," with an enemy's bayonet stuck in their guts and their bayonets sunk into their dead enemies.[26]

The veteran Continental troops drove the British through their neat rows of canvas tents, back toward the brick mansion with its big, walled gardens. The British general, Alexander Stewart, had ordered a major to occupy that mansion "to check the enemy, should they attempt to pass it."[27]

As the Maryland and Virginia troops drove toward the mansion, a mad race ensued to get inside that building first. The British troops won, pushing the door closed against a tide of Americans trying to shoulder it open. Hungry, thirsty American troops surging through the neat rows of the British camp began plundering the tents for food, drink, and clothes.

British marksmen opened fire from the mansion's windows, blasting their own campground with deadly fire.

Colonel Williams wrote:

Everything now combined to blast the prospects of the American commander [Greene.] *The fire from the house showered down destruction upon the American officers; and the men . . . perhaps thinking the victory secure and bent on the immediate fruition of its advantages, dispersing among the tents, fastened upon the liquors and refreshments they afforded, and became utterly unmanageable.*[28]

Much of Greene's cavalry had gotten tangled up in the "black jack" bushes on the river side of the mansion, and British troops raked them over, killing Col. William Washington's horse. Washington hit the ground hard, was bayoneted, and then captured.

After nearly four hours of fighting, Greene had seen enough. He pulled his men back, leaving an advance piquet, or guards, to keep an eye on the battlefield. The rest of his troops, some bloody, all wet with sweat and grimy with gunpowder, walked the seven miles to the nearest well at Burdell's Plantation, where they had camped the night before.

In terse orders that evening an exhausted Greene wrote: "The Troops will Encamp as they lay last Night & refresh themselves. The Wounded are to be carefully Collected & dressed, & the Prisoners of War sent off."[29]

❦   ❧

The next morning, September 9, 1781, Greene had more to write about the Battle of Eutaw Springs. And in his writings to South Carolina Gov. John Rutledge, he claimed victory: "We have had a most Obstinate and Bloody action. Victory was ours."[30]

Greene made the same claim the next day in a letter to the president of the Continental Congress, Thomas McKean:

We collected our Wounded, except such as were under command of the fire of the House, and retired to the ground from which we marched in the morning, there being no Water nearer, and the Troops ready to faint with the heat . . . I left on the field of action a strong Picquett, and early in the Morning detached General Marion and Lt Colonel Lee with the Legion Horse between Eutaw and Charles Town, to prevent any reinforcements from coming to the relief of the Enemy.[31]

When British Gen. Alexander Stewart read Greene's claim of leaving advanced guards on the battlefield, he was livid. Stewart wrote to Lord Cornwallis: "in short his Letter is full of lies." Stewart, too, claimed victory at Eutaw Springs. But he did not stick around to savor it.[32]

As a chill rain fell on the day after the battle, Stewart ordered his men to break one thousand muskets that they would no longer need; the British threw those muskets into Eutaw Springs. They also stove in twenty to thirty barrels of rum and poured it on the ground, in order to lighten the load for a fast retreat toward Charleston.

Stewart left Eutaw Springs with at least 40 percent fewer men than he'd had at the start of battle. He had lost at least 866 men out of less than 2,000: 85 dead on the field, 781 wounded or missing. This represented the greatest percentage of losses suffered by any army during the war.

Greene lost a quarter of his force: 139 killed, 375 wounded, at least 8 missing. In a report to North Carolina's governor, Greene, a veteran of ten battles from Harlem Heights to Guilford Courthouse, called the Battle of Eutaw Springs "by far the most bloody and obstinate I ever saw."[33] As for who won, arguably the "honors" of that day belonged to Stewart as his troops camped on the field; but as in all of Nathanael Greene's so-called defeats, he won by losing.

As soon as Stewart marched from Eutaw Springs on September 9—leaving seventy wounded men besides his broken muskets and stove-in rum casks— Greene pursued. He chased the British troops to Fergusons Swamp, about thirty miles from Charleston, where Stewart's troops linked with reinforcements from the city. Greene broke off the chase, writing to the president of Congress "we shall halt a Day or two to refresh; and then take our old position in the High Hills of the Santee."[34]

On the march back to the High Hills, the American Army stepped along the River Road, swinging through Eutaw Springs at 8 a.m.; Greene gave his men a chance to pause on the battlefield and reflect.

❦   ❧

Soon after he reached the High Hills of the Santee on September 16, 1781, Greene responded to a weeks-old letter from the Marquis de Lafayette; in his letter, Lafayette reported happy news: A French fleet had sailed into the Chesapeake Bay, giving the allied forces control of Virginia's coastline.

And in a postscript, Lafayette dropped this bombshell: Lord Rawdon, who had chased Greene off Hobkirk's Hill and away from Ninety-Six, had been captured while sailing home to England. He was now a prisoner aboard the French fleet. Lafayette gloated: "Lord Rawdon is certainly on Board a Ship in the James River and I shall Have the pleasure of Seeing Him in a few hours."[35]

As a captive aboard a French warship, Rawdon had a ringside seat to the most important naval battle of the war, the Battle of the Virginia Capes.

Just like they had when the French took control of Narragansett Bay in 1778, the British sent a fleet toward the Chesapeake in hopes of drawing the larger French fleet out to sea for a battle; and just as they had in 1778, the French slipped their cables to give chase on September 5, 1781.

This time, no tempest blew through to scuttle the battle; the two fleets funneled toward each other and thundered away. Both captains—the French Admiral de Grasse and the British Admiral Samuel Graves—fought a conservative, two-hour battle with only one vessel lost, the British ship *Thunderer* of seventy-four guns. For five days the fleets maneuvered within sight of each other without firing another shot.[36] Finally, his fleet intact, de Grasse sailed back into Chesapeake Bay, where he found that a smaller French fleet had arrived from Newport with six hundred marines and heavy siege cannon to assault Cornwallis's post in the deepwater port of Yorktown.

Nathanael Greene kept abreast of these developments from his camp in the High Hills of the Santee. Greene knew exactly what was unfolding: Cornwallis was trapped. He had posted his troops in Yorktown at the tip of a peninsula; Lafayette had camped his five thousand troops at the neck of the peninsula, sealing Cornwallis out on the tip. Washington and Rochambeau were hustling that way from the Hudson River with eleven thousand French and American reinforcements. The French fleet controlled the waters off the peninsula; for Cornwallis there was no way out. As Greene wrote to Gen. Anthony Wayne: "the old fox has got into the trap at last."[37]

Washington and Rochambeau rode to the outskirts of Yorktown on September 14, 1781; there they began a siege similar to the one Greene had tried to take the garrison of Ninety-Six, only on a much larger scale.

Like a bird dog, Greene had flushed Cornwallis from the North Carolina bush; and like a hunter Washington now had Cornwallis in his sights. On September 29, Greene wrote to Henry Knox: "We have been beating the bush and the General has come to catch the bird. Never was there a more inviting object to glory. The General is a most fortunate Man, and may success and laurels attend him. We have fought frequently, and bled freely, and little glory comes to our share."[38]

In early October 1781, Nathanael Greene left his army on the High Hills of the Santee and turned his horse toward Charlotte, North Carolina, a ninety-mile ride. He wanted to tour the hospitals between his camp and Charlotte, and he wanted to recruit militia from Charlotte to completely drive the Loyalists out of the low country and into Charleston.

Greene arrived in Charlotte after a long day in the saddle; he felt "unwell and very tired."[39] His hospitals were, as Col. Otho Williams had described them, "deplorable." The wounded from Eutaw Springs were "wholly without necessarys," Williams had told Greene, "some of them scarcely attended, and others wholly neglected; many had their wounds animated with fly blows [maggots]. . . . Their moans indicating pain, want and dispair impressed the Spirits of every humane Spectator."[40]

In a letter to Congress, Greene concurred: "our sick and wounded [are] in a most deplorable situation and numbers of brave fellows, who have bled in the Cause of their Country, have been eat up with maggots."

Greene returned to his camp in the High Hills of the Santee in mid-October, where he found many men sick with fever, probably malaria. His soldiers had received no pay in two years. More than a third, Greene observed, "were entirely naked with nothing about them but a breech cloth," and now they shared one tent for every ten men.[41] Yet on October 28, 1781, this camp of sickly, near-naked men, "ragged as wolves," broke out in cheers and fired all their cannon in a celebratory feu de joye: Lord Cornwallis had surrendered his army of seven thousand men, their ships, cannon, flags, and supplies at Yorktown.

Greene wrote Washington: "Nothing can equal the joy that it gives to this Country."[42]

The loss of seven thousand men at Yorktown did not force the British to surrender; in fact it prompted King George III to make a bellicose speech to Parliament, calling for "your firm concurrence and assistance, to frustrate the designs of our enemies."

The *Charleston Royal Gazette* published the king's November speech on March 2, 1782; within a week, Greene had read it, commenting to Gen. George Washington: "Your Excellency will see by the King's speech and other measures taken in Great Britain, the enemy are determined to prosecute the war."[43]

Greene did not feel ready for a renewal of warfare on the scale of Guilford Courthouse and Eutaw Springs. "We have 300 men now without arms," he complained in that same letter to Washington, "and twice that number so naked as to be unfit for any duty but in cases of desparation. Not a rag of clothing has arrived to us this winter. Indeed our Prospects are really deplorable."

To raise troops, Greene proposed arming and training slaves in Georgia and South Carolina. In exchange for fighting, the slaves would win their freedom. Before the war, slaves outnumbered whites in South Carolina by about 100,000 to 70,000. "The natural strength of this country in point of numbers, appears to me to consist much more in the blacks, than the whites," Greene wrote to South Carolina Gov. John Rutledge. "That they would make good Soldiers I have not the least doubt."[44] Greene had seen black soldiers fight at Monmouth and had commanded the segregated First Rhode Island Regiment when they held off the Hessians near Newport. He knew that they could fight.

Greene made a similar pitch for arming slaves to the Georgia legislature; they tabled it without even a discussion. South Carolina's legislature, spurred by the abolitionist Col. John Laurens, son of a former Congressional president, at least discussed Greene's proposal—before rejecting it by a vote of "12 or 15 . . . for it and about 100 against."

"Genr Greene favored it—wished for its success," noted one participant in the debate. "The northern people I have observed, regard the condition in which we hold our slaves in a light different from us. I am much deceived indeed, if they do not secretly *wish* for a general Emancipation, if the present struggle was over."[45]

South Carolina did offer to send unarmed slaves to the Continental Army as servants and artisans, but with two catches: They'd retain their status as slaves, and they would count toward the state's quota of armed men. Greene felt this was preposterous, and the matter died.

While the American states, outside of Greene's native Rhode Island, refused to arm slaves, he knew that the British in Charleston were doing it. To buttress his argument Greene wrote Gov. John Rutledge of South Carolina:

> *The* [British] *army are now arming a considerable body of negroes and I am well informed that they determine to compleat them to the number of 3,000 for the defence of Charlestown should it be necessary nor can we doubt of the measures being approved by british Administration when Lord Sandwich declared in Parliament that the Ministry would avail themselves of every thing that God and Nature had put in their power to crush this rebellion.*[46]

The British never did arm three thousand slaves, far from it; the actual number was closer to seven hundred, including two outfits of mounted dragoons that operated on the outskirts of Savannah. Most of the fiercest fighting of 1782 took place around Savannah, where Gen. Mad Anthony Wayne's troops killed a leader of the Black Dragoons called General March. Unlike the all-slave First Rhode Island Regiment, which was led by whites, Britain's black troops served under black officers, such as March. About ten weeks after March's death the British abandoned Savannah, leaving them in possession of just two cities in the United States: New York and Charleston.

❦   ❧

In late October 1781, the schooner *Adventure* slipped into Newport Harbor; it had sailed directly from Virginia's York Peninsula, and its captain brought the news that Cornwallis had surrendered to Washington at Yorktown. Within a week of getting the news at her farm in Westerly, Caty Greene had packed her two-horse carriage with the Greene coat-of-arms painted on the doors for a long trip through a war-wrecked country to the Deep South.

Caty, a 27-year-old mother of four, had not seen her husband in nearly two years. When they'd last seen each other at Morristown, he'd been on the outs with Congress after his resignation from a quartermaster's department that was in shambles. Now he was lionized at home and abroad as the Conqueror of the South.

With the South somewhat placated, Caty was determined to see her husband, who was then moving his troops into the swamps of the Carolina low country, nearer to the British garrison at Charleston. His march through the flooded Four Hole and Cypress Swamps were "the most disagreeable" he had ever made.

Caty's trip would be a hard, hazardous journey of more than a thousand miles. For company on the first leg of her trip, Caty had Billy Blodget, a funny, Falstaffian character who'd been a major in the Continental Army; she also brought her six-year-old son, George Washington Greene.

Greene heard of Caty's planned journey in mid-November, and he could not believe it:

"I am told Mrs. Greene is coming to the southward;" he wrote Henry Knox on December 10, 1781, "but I can not give much credit to it, as the under taking is so arduous, and I have painted to her the dangers and difficulties in such strong colours. However I left her at liberty to follow her own inclinations, and perhaps her wishes has got the better of her prudence."[47]

By the time Greene wrote that letter, his wife had already been in Philadelphia for three weeks; she'd arrived "in charming health," Knox reported, and planned soon "to wing her Way to the High Hills of the Santee" with young George.[48]

Those plans went awry. She fell ill; a Christmas Eve blizzard socked in Philadelphia, immobilizing carriages. Then there was the issue of taking the boy George Washington Greene into what was still a hot war zone. Col. Charles Petit, a wealthy Philadelphia lawyer and a good friend of the Greenes, persuaded Caty to leave the boy in his care.

Caty's illness lingered for weeks. She finally rode out of Philadelphia on January 15, 1782, rolling over frost-hardened roads now in the company of Maj. Ichabod Burnet, one of Greene's closest aides, though at times a grouchy and impatient travel companion.

"The severity of the weather and the excessive badness of the roads caused many unexpected delays," Burnet wrote Greene.[49] An ice-clogged river prevented ferry passage, forcing Burnet and Caty to spend a week at Mount Vernon, George Washington's palatial spread on the Potomac. Neither George nor Martha Washington was there—Martha had just lost her only son,

John Parke Custis, who contracted dysentery in camp outside Yorktown. Martha was then grieving his loss in Philadelphia.

After twenty days on the road, Caty and Ichabod Burnet reached Fredericksburg, Virginia:

"Mrs. Greene bears all the fatigue and delay with her usual fortitude and cheerfulness," Burnet reported to Greene. "She is yet undetermined what route to pursue, but will proceed, after refreshing her horses a day or two at this place."

A "day or two" at Fredericksburg turned into nine; the local leaders demanded that the wife of the great General Greene stick around for a George Washington's birthday bash. The ball "was brilliant," the *Maryland Gazette* reported, "being composed of sixty-odd ladies and an equal number of gentlemen. Mrs. Greene danced with General [Alexander] Spotswood."

She hit the road again on February 13, 1782; after five weeks of wagon wheels churning through the red dirt roads of Virginia and North Carolina, she drew within a few days' ride from Greene's camp.

Burnet found shocking conditions in the South. He wrote to Col. Clement Biddle, a mutual friend of Burnet's and Greene's in Philadelphia, that Loyalist militiamen "are numerous and their Situation so desperate that they confine themselves to their private haunts and conceal themselves in the Swamps from which they issue forth and murder and rob every person on the road."

Greene's army he found "in a most lamentable situation," without "money[,] perfectly naked[,] fed very scantily with Rice and poor Beef[,] without Rum and what is much worse in a most discontented situation."[50]

Greene's own assessment of his army in the spring of 1782 was: "Several hundred men had been as naked as they were born except a Clout about their middle for more than four months and the Enemy in force within four hours march of us all the time."[51] On March 24 Greene moved his army to a thicket on the Ashley River.[52] From there, Greene could better pinch off the flow of goods from the countryside to the British garrison in Charleston. With his wife coming any day now, Greene ordered: The new camp is to be kept clean. Tents must be "pitched regular and Vaults [or latrines] immediately dug."

The next day, March 25, 1782, Greene received word that Caty was drawing near; he rode out twelve miles to greet her, giving her a hug for the first time in twenty-three months. He wrote to Biddle:

Can you believe it that Mrs. Greene is at Camp in South Carolina? However improbable the thing the fact is so; and I as happy as heart can wish. Poor Girl she has had a most horid time on the way, bad roads, bad accommodations and frequent alarms, and continual delays. . . . I feel myself under great obligations for her for persevering under such a variety of difficulties to come and see me. You know I am one of the old fashioned sort of people fond of my sweetheart; and therefore must be supremely happy at meeting.[53]

Lt. William McDowell was posted on advanced guard duty that May morning in 1782, stopping all foot and horse traffic approaching a bridge spanning the Ashley River in South Carolina. On the other side of that bridge lay the American Army's base camp, and no one was to cross without permission.

Around 2 p.m. a British officer in his scarlet coat rode toward the bridge with a white flag of truce fluttering over his head. The officer identified himself as Major Francis Skelly, an aide to British Gen. Alexander Leslie, now the commanding officer of all British troops in the South. He said he came on business "of consequence to both armies."

McDowell sent that day's field officer to fetch his commander, Maj. Gen. Nathanael Greene, who was in no hurry to meet with the British major; Greene left him cooling his heels at the bridge until sunset.

"While he remained with me, we had a good deal of conversation," McDowell wrote in his journal. "He hop'd that matters were on a rare footing for peace; he hop'd that we would soon have the pleasure of drinking a glass of wine and taking each other by the hand in peac[e]able terms."[54]

Greene eventually came down and met with Skelly in an outpost; he handed Greene some official-looking documents fresh off the boat from England: a March resolution of the British House of Commons, and King George III's reply to it.

Greene read the House's resolution, calling for an end to "offensive War on the Continent of North America." King George concurred, writing that he wished "harmony between great Britain and the revolted colonies."

Skelly offered Greene a ceasefire; if American troops would not fight, the British troops would also cease.

If anyone was ready for peace it must have been Nathanael Greene. Of all the generals in the Continental Army only three had served since the 1775 siege of Boston: Washington, Knox, and Greene. Of those, Greene had seen far more hardship, battle, and bloodshed. Indeed, the story of Nathanael Greene's life during the war reads as a biography of the American Revolution itself.

Greene dismissed Skelly around 8 p.m. He slept on it that night. And then Nathanael Greene rejected this peace proposal. He wrote Congress, spelling out his reasons for rejecting the ceasefire: If America stopped fighting, England could turn more resources against France, which was not fair to America's trusted ally; also a ceasefire would lull Americans into a false sense of security, making it more difficult to negotiate a "peace with honor."

So the fighting continued, not as much as before but enough to end the life of a son of a former Congressional president: On August 27, 1782, Col. John Laurens died in a rice paddy as he led a reckless attack on British ships that had sailed up the Combahee on a foraging expedition.

"Poor Lawrens has fallen in a paltry little skirmish," Greene wrote to a friend. "This State will feel his loss; and his father will hardly survive it."[55]

By September 1782, British bullets had ceased killing American soldiers, but malaria dropped them in droves. Many thought that the summertime fevers of the South sprang from swamp vapors rising in the morning mist. Sick soldiers became such a problem that Greene moved his camp seven miles from Bacon's Bridge to Ashley Hill, South Carolina, in hopes that higher, drier ground would stem the fever. Still it spread, so that by September more than half the men, including Greene, suffered from "malignant fever."

Greene reported: "alas we have buryed upwards of two hundred of our fine fellows. A loss which we feel most sensibly as well from the smallness of our numbers as from the manner of their deaths. Had they fallen in the field it would have been nothing; but to dye in hospitals is truly distressing."[56]

To avoid the sickness Greene's wife, Caty, in company with a few ill officers, sailed over to Kiawah Island, near Charleston. Part of this party, Capt. William

Pierce, reported to Greene: "I feel much benefited already by the salts, and everyone here seems to have improved by them . . . Mrs. Greene who is the very picture of health, sits, observes, and laughs at all about her."[57]

Finally on December 13, 1782, word came that the British would sail next day from Charleston, their last stronghold in the South.

"It is one of the most pleasing events of my life," Greene wrote of the evacuation.[58] To Jeremiah Wadsworth he recounted the odds that he faced in chasing the British from the South:

> [T]*he enemy had upwards of 18000 regular troops in the southern department last year* [plus 3,000 militia and nearly 1,000 black soldiers]. *Upwards of 10000 of these were in South Carolina and Georgia. . . . I believe when it is known our force amounted to little more than 2000 Men it will be difficult to account how the enemy have left this Country.*"[59]

On December 14, 1782, two years after taking the Southern command, Greene rode into Charleston behind thirty dragoons; behind him came about 150 people, members of city government, his officers, and eminent citizens. They were trailed by 180 cavalry, a huge party of men and horse marching into the newly freed city.[60] Greene, his wife, and his military aides moved into the former governor's mansion in "Charlestown," which was renamed Charleston to make it sound less British. The house was a grand, three-story structure with gingerbread trimming on the two-tiered verandah.

Naturally the local leaders wanted to host a ball to celebrate the city's liberation; Greene was cool on the idea, but urged his officers to go as "a generous return for the respect intended. . . . we must[,] we must take it as it is offered."[61]

Col. Thaddeus Kosciuszko turned his skills as a military engineer to festooning Dillon's Long Hall with magnolia leaves sprouting paper blossoms. The ball was held on January 2, 1783; Caty attended, but Greene did not. "It was elegant and pleasing;" he wrote, "but you know I have not the higher relish for these amusements."[62]

Even with the British gone, Greene had much on his mind. The war was not officially over; he still had an army to clothe and feed, and it was faring badly.

"I wish you a happy newyear," he wrote on January 1, 1783, to Gen. Mordecai Gist. "If the year continues as badly as it has begun we shall end badly as we have nothing to eat for man or beast."[63] Greene was not exaggerating. Hungry men with guns are a dangerous force, and they began plundering. Greene complained of his men taking "meat out of the Market" in Charleston "at the point of the bayonet."[64]

The hardships of Greene's troops were well-known to Congress. Supplies sent toward Greene's troops from Philadelphia tended not to reach their destination—armies in between snatched them up, or teamsters hired to deliver them claimed items such as shoes had fallen from broken casks while en route.[65] Gen. Benjamin Lincoln, now the secretary of war, wrote in the fall of 1782 that Greene could strike any deal that he saw fit to buy clothes for his troops.

The nation's superintendent of finance, Robert Morris, followed Lincoln's lead, granting Greene authority to negotiate Army contracts in Georgia and the Carolinas. Greene's problem was that no reputable contractor could promise to supply the great quantities of winter clothing and provisions that Greene needed. Joseph Kershaw, who essentially owned the town of Camden before the war, said he couldn't fill the contract because "the Stocks of the Country around for A great distance [are] almost totally destroy'd.[66]

❦   ❧

Morris advertised seven contracts for supplying the Southern army and only one merchant, John Banks with the Virginia firm of Hunter, Banks, and Co., bid on the contract. Greene agreed to do business with Banks.

In November Greene gave his officers a two-month advance in pay so they could buy clothes. The advance was not in cash—Greene didn't have much, if any, but in "drafts" or bills against the United States with Morris as their agent. The merchants in Charleston did not want to accept these speculative drafts in exchange for good clothes, so Banks concocted a complicated scheme: The bills on Morris would be used to buy tobacco in Virginia, where growers would accept the drafts in exchange for tobacco, a real, durable good. The tobacco would then be shipped to British islands in the West Indies, where cash from its sale would be given to the merchants that had sold clothing to Banks. This scheme violated Virginia's policy of doing business with the enemy.[67]

Banks had as partners two American majors—Ichabod Burnet and Robert Forsyth. They used the military mail to send their bills, and a general in Virginia ripped open their letters, exposing their illegal scheme. In one of the letters Banks had dropped Greene's name, writing: "I find General Greene an exceedingly agreeable man; and from hints dropt already, expect his proposals for an interest in a [mercantile] house we may establish in Charleston."[68]

When Virginia officials heard of the scheme they banned the tobacco sales to Banks. Now Banks had no way to pay those merchants and his credit took a hit. Greene's reputation also took a serious blow: If Greene had hinted to Banks that he wanted to join the business that he had personally contracted to supply his troops, then he was guilty of profiteering from the very men he commanded. Greene learned of Banks's claim from Virginia's governor, Benjamin Harrison, and denied it in the strongest possible terms, going so far as to make Banks sign an affidavit declaring that Greene had never said any such thing.

Banks wasn't selling only clothing to Greene's troops; he also supplied sundry necessities such as beef, candles, and soap. In the spring of 1783 his credit dried up, and Banks could buy no goods to sell to the Army. With no provisions coming into camp, the First and Third Continental dragoon companies began to ride out in mutiny. Their major, John Swan, stopped them and asked why they were committing mutiny.

"I was informed by the sergeants that they had been starving for several days," Swan reported to Greene. "In this Situation I was at a Loss how to act. Their Complaints were in many instances too true."[69]

Swan convinced his dragoons to stay, but Greene needed to do something drastic or his troops would disband and plunder the countryside en route to their homes. In order to keep supplies flowing, Nathanael Greene pledged his personal bond for 30,000 pounds sterling to cover debts to merchants who had sold clothing to his army through Banks.[70] As part of the deal Greene expected Banks to use money that he made from the contracts to pay debts owed to the merchants.

In signing that agreement, Greene had essentially agreed to cover the costs of clothing an entire army. He had seen the Marquis de Lafayette make a similar magnanimous gesture, guaranteeing 1,550 pounds to clothe troops marching south in 1781; but the Marquis was a French aristocrat who drew a salary of 18,000 pounds per year for doing nothing. Greene, on the other hand, was broke. Almost all of Greene's wartime investments had gone bust—his privateers had made fortunes then lost them; the Batsto iron furnace in New Jersey had not turned a profit. His one asset was real estate. Thanks to the appreciative legislatures in the Carolinas and Georgia, he had plenty of land: All three states had voted to give him huge tracts. South Carolina and Georgia gave him fallow but promising plantations confiscated from exiled Tories.

South Carolina gave Greene a plantation called Boone's Barony, some 6,600 acres on the Edisto River. The legislature authorized an expense of 10,000 guineas to buy the land. They spent less than that, and Greene successfully petitioned to use the rest of the money to buy the plantation's "Negroes," or slaves. Certainly slavery would have been nothing new to Nathanael Greene. In 1750, when he was eight, one in ten people in his native state of Rhode Island was enslaved, with a particularly heavy concentration of slaves in Newport, a city he knew well. His wife, Caty, probably grew up with four slaves in her uncle's house, and Nathanael and Caty "owned" Africans, such as a house slave named Christa, during the war.[71]

In his petition of February 26, 1783, Greene argued that he should receive the Boone's Barony slaves because:

> *The land without the means of cultivation will be but a dead interest. Those negroes belonging to the estate will be of more value to me than to any body else, but it will be enitrely out of my power to purchase them unless the State will make the conditions of pay favorable to my wishes. . . .*
>
> *I have a dependant family and children to educate which I hope will apologize for this proposition.*[72]

The Georgia plantation, Mulberry Grove, looked particularly promising: more than 1,300 acres, much of it "fine River Swamp" for cultivating rice on the Savannah River, plus a "very elegant House."

The value of both plantations lay in the crops they could produce, chiefly rice. From his headquarters in Charleston, Greene began buying more slaves to work his plantations. He spent more than five thousand pounds sterling for more "Negroes," whom he enslaved at Boone's Barony.[73]

Warner Mifflin, a Philadelphia Quaker who freed all of his slaves before the war, pressed Greene on the subject of slavery, pointing out the obvious contradiction that Greene had fought for liberty and was now practicing slavery. Mifflin had read the letter that Greene had written to the Quaker, Abel Thomas, while encamped at Ninety-Six. "[A]nd as thou mentioned a hope you should fix

Liberty on so broad a basis that it would be lasting . . . thou said nothing respecting Black People," Mifflin wrote, "yet as the Grand Strugle was for Liberty and thou took thy Commission from Congress who had in their Declaration [of Independence] set forth in such clear terms its being the Natural right of all men should thou after all by thy Conduct countenance slavery it would be a stigma to thy Character in the Annals of History if the Historians of the present day should do justice in transmitting to Posterity the transactions thereof."[74]

Greene responded: "On the subject of slavery, nothing can be said in its defence."[75] Then he attempted to offer not so much a defense as an excuse: "The generosity of the southern states has placed an interest of this sort in my hands, and I trust their condition will not be worse but better. They are, generally, as much attached to a plantation as a man is to his family; and to remove them from one to another is their great punishment."

He continued to enslave hundreds of people for the remaining three years of his life.

§   §

On April 16, 1783, somewhere around 11 a.m., an express rider galloped up to the John Rutledge mansion with an urgent message for Maj. Gen. Nathanel Greene: A ship from Paris had brought news to Philadelphia that negotiators from the United States of America had signed preliminary articles of peace with Great Britain. The war was over.[76]

Copies of King George III's speech to parliament arrived soon after: "I did not hesitate," said the king, "to go the full length of the powers invested in me, and offer to declare them FREE and INDEPENDENT STATES, by an article to be inserted in the Treaty of Peace."

Greene took up his quill and wrote to Washington: "I beg leave to Congratulate your Excellency upon the returning smiles of peace, and the happy establishment of our Independence. This important event must be doubly welcome to you who has so successfully conducted the War, thro' such a variety of difficulties to so happy a close."[77]

Greene had sacrificed as much as, and, arguably, more than Washington. In every aspect of life that is most dear to a man, Greene had suffered: in his health, his marriage, and his finances.

Almost immediately, Greene's thoughts turned to home. He wrote John Collins, a Rhode Island Congressman: "I feel for Rhode Island what I cannot for any other spot on Earth. What is it that recals this attachment; and how is [it] that neither time nor change of place can alter its Steady Operation."[78]

It would be many months of hot and tedious living before Greene could get away; he faced a near mutiny when the First Cavalry deserted, riding off with the camp's best horses; then his malarial fever flared again, leaving him "almost blind with sore eyes." Caty sailed for Rhode Island on a troop ship in early June, but he had to stay until the last man marched for home. In the eleven months from the time he took command of the Southern army in December 1780 until his final push into the low country outside Charleston the following November, Greene and his men had fought three major battles, excluding the tortuous siege of Ninety-Six, and had ridden or marched 2,600 miles.[79]

Greene gave his final orders on June 21, 1783; adjutants would usually stand before their men and read the day's orders, but on this day Greene made the farewell address to his men:

> To review scenes that are past, and look over incidents of the war, must be interesting to the feelings of every soldier. To call to mind a train of sufferings, and run over the many dangers we have passed in the pursuit of honor, and in the service of our country, affords a pleasing prospect for contemplation.
>
> The general joined this army when it was in affliction, when its sprits were low, and its prospects gloomy. He now parts with it crowned in success, and in full triumph. We have trod the paths of adversity together, and have felt the sun-shine of better fortune. We found a people overwhelmed with distress, and a country groaning under oppression. It has been our happiness to relieve them—The occasion was pressing, the attempt noble, and the success answerable. In this it has been the General's good fortune to point the way, but you had the honor to accomplish the work. Your generous confidence, amidst surrounding difficulties; your persevering tempers, against the tide of misfortune; paved the way to success; and to these are the people indebted for the repose they now enjoy.[80]

NINE

Mulberry Grove

The last military transport ship left Charleston on July 29, 1783, leaving Maj. Gen. Nathanael Greene in a pensive mood. He wrote to his friend, Charles Petit: "All the Soldiers have embarked and sailed for their respective States; and I am left like Samson after Delilah cut his locks. I am become quite like another man."[1]

The summer felt hotter than any he had ever seen; temperatures hit the high nineties day after day, and as he tended to the final acts of closing out his army's accounts, Greene's patience snapped. His wife, who had gone on before him to escape the heat, was then in Philadelphia, where she was often seen at parties on the arm of Gen. Mad Anthony Wayne, a war hero celebrating in the city without his wife.[2] Caty spent freely, buying silks, a pair of horses, and much more. In a letter to Caty, Greene wrote:

Petit . . . writes that he has got you a pair of horses to your liking, and a Phaeton [a kind of carriage] and that a Chariot is making and that the amount of the whole will be upwards of 1400 Dollars. He adds also that he will want the money the moment I arrive. How or where to get it god knows for I dont. Col Wadsworth informs me all my stocks put into his hands have been lost; and that out of upwards of a thousand pounds put into his hands four years ago, I have not fifty left. . . . I had rather live in a cave than be under so much perplexity.[3]

Like many military men, Greene found the transition to civilian life very hard. He rolled out of Charleston on August 14, bound for Rhode Island by coach. Bells rang throughout Philadelphia to announce and honor Greene's arrival there on October 4; he then rode with Washington from Trenton to Princeton—a trip made in very different circumstances than the time they'd skulked out of town on a stumpy back road through a freezing night. Congress was meeting in Princeton, removed there from Philadelphia to avoid armed mobs of soldiers demanding their pay. As he was still officially in military service, Greene asked Congress for permission to go home: "It is now going on Nine years since I have had an opportunity to visit my family or friends or pay the least attention to my private fortune," he petitioned. "I wish therefore for the permision of Congress to return to Rhode Island."[4]

In resolving that "Major General Greene hath permission to visit his family at Rhode Island," Congress took the additional step of granting Greene two engraved cannon "taken from the British Army at the Cowpens, Augusta, or Eutaw" Springs.[5] He never did get them.

Business detained Greene in Philadelphia as he attempted to clear up some accounts. Here he learned that the firm of Hunter and Banks had not used any of their profits from the Army contracts to repay the merchants whom Greene had promised to pay in case of default.[6] John Banks had diverted that money into other ventures and Greene was on the hook for the 30,000 pounds sterling that he had guaranteed to feed and clothe his army.

From the City of Brotherly Love, Greene took care of some plantation business: buying slaves. He'd received a letter from his slave broker telling him that the prices Greene wanted to pay for people were way too low:

"[C]ommon field Negroes sold at St. Augustine from 50 pounds to 70 pounds Sterling, and on Credit they sell of course much higher. The lowest terms that any have been offerd at were 70 pounds pr head for a Gang of 72, viz. 25 Men, 24 Women & 23 Children.

There are several other Gangs for Sale, but they expect higher Prices." With more money Penman could buy a "gang" of 70 slaves "of which 50 are Workers, and the rest Children some of which are nearly fit for the Hoe."[7]

Greene wrote back from Philadelphia that he would be willing to pay more, but not more than seventy pounds per person, and "The Negroes must be sound, not old, and the property unquestionable. I beg you will engage the Negroes as soon as possible and have them conveyed to my estate in Georgia."[8]

Greene bought fifty-eight slaves for his Georgia plantation, though he later groused upon inspecting them that "many are small."[9]

＊　＊

Late in the drab month of November 1783, a sailing ship ghosted into Newport Harbor in the darkness. Nathanael Greene, by now the storied Conqueror of the South, stepped off the ship without fanfare. He walked or rode a carriage to his new home, a house his wife had rented in "The Point" section of Newport, a damp and chilly neighborhood on the waterfront.

Greene quickly determined that the house "will not answer well for the Winter" and set out to find one on higher ground. Newport was then a depressing place; before the war, Paul Revere called it "the garden of America" for its fruit orchards and fertile fields.[10] Now there was barely a single tree standing on the whole of Aquidneck Island. During the three years of British occupation, troops had cut orchards and burned fruit trees as firewood; they ripped the planking off the wharves and burned it, also to keep warm; they torched houses on the waterfront and pulled them down on the hills to create better firing lines for their cannon.

Most of the houses in nearby Bristol and Warren were still burned-out shells from the British raid of 1778. Much of the long and narrow nation of the United States bore the marks of England's scorched-earth campaign: Bedford-Fairhaven in Massachusetts; New London-Groton, Connecticut; Esopus, New York; Springfield, New Jersey; Georgetown, South Carolina. Coastal cities such as New York and Charleston stood burned and shelled from the war, while along the mountainous frontier, American armies had laid waste to Indian villages from the Adirondacks of New York through the Cherokee and Creek settlements in the Appalachians of Georgia.

For Greene there was no homecoming fanfare. There were the predictable encomiums from the General Assembly and committees from local towns. They all offered good words and the best of luck, but no one offered what Greene needed most: money. In attempting to rebuild his life in a war-wracked country, Greene felt enormous economic pressure. He lived with bad credit in a bad house, and in January, the new year of 1784 brought him bad news: A hurricane had wiped out his Boone plantation's rice crop.

That winter was one of the worst of the century. Greene slipped on ice and "hurt the vessels of the stomach," he complained to Charles Petit. "I was seized with deadly pain" that spread into his chest and lasted well into spring.[11]

Also, for the fifth time in seven years, Caty was pregnant. "Mrs. Greene['s] situation has prevented my visiting Boston," Greene wrote to Henry Knox in early March 1784. "I expect her to put to bed every hour."

Three weeks later he wrote Knox again, "Mrs. Greene is not yet in bed but in hourly expectation. My little flock engross my attention and the little prattlers find some new avenues to the heart every day."[12]

Before his November homecoming, Greene had not seen his wife since she left Charleston on the brig *Christiana* on June 7, so by mid-March—nine months later—he naturally expected the baby to be born at any moment. The human gestation period is about 280 days, which, assuming conception on the last day they could have seen each other in South Carolina, would have brought the birth on March 12.

In a letter of April 15, he was still waiting.

Finally on April 17, 1784, a healthy baby girl named Louisa Catharine Greene was born. From Newport Greene wrote to his business partner and former assistant quartermaster, Col. Charles Petit: "I imagine you will be equally surprised to find me here as not having heard from me before. Mrs. Greenes not getting to bed as early as she expected prevented my setting out for the Southward[,] and a very disagreeable complaint in my breast has forbid my writing."[13]

Caty's putative term of 315 days (1784 was a leap year) was almost a smoking gun for infidelity. A rumor swirled that Greene "had made application for a divorce from his wife, because she had been unfaithful to his bed in his absence." Isaac Briggs, a Georgia inventor and politician who owned land near Greene's in

Georgia, took it upon himself to investigate this rumor on a trip to Newport. He
reported:

> *I made inquiry concerning this report and found 'twas all a lie. . . . A lady*
> *who is superior to the little foibles of her sex, who disdains affectations, who*
> *thinks & acts as she pleases, within the limits of virtue and good sense,*
> *without consulting the world about it, is generally an object of envy and*
> *distraction.—such is Lady Greene* [Caty.]*—She confesses she has passions*
> *& propensities & that if she has any virtue 'tis in resisting and keeping*
> *them within due bounds. . . . In short she is honest & unaffected enough to*
> *confess that she is a woman, & it seems to me the world dislikes her for*
> *nothing else.*[14]

In May 1784, Nathanael Greene left his wife and their five children in their
rented house near the Newport wharves and set out for Philadelphia; he hoped
to settle his Army accounts with Congress. He had no luck. The war had
saddled Congress with a national debt of 30 million dollars, and the federal
government had no power to tax the states to pay for it.[15]

Bad news too came up from Charleston in the form of a letter written by the
overseer of Boone's Barony. "You have been very unfortunate in yr horses. The
Bays are both dead of the Farcy and one of the Chestnuts of the Bots. Your
carriage is Ruind by being exposd to the Weather. . . ."[16] And the overseer had
saddled Greene with more debt to buy "58 Negroes."

Greene sailed back to Newport on June 7. Again bad news, this time
from Philadelphia, caught up with him there: John Banks had no way of paying any of his bills. Banks "is in a bad way," a friend wrote from Philadelphia.
"I hope not ruind intirely in purse; but I am apprehensive too much so in
character."[17]

Then came a letter from a London firm called Newcomen and Collett,
dunning Greene for money for the clothing they had sold to Banks to clothe
Greene's army at Charleston. Greene answered that he was broke so the
company should badger Banks. Greene wrote that he had told Banks: "[H]e &
I would not live long in the same World if he brought me into difficulties in the
matter, and I will follow him to the ends of the Earth for Satisfaction. I am now
going to Charleston and shall be glad to hear from you there."[18]

Greene shipped out of Newport aboard a sloop that he partially owned, the *Charleston Packet*, arriving in the oppressive heat of South Carolina on August 1, 1784. Almost immediately he was hit with demands for the loans he had guaranteed to feed and clothe his army. Banks turned out to be quite a con man. He told the overseer of Greene's Boone plantation that he'd settled all debts with Greene, was acting as his attorney, and that Greene had instructed the overseer to give Banks some money. This the overseer did, before Banks fled town, leaving behind twenty lawsuits and several judgments against him.[19]

The debt for Banks's Army purchases weighed heavily on Greene as he wrote from Charleston to his brother Jacob:

> *My heart is too full and my situation too distressing, to write much. . . . My situation is truly afflicting! To be reduced from independence to want, and from the power of obliging my friends, to a situation claiming their aid. . . . My heart faints within me when I think of my family.*[20]

In September 1784, Nathanael Greene set out from Charleston bound for North Carolina to find John Banks. From Charleston, Greene wrote to Caty: "Banks has been such a peculiar curse to me that I am almost led to beleive that Providence has designed him for a scourge for some of my evil deeds. . . . I verily believe if I was to meet him I should put him to death. He is the greatest Monster and most finished vilian that this age has produced."[21]

Greene was not the only angry man on Banks's heels. Patrick Carnes, a former officer in Light-Horse Harry Lee's legion was tracking Banks for selling him a set of slaves that Banks had already sold to someone else; Robert Forsyth, a business partner of Banks's and later a federal marshal, was also on his trail.[22]

Greene traced Banks to Washington, North Carolina, a small town on the Pamlico Sound. Greene arrived in Washington on October 1, and John Banks turned up dead around the same time. As soon as he got to town Greene wrote to Forsyth: "I arrivd here yesterday and found John Banks dead and buried."

Greene reported the same story to Hugh Rutledge: "John Banks is dead and buried. He was buryed two days before my arrival. My prospects are now worse than ever."[23]

Decades later Banks's brother and business partner, Henry Banks, wrote a pamphlet claiming that Greene or an aide strangled John Banks.[24] If Banks was murdered, and it's far from certain that he was, there was no lack of suspects; and when Banks died he took with him Greene's last hope of reimbursement.

Greene pressed on from the little town of Washington, riding into Richmond, Virginia, on a borrowed horse. He'd come hoping to clear up his heavy debts, but his meeting with a lawyer had not gone well. He left Richmond for home in late October, saddled with the real possibility that he may go to jail as a debtor. Before leaving town Greene wrote Robert Forsyth, who was both his friend and a former business partner of Banks's: "I leave this place with a heavy heart, the business which brought me here hangs still over my head like a threatening Cloud which embitters every moment of my life."[25]

❧   ❧

The last full year of Nathanael Greene's life, 1785, began badly. In January he shipped from Newport bound for Charleston. The ship he was on, *Union*, was just a few days out from port when a winter storm knocked it down. Seas broke over the deck and "washed the Captain with such force against the Chains as to dislocate his Leg, and greatly injured the first Mate," according to the *Newport Mercury*. Greene, an experienced hand on a ship and a combat veteran, stayed cool. "While the ship was on her Beam-ends, the Hon. Major-General Greene . . . by an Exertion and presence of Mind peculiar to himself, was greatly instrumental" in righting the ship.[26]

The *Union* limped into Charleston on January 28, her rigging a mess of snapped spars and tangled sheets. Ashore, Greene quickly learned that heavy rains had flooded his ripened rice crops, leaving him with just a fraction of what he'd expected to sell. Then a Georgia cavalry captain who'd served under Greene in the Southern army, James Gunn, challenged Greene to a duel. Gunn felt that Greene had insulted him two years previously by refusing to let him keep federal horses as his personal property when the army broke up. Greene was in Savannah, preparing to inspect his plantation near there, when, in late February, he received a threatening letter. Gunn, who also owned a plantation on the Savannah River, was near enough to act on his threats.

Greene responded politely that it was "foreign to my intention to offer you or any other Officer an insult." That did not satisfy Gunn, who wrote that with both men now claiming civilian status, Greene no longer had the

> *power to do me an Injury notwithstanding you may feal a disposition to do so. Consequentially as I feal myself equally Independent with you: there can be no acceptation taken: nor can you object to meeting me with your friend, provided with Arms necessary on those occasions at 4. oClo. this afternoon, on Mr. Campbells plantation opposite to Savannah, to render that satisfaction, which is due to Injured reputation.*

Gunn had challenged Greene to bring a second and pistols to a duel, that afternoon, across the Savannah River in South Carolina. In a terse response that day, March 2, Greene refused the challenge. He wrote: "I will never establish a precedent for subjecting superior officers to the call of inferior officers for what the former have done in the execution of their public duty."

Greene's reasoning was sound; every officer of the past two centuries would be thankful to him for refusing to set the precedent of dueling with aggrieved subordinates. Still, declining the duel gnawed at him; more than a month after Gunn's challenge it weighed on Greene's mind as he wrote George Washington:

> *If I thought my honor or reputation might suffer in the opinion of the World and more especially with the Military Gentlemen I value life too little to hesitate a moment to answer the challenge. But when I think of the nature of the precedent and the extent of the mischief it may produce I have felt a necessity to reject it.*

Washington wrote Greene that he had done the right thing:

> *[Y]our honor and reputation will not only stand perfectly acquited for the non-acceptance of his challenge, but that your prudence and judgment would have been condemnable for accepting of it, in the eyes of the world, because if a commanding officer is amenable to private calls for the discharge of public duty, he has a dagger always at his breast, & can turn neither to the right nor to the left without meeting its point.*[27]

Even with Washington's approval, the Gunn affair rankled Greene. He took to carrying a concealed pistol in case Gunn tried anything. "If he should," Greene wrote a friend, the Connecticut merchant Jeremiah Wadsworth, "he should take a sudden leap."[28]

&   &

In a rented house on a hill in Newport, Caty Greene delivered a baby girl, her sixth child. Nathanael Greene was not home for the birth, having sailed to New York in hopes of settling some of his debt.

Greene sailed back into Newport just days after the baby's birth in mid-August 1785. He brought a houseguest, the Baron von Steuben, who had earned fame at Valley Forge for teaching Americans how to fight as unified battalions, enabling them to stand toe-to-toe with the British at Monmouth. Now Steuben was as destitute as Greene; he was so broke he had sold even his watch and silver forks to support his troops in Virginia.[29]

The Greenes now lived on a hill in Newport, where they'd moved to be above the dank air near the city's wharves. The rent cost $85 more per year, money Greene could ill afford, but he hoped the more healthful air would cut down on his doctor's bills. His hopes were in vain; soon after Greene got home all of the children came down with whooping cough. On August 30, Greene wrote to Wadsworth, sadly reporting the death of the baby, Catherine:

> *Since I wrote you last Tuesday I had the misfortune to loose my youngest Child with the throat distemper. Mrs Greene is very poorly and my two little Girls very sick with the hooping Cough. Patty is so bad with it as to be dangerous. Cousin Griffin arrived from New York and now lays sick with fever at my house.*[30]

Two days later, Greene got hit with a demand for payment of 1.1 pounds for a baby-size coffin.[31] Word spread through town that the Greenes planned to move to their Mulberry Grove plantation in Georgia; Greene groused "People knowing that I am going away harass me death for a number of little debts."

The family—five children plus a tutor, the Yale-educated Phineas Miller—sailed on October 14, 1785. When Block Island slipped astern, Nathanael Greene saw the last that he ever would see of his beloved Rhode Island.

After a sixteen-day sail Nathanael Greene wrote from Charleston:

The passage was long and disagreeable, Catys sufferings inexpressible. Her fears magnified the smallest dangers into certain ruin. However we had two Gales in one of which we lost a man over board that were not pleasant and not altogether free from danger. Caty was so affrighted during their greatest violence that she almost loose her senses.[32]

At Savannah, the Greenes and the tutor unloaded their carriages from the ship and drove the Augusta Road a dozen miles upriver to their new home, the Mulberry Grove plantation on the Savannah River. Before the State of Georgia confiscated the place and gave it to Greene, the estate had belonged to a British lieutenant-governor, John Graham, who had lived in a stately house in a grove of mulberry trees.

Greene had sent carpenters to Mulberry Grove the previous spring to spruce up the estate. Now in November, many windows were still shattered in the house, the greenhouses, and bird coops. And the place was grimy. Still, Greene was pleased with what he saw. The grounds held a coach house and stables, an out kitchen for cooking in the summer heat, a long poultry house, and a smokehouse.

One complication marred Greene's arrival: The overseer had sent a slave out to keep cattle from grazing in the rice, and the slave had built a fire—possibly to chase away the "rice birds" or bobolinks—and it burned out of control. Fire ate up a field of harvest-ready rice worth two hundred pounds sterling. Another forty-five barrels Greene sent downriver to Savannah were ruined when the ship sunk while tied to the docks. So far Greene's plantations had lost rice to flood and fire while yielding precious little for market.

In March 1786, Greene wrote a letter to Henry Knox that sounded as plaintive as a country-western song:

My family is in distress and I am overwhelmed with difficulties and God knows where or when they will end. I work hard and live poor but I fear all this will not extricate me. . . . Mrs. Greene is just ready to lay in. [For the seventh time in eleven years she was pregnant.] *And the children have just got out of the small pox by inoculation. . . . Mrs. Greene joins me in affectionate compliments to you and Mrs Knox. She is transformed from the gay Lady to the sober house wife.*[33]

Portrait of Caty Greene drawn from life probably when she was in her mid-fifties. After Nathanael Greene's death she married her children's tutor, Phineas Miller. She died in 1814 at age sixty. Attributed to James Frothingham (American, 1786–1864). Catharine Littlefield Greene Miller, c. 1809. Oil on panel. 32 ³⁄₄ x 25 ³⁄₄ in. Telfair Museum of Art, Savannah, Georgia. Museum purchase,1947.

In docketing this letter Knox scrawled: "This is the last letter I ever received from my truly beloved friend Genl. Greene."

❧   ❧

E. John Collett was a very good businessman—polished, polite, and persistent as the devil. He represented the London house of Newcomen and Collett, one of two businesses that had supplied an American Army contractor with clothes for the southern troops; now, three years after the war, he wanted payment for those clothes, payment that Maj. Gen. Nathanael Greene had guaranteed from his personal funds.

Collett was aware that in trying to collect from Greene he was dunning an American hero; in his first collection letters his tone was almost apologetic, but still—a deal was a deal and he counted on Greene's honor.

Collett sailed from London to collect that debt; upon arriving in Charleston in early March he wrote a letter that Greene either did not receive or ignored. Collett wrote again; this time Greene responded, and although the letter does not survive it is obvious from Collett's next letter—written from Savannah—that Greene laid out a litany of hardships that prevented his paying. Collett responded: "I am very Sensible Sir of the disagreeable Situation in which you are placed, & I assure you it is by no means my intention to add to your difficulties. . . . I am now in Savannah, where I shall await your answer."[34]

Despite his hardships, Nathanael Greene managed to keep a sense of humor and, at least on one April morning, a modicum of optimism. Writing to Ethan Clarke, a Newport merchant who married Greene's former heartthrob, Nancy Ward, he described a calamitous day on Mulberry Grove: His hugely pregnant wife, Caty, had turned her ankle, fallen, and bruised her hip.

Then the housekeeper's son took a horse kick to the face "and had his upper lip cut through his jawbone from his nose downwards and the end of his nose split open." Greene took up needle and thread and sewed the wound himself. "I am in hopes it will not disfigure him greatly, but cannot pronounce positively it bled so freely as to render the operation difficult."

While he was sewing the boy's bloody face the family tutor yelled that Patty, Greene's oldest daughter at age nine, had taken a sort of fit.

Here we had a serious call for all our medical knowledge and I hardly know
which is the greatest quack Mrs Greene or me. [Patty] *lay in a lifeless situa-*
tion for two hours until I got a puke to operate which restored vital heat and
activity to the circulating fluids. . . . The accidents of yesterday made me
think of Job[']*s Messengers. The family all well at noon and in the evening*
one half of it laid by the heels.

And yet, Greene wrote Clarke, his life was good. Through a settlement with
the estate of John Banks, he now owned all of Cumberland Island, an eighteen-
mile-long sea island near the Florida border. Greene planned to escape the heat
of a lowland summer by moving his family there.

"The garden is delightful," he wrote Clarke from Mulberry Grove. "The
fruit trees and flowering shrubs forms a pleasing variety. We have green peas
almost fit to eat and as fine Lettice as you ever saw. The mocking bird serenades
us evening and morning."

His orchards were fragrant with blossoms of apples, pears, peaches and apri-
cots, nectarines, plumbs, figs, oranges. "And we have strawberries that are three
inches around."

Yet, Greene wrote in a more melancholy vain, "it is a great deduction from
the pleasures we shall feel from the beauties and conveniences of the place that
we are obliged to leave it before we shall have tasted of several kinds of fruit."[35]
Greene meant that he'd never taste the fruit of his orchards because he'd be on
Cumberland Island when it ripened. In fact he never ate of his fruits, for not
long after the bloom fell from the branch, Nathanael Greene would be dead.

❦   ❦

Meanwhile, E. John Collett would not be denied; Nathanael Greene owed him a
fortune, and he was bound to collect. On May 10, 1786, he sent a messenger up
the Savannah River to deliver a collection letter to Greene's plantation. When,
Collett wanted to know, could Greene meet him face to face to discuss the debt?

Greene knew he could postpone Collett no longer; he packed his carriage
and turned his horses down the Augusta Road to Savannah. Caty rode with
him; she wanted to get off their isolated plantation for a while. She felt weak, the
result of having a full-term miscarriage after her bad fall.

About a mile from town, it occurred to Greene that his old comrade, Gen. Mad Anthony Wayne, was supposed to ride over from his nearby plantation for dinner that night. Despite their public dalliances up in Philadelphia, Greene never expressed any jealousy about Wayne and his wife; around this time, however, he did express concerns to Jeremiah Wadsworth about Caty's apparent attraction to the tutor Phineas Miller, a much younger man.[36] Greene thought about turning around to write Wayne a message saying not to come, but with his wife's weakened condition he did not want to prolong the carriage ride.[37]

In Savannah, Greene tried to hammer out a deal with Collett in which he'd pay some of his debts. The two men agreed to meet again in a month, and on June 12, 1786, the scene repeated itself: The Greene carriage rolled down the sandy, shady Augusta Road carrying Nathanael and Caty into town so Greene could meet Collett to finalize a debt schedule.

The Greenes spent that night at the riverfront home of Nathaniel Pendleton, a former aide-de-camp of the general's who had narrowly saved Greene from capture at the Battle of Guilford Court House. The next morning, Greene and his wife left early for Mulberry Grove, intending to breakfast up the river with William Gibbons; he owned the plantation next to Greene's and sometimes acted as Greene's lawyer, even though his father was suing Greene for ownership of a portion of Mulberry Grove. After noon, the Greenes and Gibbons walked his plantation to see how Gibbons's rice was getting on. An eighteenth-century rice plantation in mid-summer was a miserable place, with slaves shin-deep in muck hoeing aquatic weeds from the stinking, stagnant swamp waters that nurtured the rice.

When he resumed his carriage ride home, Greene complained to his wife of a headache; he slept on it, and the next morning, a Wednesday, it still hurt. That Thursday, June 14, his chronic eye pain flared again, behind both eyes. His forehead swelled painfully.

Pendleton rode into Mulberry Grove that evening, and was alarmed at what he saw. Greene seemed depressed and wouldn't or couldn't join in the conversation. A call went out for the local doctor, John Brickell; he arrived, drew a little blood, and administered some medicine. That didn't work. Still Greene's forehead swelled. Brickell called in a consultant, Dr. Donald MacLeod; he "blistered" the temples and drew blood freely, but Greene's entire head continued to swell until he fell into a stupor.

MacLeod dashed off a note to Anthony Wayne: "Gen Greene, I am distressed to inform you is just about closing the chapter of his life. As you may wish to be here at this unhappy moment, I thought it a duty to inform you. Mrs. Greene's Situation is not to be described."[38]

Wayne came and kept a bedside vigil of his comatose friend. On Monday morning, June 19, 1786, Nathanael Greene drew his last, shallow breath. He was forty-three years old.

In the light of a mid-summer morning Wayne dipped his quill and in a quivering hand wrote to James Jackson, a former colonel in the Georgia dragoons:

> *I have often wrote you but never on so distressing an occasion. My dear friend General Greene is no more. He departed this morning at 6 o'clock a.m. He was great as a soldier, greater as a citizen, immaculate as a friend. His corpse will be at Major Pendleton's this night. . . . Pardon this scrawl; my feelings are but too much affected because I have seen a great and good man die.*[39]

The next morning they brought the general's body by boat downriver to Savannah. The estate that had been confiscated from the Tory Lt. Gov. John Graham came with a burial plot in Colonial Cemetery, where Greene would be interred. As the boat bearing Greene's corpse sailed silently by, ships in Savannah Harbor struck their colors to half-mast. In town, merchants drew their shutters against the summer sun and closed business for the day.

Around 5 p.m., pall bearers carried Greene's casket from Major Pendleton's riverfront house. A troop of horse-guards led the funeral parade, the hooves thudding through the quiet, sandy streets of Savannah up to Colonial Cemetery. Artillery rolled behind the horses; infantry soldiers flanked the coffin. Over and over a band played the sad, repetitious notes of "The Dead March." Once a minute, the guns of distant Fort Wayne boomed.

As no preacher could be found anywhere in Savannah, a judge read a funeral service, ironically the service of the Church of England. The infantry parted for the pallbearers, who stooped to slip Greene's body into a low vault. The artillery fired a salute of thirteen guns that echoed along the river and faded. No one thought to put a marker on the plain, brick tomb.

NOTES

PROLOGUE

1. *Savannah Morning News*, March 3 and March 6, 1901. These articles contained details of the lamplight, the stench, and Gardner's hat.

2. Asa Bird Gardner, ed., *Remains of Major-General Nathanael Greene* (Providence, RI: E. L. Freeman & Sons, 1903), 32–33. Much of this chapter was recreated from this odd little book commissioned by the Rhode Island General Assembly. Besides Gardner's eyewitness report it contains sworn affidavits from the parks department laborers who assisted the search.

3. George Washington Greene, *The Life of Nathanael Greene*, 3 vols. (New York: Hurd and Houghton; Cambridge: Riverside Press, 1871), 1:25.

4. Ibid., 1:26. In describing Greene's eyes as kindling "under excitement to an intense and flashing light," Greene's grandson, George Washington Greene, added this footnote: "Lest the reader should tax me with exaggeration, I hasten to add that this peculiarity was told me by my uncle, colonel Samuel Ward."

5. Greene's father logged Nathanael Jr.'s birth date as "the twenty-seventh day of the fifth month, 1742," which led to the impression that Greene was born in May. As was Quaker custom, Greene Sr. employed the civil year, which began on the day of the Annunciation, March 25, not the historical year, which begins more than three months earlier on January 1. Further confusing Greene's birth date was the adoption of a new calendar in Great Britain and America in 1752. Under the "new style" calendar, used to the present day, Greene was born on August 7, 1742, making him forty-three at the time of his death. Gardner, *Remains of Major-General Nathanael Greene*, 70–73.

6. See, for example: Alexander Hamilton's eulogy of Nathanael Greene delivered on July 4, 1789 in *The Papers of Alexander Hamilton, Vol. 8*, eds. Harold C. Syrett

and Jacob Cooke (New York: Columbia University Press, 1961–1987); Mark M. Boatner III, *Encyclopedia of the American Revolution* (Mechanicsburg, PA: Stackpole Books, 1994), 1018–1019; and Gardner, *Remains of Major-General Nathanael Greene*, 156.

ONE   WAR, WAR BOYS!

1. Elaine Forman Crane, *A Dependent People: Newport, Rhode Island in the Revolutionary Era* (New York: Fordham University Press, 1992), 87–88. Newporters even tarred and feathered one treasury office worker who tried to enforce customs laws.

2. The *Fortune*'s capture was recreated from the testimony of Rufus Greene before the King's Commission to Investigate the Destruction of the *Gaspee*, East Greenwich, RI, January 14, 1773. Original manuscripts of this and all King's Commission testimony are housed in the Rhode Island Secretary of State, Archives Division, Providence, RI. Also available in Hon. William R. Staples, *The Documentary History of the Destruction of the Gaspee* (Providence, RI: Knowles, Vose, and Anthony, 1845), 34. King's Commission testimony also available online at http://www.gaspee.org.

3. Quakers do not actually preach, but the spiritual leader of a meetinghouse is often referred to as a Quaker preacher. Nathanael Greene's descendants still refer to Greene's father as a Quaker preacher.

4. Greene, *Life of Nathanael Greene*, 1:53.

5. Ibid., 1:54–56.

6. Ibid., 1:67. Nancy Ward's daughter eventually married one of Nathanael Greene's sons and had a son, George Washington Greene, author of *The Life of Nathanael Greene*. In this sentence G. W. Greene is describing his grandmother's eyes.

7. Staples, 55.

8. Letter of Darius Sessions to Gov. Joseph Wanton, June 11, 1772, Rhode Island Secretary of State, Archives Division, Providence, RI.

9. Dennis M. Conrad, Richard K. Showman, and Roger N. Parks, eds., *The Papers of Nathanael Greene*, 13 vols. (Chapel Hill: University of North Carolina Press, 1976–2006), 1:53. Hereafter *PNG*.

10. *PNG*, 1:34. Dudingston appealed and won a reduction to three hundred pounds. He was ordered to be held "safely secure in our Goal in Newport" until the money was paid. Collector Charles Dudley posted the money "as Bail to William Duddingston."

11. *PNG*, 1:38–39.

12. *PNG*, 1:41–42.

13. *PNG*, 1:37.

14. *PNG*, 1:52.

15. *PNG*, 1:55.

16. *PNG*, 1:69–70. The original manuscript is "Friends Minutes," vol. 5, 1751–1806, Rhode Island Historical Society, Providence, RI.

17. *PNG*, 1:50.

18. *PNG*, 2:104, n. 4.

19. *PNG*, 1:47–48.

20. Greene, *Life of Nathanael Greene*, 1:12–13.

21. Ibid., 1:27.

22. Laurence Sterne, *Tristram Shandy* (New York: Random House, 1948), 106.

23. *PNG*, 1:15.

24. *PNG*, 1:61.

25. John F. Stegeman and Janet A. Stegeman, *Caty: A Biography of Catharine Littlefield Greene* (Providence, RI: Rhode Island Bicentennial Foundation, 1777).

26. H. W. Brands, *The First American: The Life and Times of Benjamin Franklin* (New York: Anchor Books, 2000), 258–260.

27. Stegeman and Stegeman, 10.

28. *PNG*, 1:64. This marked the only time in all of his writings that Greene referred to Caty as "Kitty."

29. *PNG*, 1:65.

30. Boatner, 632.

31. Greene, *Life of Nathanael Greene*, 1:76.

32. Greene, *Life of Nathanael Greene*, 1:51.

33. *PNG*, 1:68.

34. Wanton Casey, Kentish Guards charter member, described the uniforms in a letter written in 1836. Archived at the Rhode Island Historical Society, Providence, RI.

35. *PNG*, 1:78.

36. *PNG*, 1:75–76.

37. *PNG*, 1:77.

38. Benson J. Lossing, *Reflections of Rebellion: Hours with the Men and Women of the Revolution* (1889; Charleston, SC: History Press, 2005).

39. Frederick Mackenzie, *The Diaries of Frederick Mackenzie*, 2 vols. (Cambridge: Harvard University Press, 1930), 1:24, and Boatner, 631. Militia generally carried thirty-six to forty rounds per man. The British suffered about 250 casualties and it's estimated that one bullet out of three hundred fired hit its mark (Boatner, 631), which would require 75,000 shots fired to hit 250 men. The shooting began at the North Bridge before 11 a.m. and concluded as the British troops drew up on the heights above Charlestown Neck around 7 p.m., some 8

hours, or 48,000 seconds, later. At the height of the firing around Meriam's Corner, American militia and minutemen must have been firing multiple shots every second along the length of the British column.

40. Mackenzie, 1:20–22.

41. Greene, *Life of Nathanael Greene*, 1:77.

42. Ibid., 78.

43. Ibid.

44. The first editor of the *Papers of Nathanael Greene*, Richard K. Showman, made a persuasive argument that Greene never served in the Rhode Island General Assembly, concluding "Perhaps some time a document will be found that settles the matter" (see PNG, vol. 1, pp. xvi–xviii). The addenda of the thirteenth and final volume of the *Papers* includes such a document on pages 707–708, in which Greene writes to Moses Brown in 1770 about an issue (the appointment of judges) currently before Greene in the General Assembly.

45. Joseph Jencks Smith, ed., *Civil and Military History of Rhode Island, 1647–1800* (Providence, RI: Preston and Rounds Co., 1900), 305.

TWO   MAD, VEXT, SICK AND SORRY

1. *PNG*, 1:89.

2. *PNG*, 1:82–83.

3. *PNG*, 1:86.

4. *PNG*, 1:90. *Memoirs Concerning the Art of War*, by Comte de Saxe, France's marshal-general, had recently been translated from French into English. It was a work that Greene's friend, Henry Knox, was recommending, and it's possible that Greene bought his copy from Knox's bookstore.

5. Samuel F. Batchelder, "Cambridge Historical Society Proceedings for 1925," vol. 18, 1925, 46.

6. A. J. Langguth, *Patriots* (New York: Simon & Schuster, 1988), 299.

7. Boatner, 1168.

8. *PNG*, 1:94.

9. George F. Scheer and Hugh F. Rankin, *Rebels and Redcoats* (New York: Da Capo Press Inc., 1957), 82.

10. Fred W. Anderson, "The Hinge of the Revolution: George Washington Confronts a People's Army, July 3, 1775," *Massachusetts Historical Review* 1 (1999).

11. *PNG*, 1:93.

12. Within six months of meeting Gen. Charles Lee, Greene observed: "His temper scarce admits of a proper medium to form a just estimate of people and things." *PNG*, 1:12.

13. *PNG*, 1:100.

14. *PNG*, 1:106.

15. *PNG*, 1:123–124.

16. *PNG*, 1:168, and David McCullough, *1776* (New York: Simon & Schuster, 2005), 12.

17. Ernest F. Henderson, *A Short History of Germany*, vol. 2 (New York: MacMillan, 1902), 179.

18. *PNG*, 1:167.

19. *PNG*, 1:177.

20. *PNG*, 1:173.

21. *PNG*, 1:193.

22. Though Caty had been in camp outside Boston while pregnant, she was in Rhode Island with her newborn when summoned to her ill husband's bedside. It is not definitively known whether she delivered their first child, George Washington Greene, in camp or in Rhode Island. *PNG*, 1:193.

23. McCullough, *1776*, 80.

24. *PNG*, 1:178.

25. *PNG*, 1:208.

26. *PNG*, 1;215.

27. *PNG*, 1:222

28. Richard M. Ketchum, *The Winter Soldiers* (1973; New York: Henry Holt and Co., LLC, 1999), 89.

29. Theodore Thayer, *Nathanael Greene, Strategist of the American Revolution* (New York: Twayne Publishers, 1960), 95.

30. *PNG*, 1:288.

31. McCullough, *1776*, 192.

32. *PNG*, 1:291.

33. *PNG*, 1:292–93.

34. *PNG*, 1:296, and Greene, *Life of Nathanael Greene*, 1:214.

35. *PNG*, 1:297–98.

36. Gardner, *Remains of Major-General Nathanael Greene*, 150.

37. Scheer and Rankin, 182.

38. *PNG*, 1:300.

39. *PNG*, 1:300. Greene's sanguine account of his first combat was a concise six sentences.

40. *PNG*, 1:300–302.

41. Mackenzie, 1:60.

42. *PNG*, 1:305.

43. *PNG*, 1:303.

44. Mackenzie, 1:165.

45. *PNG*, 1:342–343.

46. *PNG*, 1:344.
47. *PNG*, 1:351.
48. *PNG*, 1:352.
49. Mackenzie, 1:111–112.
50. *PNG*, 1:352.
51. *PNG*, 1:359–60.
52. Ketchum, 139.
53. Mackenzie, 1:113.
54. Ketchum, 139.
55. *PNG*, 1:365.

THREE   THEIR ETERNAL HONOR

1. Scheer and Rankin, 207.
2. *PNG*, 1:368.
3. *PNG*, 1:375.
4. McCullough, *1776*, 263, and Ketchum, 204.
5. Both quotes from Ketchum, 245, 204.
6. Scheer and Rankin, 211.
7. Thomas Paine, "The Crisis," in Bruce Kuklick, ed., *Thomas Paine Political Writings* (Cambridge: Cambridge University Press, 1989), 41.
8. Ketchum, 248.
9. Langguth, 411.
10. Scheer and Rankin, 212, quoting the journal of Col. John Fitzgerald.
11. Boatner, 1115.
12. Scheer and Rankin, 216.
13. Catharine R. Williams, *Biography of Revolutionary Heroes Containing the Life of Brigadier Gen. William Barton and also of Captain Stephen Olney* (Providence, RI: Published by the author, 1839), 192.
14. *PNG*, 2:4.
15. Greene, *Life of Nathanael Greene*, 1:302.
16. Langguth, 426. The phrasing of Erskine's quote varies from account to account, but the gist of it is that Erskine, concerned that Washington would escape, advocated a nighttime attack.
17. Oft-cited quote, including in Ketchum, 92.
18. Ketchum, 298, and McCullough, *1776*, 288.
19. Langguth, 427. Before he succumbed to his wounds, Mercer regained consciousness and reported that he'd heard British troops declare him dead.
20. Greene, *Life of Nathanael Greene*, 306.
21. Scheer and Rankin, 218.

22. Ketchum, 308.

23. Scheer and Rankin, 219.

24. Ketchum, 313. The doctor was Benjamin Rush, briefly a surgeon general before clashing with Washington and others.

25. *PNG*, 2:6.

26. *PNG*, 2:7.

27. *PNG*, 2:50.

28. *PNG*, 2:32, 58.

29. *PNG*, 2:31.

30. *PNG*, 2:47.

31. *PNG*, 2:47.

32. *PNG*, 2:50.

33. *PNG*, 2:54.

34. *PNG*, 2:72.

35. *PNG*, 2:67.

36. *PNG*, 2:67.

37. John Russell Bartlett, *Rhode Island Colonial Records*, vol. 8, 1862, 263. RI Secretary of State Archives Division, Providence.

38. Mackenzie, 1:150.

39. *PNG*, 2:86.

40. *PNG*, 2:121.

41. Boatner, 606.

42. For a good understanding of the du Coudray affair see John Adams to Greene, *PNG*, 2:69–71; Greene to Adams, *PNG*, 2:98–99; Greene to John Hancock, *PNG*, 2:109; Adams to Greene, *PNG*, 2:111–114; and Greene to Hancock, *PNG*, 2:123–125.

43. Boatner, 592.

44. *PNG*, 2:200.

45. *PNG*, 2:147.

46. *PNG*, 2:154–55.

47. *PNG*, 2:159.

48. W. J. Wood, *Battles of the Revolutionary War 1775–1781* (New York: Da Capo Press Inc., 1990), 108.

49. Scheer and Rankin, 239.

50. Scheer and Rankin, 237.

51. Scheer and Rankin, 239.

52. *PNG*, 2:156.

53. *PNG*, 2:471.

54. *PNG*, 2:167–69.

55. *PNG*, 2:172.

56. *PNG*, 2:173.

57. Ibid.

58. Scheer and Rankin, 246.

59. *PNG*, 2:188.

60. *PNG*, 2:247.

61. Greene, *Life of Nathanael Greene*, 481.

62. Greene, *Life of Nathanael Greene*, 468.

63. *PNG*, 2:171.

64. Greene, *Life of Nathanael Greene*, 1:489.

65. Williams, 223.

66. *PNG*, 2:190.

67. Jeannette D. Black and William Greene Roelker, eds. *A Rhode Island Chaplain in the Revolution: Letters of Ebenezer David to Nicholas Brown, 1775–1778* (Providence, RI: The Rhode Island Society of the Cincinnati, 1949), 68.

68. Joseph Plumb Martin, *A Narrative of a Revolutionary Soldier: Some of the Adventures, Misgivings, and Sufferings of Joseph Plumb Martin* (1830; New York: Signet Classic, 2001), 73.

69. *PNG*, 2:197.

70. *PNG*, 2:198.

71. Martin, 80.

FOUR   SORE WITH THE HARDSHIPS

1. Martin, 88.

2. *PNG*, 2:228.

3. *PNG*, 2:240.

4. Boatner, 1137.

5. Martin, 89.

6. Scheer and Rankin, 304.

7. *PNG*, 2:261.

8. Scheer and Rankin, 303.

9. *PNG*, 2:281.

10. *PNG*, 2:283.

11. *PNG*, 2:285.

12. *PNG*, 2:242.

13. *PNG*, 2:293.

14. *PNG*, 2:195.

15. *PNG*, 2:279.

16. *PNG*, 2:260.

17. *PNG*, 1:325.

18. *PNG*, 2:294.
19. *PNG*, 2:309.
20. *PNG*, 2:326.
21. *PNG*, 3:427.
22. *PNG*, 2:327.
23. *PNG*, 2:315.
24. *PNG*, 2:277.
25. Scheer and Rankin, 305–06.
26. Scheer and Rankin, 308.
27. Scheeer and Rankin, 308.
28. *PNG*, 2:353. For condition of roads see *PNG*, 2:335–36.
29. Scheer and Rankin, 315.
30. Scheer and Rankin, 313.
31. *PNG*, 2:406.
32. Greene was heading back to Valley Forge after riding up to Fishkill, New York, probably in a vain attempt to convince a deputy quartermaster to stay on the job. See *PNG*, 2:393.
33. *PNG*, 2:392–93.
34. Boatner, 236.
35. *PNG*, 2:446, 471.
36. *PNG*, 2:445–47.
37. *PNG*, 2:450.
38. Martin, 109–111.
39. Quoted in multiple sources, including Scheer and Rankin, 330, and Boatner, 722.
40. Many analysts, including the American Capt. Stephen Olney and the British Gen. Henry Clinton, argue that Lee's decision to retreat was correct. But after the battle Lee pestered Washington with a series of insubordinate letters, one of them referring to Washington's "tinsel dignity," leading to a court martial's valid finding of guilty on a charge of disrespect. See *PNG*, 2:456; Catharine R. Williams, *Biography of Revolutionary Heroes Containing the Life of Brigadier Gen. William Barton and Also of Captain Stephen Olney* (Providence, RI: Published by the author, 1839), 257.
41. *PNG*, 2:451.
42. Martin, 115.
43. Boatner, 724.
44. Caroline Cox, *A Proper Sense of Honor: Service and Sacrifice in George Washington's Army* (Chapel Hill, NC: University of North Carolina Press, 2004), 163.
45. Ron Chernow, *Alexander Hamilton* (New York: Penguin Books, 2004), 114–115.
46. Greene, *Life of Nathanael Greene*, 2:109.
47. *PNG*, 2:456–458.

48. Edward G. Lenge, *General George Washington: A Military Life*. (New York: Random House, 2005), 313–318. Around the time of the Monmouth battle, Washington asked for a return of "negroes in the American Army" and learned that he had 755 black soldiers. With the troops of the First Rhode Island Regiment added to that total, about 6 percent of Washington's Army was black.

49. *PNG*, 2:346.

50. Mackenzie, 1:257.

51. *PNG*, 2:465.

52. *PNG*, 2:345.

53. *PNG*, 2:466–67.

54. *PNG*, Vol.:472.

55. *PNG*, 2:467.

56. Mackenzie, 2:318–19.

57. Paul F. Dearden, *The Rhode Island Campaign of 1778: Inauspicious Dawn of Alliance* (Providence, RI: Rhode Island Bicentennial Foundation, 1980), 48.

58. Mackenzie, *Diary*, 2:319.

59. Dearden, 48–49.

60. *PNG*, 2:478.

61. Dearden, 50.

62. Dearden, 39.

63. Mackenzie, 2:330.

64. Scheer and Rankin, 339.

65. Dearden, 94, and Scheer and Rankin, 341.

66. Mackenzie, 2:341.

67. Dearden, 74.

68. Dearden, 75.

69. Mackenzie, 2:341–42.

70. Mackenzie, 2:345–46.

71. *Order Book of the American Forces in the Battle of Rhode Island*, 1778, Redwood Library, Newport, RI.

72. Ibid.

73. Greene, *Life of Nathanael Greene*, 2:114.

74. Mackenzie, 2:361.

75. Mackenzie, 2:354.

76. Greene, *Life of Nathanael Greene*, 2:117. Lafayette told this anecdote in an interview with George Washington Greene.

77. *PNG*, 2:480–82.

78. Ibid.

79. Greene, *Life of Nathanael Greene*, 2:118.

80. *PNG*, 2:487–490.

81. Dearden, 103.

82. *PNG*, 2:491–92.

83. Dearden, 106–107.

84. *Order Book of the American Forces.*

85. Dearden, 104.

86. *PNG*, 2:499–501.

87. Mackenzie, 2:380–381.

88. For disposition of troops see Mackenzie, 2:381.

89. Greene, *Life of Nathanael Greene*, 2:128–29.

90. *PNG*, 2:502.

91. *PNG*, 2:504–505.

92. Mackenzie, 2:389.

93. *PNG*, 2:502.

94. *PNG*, 1:81.

95. *PNG*, 2:506.

96. *PNG*, 2:505.

97. *PNG*, 2:519–20.

98. *PNG*, 2:526–27.

99. *PNG*, 2:528.

100. Stegeman and Stegeman, 207.

101. *PNG*, 2:540–41.

102. *PNG*, 2:543.

103. *PNG*, 3:122.

104. *PNG*, 3:125–26.

105. *PNG*, 3:131.

106. *PNG*, 3:144–45.

107. John Buchanan, *The Road to Guilford Courthouse* (New York: John Wiley & Sons, Inc., 1997), 145.

108. *PNG*, 3:123.

109. *PNG*, 4:26.

110. Scheer and Rankin, 353.

111. *PNG*, 3:256.

112. *PNG*, 3:412.

113. Stegeman and Stegeman, 133–39.

114. *PNG*, 3:403–405.

115. *PNG*, 3:353.

116. *PNG*, 3:49.

117. *PNG*, 3:354.

118. *PNG*, 4:498.

119. *PNG*, 5:12–13.

120. *PNG*, 5:122–123.

121. *PNG*, 5:135.

FIVE   TREASON OF THE BLACKEST DYE

1. *PNG*, 5:139. Snow was reported by Col. Robert Parker, Greene's friend; he was killed by British cannon in Charleston the following May.

2. *PNG*, 5:230.

3. *PNG*, 5:236.

4. *PNG*, 5:237.

5. *PNG*, 5:243.

6. *PNG*, 5:353.

7. *PNG*, 5:429.

8. Marian Sadtler Hornor, ed., "A Washington Affair of Honor, 1779," *Philadelphia: The Pennsylvania Magazine of History and Biography* 65, no. 3, July 1941.

9. *PNG*, 5:550.

10. Martin, 157.

11. *PNG*, 6:6.

12. *PNG*, 6:9.

13. *PNG*, 6:35.

14. Scheer and Rankin, 374.

15. *PNG*, 6:41, 38.

16. Scheer and Rankin, 392.

17. Scheer and Rankin, 390.

18. For a good summation of the ethnic, political, and economic fissures of the South, see John Buchanan, *The Road to Guilford Courthouse* (New York: John Wiley & Sons, Inc., 1997).

19. Ibid., 22.

20. Ibid., 46

21. *PNG*, 6:14.

22. Boatner, 212. British reports showed 5,466 Americans captured at Charleston, but that number included the sick and wounded, along with others unfit for duty. See Carl P. Borick, *A Gallant Defense: The Siege of Charleston, 1780* (Columbia, SC: University of South Carolina Press, 2003), 222.

23. *PNG*, 6:150–155.

24. *PNG*, 6:78.

25. *PNG*, 1:224.

26. *PNG*, 6:233.

27. *PNG*, 6:237.

28. Charles Royster, *A Revolutionary People at War: The Continental Army and American Character, 1775–1783* (Chapel Hill: University of North Carolina Press, 1979), 80–82.

29. Buchanan, 172.

30. *PNG*, 6:267.

31. John B. Hattendorf, *Newport, the French Navy, and American Independence* (Newport, RI: The Redwood Press, 2005), 68.

32. *PNG*, 6:289.

33. *PNG*, 6:306.

34. *PNG*, 6:308–309.

35. *PNG*, 6:320.

36. Ron Chernow, *Alexander Hamilton* (New York: Penguin Books, 2004), 141.

37. *PNG*, 6:312.

38. *PNG*, 6:314.

39. Boatner, 25–43, and Scheer and Rankin, 379.

40. *PNG*, 6:328.

41. *PNG*, 6:321.

42. Greene, *Life of Nathanael Greene*, 2:234–235. This scene written by George Washington Greene may be somewhat fanciful, but is fully supported by fact. André did admit to coming ashore disguised and without protection of a flag. See, for example, *PNG*, 6:334.

43. *PNG*, 6:335.

44. *PNG*, 6:321.

45. *PNG*, 6:328–330.

46. Scheer and Rankin, 387.

47. Ibid.

48. *PNG*, 6:339.

49. *PNG*, 6:326.

50. *PNG*, 6:347.

51. *PNG*, 6:351.

52. *PNG*, 6:397.

53. *PNG*, 3:429.

54. *PNG*, 6:385.

55. *PNG*, 6:424.

SIX   THE COWPENS

1. *PNG*, 6:402.

2. *PNG*, 6:411.

3. *PNG*, 6:416.

4. Lyman C. Draper, ed., *King's Mountain and Its Heroes* (1881; Johnson City, TN: The Overmountain Press, 1996), 169.

5. Ibid., 251.

6. Ibid., 290–292.

7. Boatner, 582.

8. *PNG*, 6:440.

9. *PNG*, 6:482.

10. To Caty: *PNG*, 6:482–83; to Washington: *PNG*, 6:486.

11. *PNG*, 6:535.

12. *PNG*, 6:512–13.

13. Greene, *Life of Nathanael Greene*, 3:71.

14. *PNG*, 6:512–13.

15. Buchanan, 188.

16. *PNG*, 6:542.

17. Boatner, 414.

18. *PNG*, 6:555.

19. Greene, *Life of Nathanael Greene*, 3:69.

20. *PNG*, 6:527.

21. *PNG*, 7:19. And Greene, *Life of Nathanael Greene*, 3:70.

22. Robert E. Lee, ed., *The Revolutionary War Memoirs of General Henry Lee* (1812; New York: Da Capo Press Inc., 1998), 227.

23. Buchanan, 72–80.

24. *PNG*, 6:551.

25. *PNG*, 6:587.

26. Boatner, 1018–19.

27. *PNG*, 6:588–89.

28. *PNG*, 6:554.

29. Lawrence Babits, *A Devil of a Whipping: The Battle of Cowpens* (Chapel Hill: The University of North Carolina Press, 1998), 24. Biography of Morgan and Battle of Cowpens compiled from multiple sources including Buchanan, Boatner, and Don Higginbotham, *Daniel Morgan: Revolutionary Rifleman* (Chapel Hill: The University of North Carolina Press, 1961).

30. *PNG*, 6:589.

31. "Redcoats, Hessians and Tories" exhibit, Charleston Museum, June 4–December 14, 2003, and William Bartram, *Travels* (New Haven, CT: Yale University Press, 1958).

32. *PNG*, 7:81.

33. *PNG*, 7:102.

34. *PNG*, 7:16.

35. *PNG*, 7:47.

36. *PNG*, 7:41.

37. *PNG*, 7:30–31.

38. Lee, 325.

39. *PNG*, 7:72–73.

40. *PNG*, 7:106.

41. Scheer and Rankin, 402.

42. Buchanan, 84.

43. Buchanan, 308.

44. *PNG*, 7:128.

45. Ibid.

46. *PNG*, 7:149.

47. *PNG*, 7:146.

48. PNG, 7: 157, note 3. Morgan later claimed to have deliberately put the Broad River at his back to keep his militia from deserting, but he'd earlier written a friend: "I did not intend to fight that day, but Intended to Cross Pacolet [Broad] River. . . ."

49. Babits, 54.

50. *PNG*, 7:152–53.

51. Scheer and Rankin, 428.

52. Babits, 31–42. Through an exhaustive analysis of pension records, Babits makes a convincing case that at the Battle of Cowpens, Morgan's troops numbered near two thousand men.

53. Banastre Tarleton, *Campaigns of 1780 and 1781 in the Southern Provinces* (1787; reprint, New York: Arno Press, Inc., 1968), 221.

54. Scheer and Rankin, 430.

55. *PNG*, 7:159–160.

56. *PNG*, 7:154–155.

57. *PNG*, 7:161, note 19.

58. *PNG*, 7:201.

59. Buchanan, 341.

SEVEN   RISE, AND FIGHT AGAIN

1. *PNG*, 7:193.

2. *PNG*, 7:219–220.

3. *PNG*, 7:220.

4. *PNG*, 7:228.

5. *PNG*, 7:242.

6. Greene, *Life of Nathanael Greene*, 3:159.

7. *PNG*, 7:251.

8. *PNG*, 7:90.

9. *PNG*, 7:295.

10. *PNG*, 7:261–62.

11. Ibid.

12. *PNG*, 7:268.

13. *PNG*, 7:266.

14. Scheer and Rankin, 439.

15. *PNG*, 7:263.

16. *PNG*, 7:283.

17. Lee, 238.

18. Lee, 249.

19. *PNG*, 7:269.

20. *PNG*, 7:293.

21. *PNG*, 7:286.

22. Lee, 245–46.

23. *PNG*, 7:287.

24. Ibid.

25. *PNG*, 7:271. Col. Edward Carrington recounted in 1809 that the American Army had just six boats at its disposal to ferry all of the troops across the Dan River. The Dan was running high at the time of the crossing, which rendered useless the "wide and shallow flats at the ferries."

26. *PNG*, 7:287.

27. Lee, 251.

28. *PNG*, 7:287.

29. *PNG*, 7:300–301.

30. Buchanan, 360.

31. Lee, 248.

32. Lee, 253.

33. *PNG*, 7:327.

34. *PNG*, 7:422.

35. Greene, *Life of Nathanael Greene*, 186–87.

36. *PNG*, 7:395.

37. *PNG*, 7:415.

38. *PNG*, 7:375.

39. *PNG*, 7:451.

40. Lee, 274.

41. *PNG*, 7:324.

42. Lee, 277.

43. Buchanan, 447.

44. Don Hagist, ed., *A British Soldier's Story: Roger Lamb's Narrative of the American Revolution* (Baraboo, WI: Ballindalloch Press, 2004), 89.

45. Lee, 278.

46. *PNG*, 7:437. "Historian/Ranger Thomas E. Baker of Guilford Courthouse has made a convincing argument that the British artillery consisted of three, six-pounders, and not three-pounders as had been previously thought."

47. *PNG*, 7:435.

48. *PNG*, 8:25.

49. Lee, 286.
50. *PNG*, 7:450.
51. Buchanan, 382.
52. *PNG*, 7:450.
53. *PNG*, 7:461.
54. *PNG*, 7:480.
55. *PNG*, 7:481.
56. *PNG*, 8:90.
57. *PNG*, 8:131.
58. *PNG*, 8:142.
59. Boatner, 919.
60. *PNG*, 8:146.
61. On the lack of officers, see Greene to Gen. Lillington, *PNG*, 7:168; and Greene to Col. Lock, *PNG*, 7:262. On officers as being the "Soul of an Army," see *PNG*, 7:301.
62. *PNG*, 8:157.
63. *PNG*, 8:159.
64. *PNG*, 8:201.
65. *PNG*, 8:160.
66. *PNG*, 8:172–73.
67. *PNG*, 8:187.
68. Dennis Conrad, the second editor of the *Papers of Nathanael Greene*, first proposed this theory for Greene's defeat on Hobkirk's Hill in a lecture delivered at the Nathanael Greene Symposium in Lugoff, S.C., on April 22, 2006. On inspection, the theory proves sound: Greene had been complaining about a lack of officers, Beatty did die early in the battle, and men who would have been under his command acted in a confused manner.
69. *PNG*, 8:168.
70. *PNG*, 8:183.

EIGHT   EUTAW SPRINGS

1. *PNG*, 8:225–227.
2. Lee, 358.
3. Draper, 374.
4. Scheer and Rankin, 459.
5. *PNG*, 8:67–68.
6. *PNG*, 8:277.
7. Buchanan, 95–96.
8. On plundering, Greene to Pickens, *PNG*, 8:350; Greene to Clarke, *PNG*, 8:356.
9. *PNG*, 8:348.

10. *PNG*, 8:358.
11. Lee, 8:374.
12. Lee, 8:375.
13. *PNG*, 8:422.
14. Lee, 378.
15. Lee, 386.
16. Scheer and Rankin, 459–60.
17. *PNG*, 9:201.
18. *PNG*, 9:36.
19. *PNG*, 8:434.
20. *PNG*, 9:38.
21. *PNG*, 7:440.
22. PNG, 9:13.
23. *PNG*, 9:257.
24. *PNG*, 9:334, and Scheer and Rankin, 462.
25. *PNG*, 9:329.
26. Lee, 469.
27. *PNG*, 9:336.
28. Scheer and Rankin, 464.
29. *PNG*, 9:305.
30. *PNG*, 9:308.
31. *PNG*, 9:328.
32. *PNG*, 9:337.
33. *PNG*, 9:355.
34. *PNG*, 9:332.
35. *PNG*, 9:280.
36. Hattendorf, 103–105; Craig L. Symonds and William J. Clipson, *A Battlefield Atlas of the American Revolution* (Mount Pleasant, SC: The Nautical & Aviation Publishing Company of America, Inc., 1986), 103.
37. *PNG*, 9:431.
38. *PNG*, 9:411–12.
39. *PNG*, 9:431.
40. *PNG*, 9:353.
41. *PNG*, 9:461.
42. *PNG*, 9:519.
43. *PNG*, 10:471.
44. *PNG*, 10:22.
45. *PNG*, 10:230.
46. *PNG*, 10:229.
47. *PNG*, 10:27.

48. *PNG*, 10:44.

49. *PNG*, 10:317.

50. *PNG*, 11:38.

51. *PNG*, 8:565.

52. *PNG*, 10:532.

53. *PNG*, 11:11.

54. *PNG*, 11:227–29.

55. *PNG*, 11:670.

56. *PNG*, 12:137.

57. *PNG*, 11;659.

58. *PNG*, 12:324.

59. *PNG*, 12:326.

60. *PNG*, 12:292.

61. *PNG*, 12:364.

62. *PNG*, 12:372.

63. *PNG*, 12:364.

64. *PNG*, 12:404.

65. *PNG*, 12:215.

66. *PNG*, 12:279.

67. *PNG*, 12:308–09.

68. Greene, *Life of Nathanael Greene*, 464.

69. *PNG*, 12:547.

70. *PNG*, 12:591.

71. PNG, 6:93.

72. *PNG*, 12:478.

73. *PNG*, 12:341.

74. *PNG*, 13:157–58.

75. *PNG*, 13;192.

76. *South Carolina Gazette and General Advertiser*, April 16, 1783.

77. *PNG*, 12:626.

78. *PNG*, 12:631.

79. Robert Leckie, *George Washington's War: The Saga of the American Revolution* (New York: HarperPerennial, 1992), 630.

80. *PNG*, 13:44–45.

NINE   MULBERRY GROVE

1. *PNG*, 13:75.

2. Stegeman and Stegeman, 106.

3. *PNG*, 13:83.

4. *PNG*, 13:137.

5. *PNG*, 13:151.

6. *PNG*, 13:566–67.

7. *PNG*, 13:135.

8. *PNG*, 13:162.

9. *PNG*, 13:381.

10. Dearden, 143.

11. *PNG*, 13:297.

12. *PNG*, 13:252, 276.

13. *PNG*, 13:297.

14. Isaac Briggs, "Three Letters," *Georgia Historical Quarterly* 12 (June 1928): 179–182.

15. *PNG*, 12:85.

16. *PNG*, 13:319.

17. *PNG*, 13:325.

18. *PNG*, 13:333.

19. *PNG*, 13:319, 356.

20. *PNG*, 13:370.

21. *PNG*, 13:386.

22. On selling the same slaves twice, see *PNG*, 13:372, note 2.

23. *PNG*, 13:401–02.

24. *PNG*, 13: 405, note 3.

25. *PNG*, 13:411.

26. *PNG*, 13:447.

27. On Gunn's challenge see *PNG*, 13:466–67 (challenge and Greene's response); *PNG*, 13:510 (Greene's letter to Washington); and *PNG*, 13:525 (Washington's response).

28. *PNG*, 13:470.

29. *PNG*, 9:533.

30. *PNG*, 13:576.

31. *PNG*, 13:578.

32. *PNG*, 13:621.

33. *PNG*, 13:668–69.

34. *PNG*, 13:686–87.

35. *PNG*, 13:676–77.

36. Stegeman and Stegeman, 136–137. Caty married Phineas Miller ten years after Greene's death.

37. *PNG*, 13:688.

38. *PNG*, 13:697.

39. Greene, *Life of Nathanael Greene*, 3:534.

BIBLIOGRAPHY

Note to reader: There are some works, listed here, from which I do not quote directly but have strongly informed my understanding of certain events in Nathanael Greene's life; as such I felt it important to include them.

Allen, Ethan. *The Narrative of Colonel Allen.* 1779. Reprint, New York: Corinth Books, 1961.

Anderson, Fred W. "The Hinge of the Revolution: George Washington Confronts a People's Army, July 3, 1775," *Massachusetts Historical Review* 1 (1999).

Babits, Lawrence. *A Devil of a Whipping: The Battle of Cowpens.* Chapel Hill: The University of North Carolina Press, 1998.

Bartlett, John Russell. *Rhode Island Colonial Records*, vol. 8, 1862. RI Secretary of State Archives Division, Providence, RI.

Bartram, William. *Travels.* New Haven, CT: Yale University Press, 1958.

Batchelder, Samuel F. "Cambridge Historical Society Proceedings for 1925," vol. 18, 1925. The Brinkler Research Library, Cambridge, MA.

Black, Jeannette D., and William Greene Roelker, eds. *A Rhode Island Chaplain in the Revolution: Letters of Ebenezer David to Nicholas Brown, 1775–1778.* Providence, RI: The Rhode Island Society of the Cincinnati, 1949.

Boatner, Mark M., III. *Encyclopedia of the American Revolution.* Mechanicsburg, PA: Stackpole Books, 1994.

Borick, Carl P. *A Gallant Defense: The Siege of Charleston, 1780.* Columbia, SC: University of South Carolina Press, 2003.

Brands, H. W. *The First American: The Life and Times of Benjamin Franklin.* New York: Anchor Books, 2000.

Briggs, Isaac, "Three Letters," *Georgia Historical Quarterly* 12, June 1928, 179–182.

Buchanan, John. *The Road to Guilford Courthouse.* New York: John Wiley & Sons, Inc., 1997.

Chernow, Ron. *Alexander Hamilton*. New York: Penguin Books, 2004.

Conley, Patrick T. *The Battle of Rhode Island August 29, 1778: A Victory for the Patriots*. Providence, RI: Rhode Island Publications Society, 2005.

Conrad, Dennis M., Richard K. Showman, and Roger N. Parks, eds. *The Papers of Nathanael Greene*, 13 vols. Chapel Hill: University of North Carolina Press, 1976–2006.

Cox, Caroline. *A Proper Sense of Honor: Service and Sacrifice in George Washington's Army*. Chapel Hill: University of North Carolina Press, 2004.

Crane, Elaine Forman. *A Dependent People: Newport, Rhode Island in the Revolutionary Era*. New York: Fordham University Press, 1992.

Crow, Jeffrey J. and Larry E. Tise, eds. *The Southern Experience in the American Revolution*. Chapel Hill: University of North Carolina Press, 1978.

Darius Sessions to Gov. Joseph Wanton. June 11, 1772. Rhode Island Secretary of State, Archives Division, Providence, RI.

Dearden, Paul F. *The Rhode Island Campaign of 1778: Inauspicious Dawn of Alliance*. Providence, RI: Rhode Island Bicentennial Foundation, 1980.

Draper, Lyman C., ed. *King's Mountain and Its Heroes*. 1881. Reprint, Johnson City, TN: The Overmountain Press, 1996.

Fields, George. Untitled Lecture. Camden, South Carolina, November 2003.

Flood, Charles Bracelen. *Rise, and Fight Again: Perilous Times Along the Road to Independence*. New York: Dodd, Mead & Company, 1976.

French, Allen. *The Day of Concord & Lexington*. 1925. Reprint, Fort Washington PA: Eastern National, 2004.

"Friends Minutes," Vol. 5, 1751–1806, Rhode Island Historical Society, Providence, RI.

Galvin, John R. *The Minute Men, The First Fight: Myths and Realities of the American Revolution*. Washington, D.C.: Brassey's, Inc., 1989.

Gardner, Asa Bird, ed. *Remains of Major-General Nathanael Greene*. Providence: E. L. Freeman & Sons, 1903.

Greene, George Washington. *The Life of Nathanael Greene*. 3 vols. New York: Hurd and Houghton; Cambridge: Riverside Press, 1871.

Hagist, Don, ed. *A British Soldier's Story: Roger Lamb's Narrative of the American Revolution*. Baraboo, WI: Ballindalloch Press, 2004.

Hattendorf, John B. *Newport, the French Navy, and American Independence*. Newport, RI: The Redwood Press, 2005.

Henderson, Ernest F. *A Short History of Germany*. Vol. 2. MacMillan: New York, 1902.

Higginbotham, Don. *Daniel Morgan: Revolutionary Rifleman*. Chapel Hill: The University of North Carolina Press, 1961.

Hooker, Richard J. *The Carolina Backcountry on the Eve of the Revolution: The Journal and Other Writings of Charles Woodmason, Anglican Itinerant*. Chapel Hill: University of North Carolina Press, 1953.

Hornor, Marian Sadtler, ed. "A Washington Affair of Honor." *Philadelphia: The Pennsylvania Magazine of History and Biography*, 65, no. 3, July 1941.

Howe, George Locke. *Mount Hope*. New York: Viking Press, 1959.

Johnson, William. *Life and Correspondence of Nathanael Greene, Major General of the Armies of the United States*. 2 vols. Charleston, SC: 1822.

Ketchum, Richard M. *The Winter Soldiers*. 1973. Reprint, New York: Henry Holt and Company, LLC, 1999.

Kimball, Gertrude Selwyn, ed. *Pictures of Rhode Island in the Past: 1642–1833*. Providence: Preston And Rounds Co., 1900.

Kuklick, Bruce, ed. *Thomas Paine Political Writings*. Cambridge: Cambridge University Press, 1989.

Langguth, A. J. *Patriots*. New York: Simon & Schuster, 1988.

Leckie, Robert. *George Washington's War: The Saga of the American Revolution*. New York: HarperPerenial, 1992.

Lee, Robert E., ed. *The Revolutionary War Memoirs of General Henry Lee*. 1812. Reprint, New York: Da Capo Press Inc., 1998.

Lengel, Edward G. *General George Washington: A Military Life*. New York: Random House, 2005.

Lossing, Benson J. *Reflections of Rebellion: Hours with the Men and Women of the Revolution*. 1889. Reprint, Charleston, SC: History Press, 2005.

Mackenzie, Frederick. *The Diaries of Frederick Mackenzie*, 2 vols. Cambridge: Harvard University Press, 1930.

Martin, Joseph Plumb. *A Narrative of a Revolutionary Soldier: Some of the Adventures, Misgivings, and Sufferings of Joseph Plumb Martin*. 1830. Reprint, New York: Signet Classic, 2001.

McCullough, David. *John Adams*. New York: Simon & Schuster, 2001.

———. *1776*. New York: Simon & Schuster, 2005.

Order Book of the American Forces in the Battle of Rhode Island, 1778, Redwood Library, Newport, RI.

Preston, Howard Willis. "The Battle of Rhode Island, August 29th, 1778," 1928. Providence: State of Rhode Island and Providence Plantations, Office of the Secretary of State, State Bureau of Information.

Quarles, Benjamin. *The Negro in the American Revolution*. Chapel Hill, NC: University of North Carolina Press, 1961, 1996.

Rankin, Hugh F. *Greene and Cornwallis: The Campaign in the Carolinas*. Raleigh, NC: North Carolina Division of Archives and History, 1976.

"Redcoats, Hessians, and Tories," exhibit, Charleston Museum, June 4–December 14, 2003.

"Research Notes on the Gaspee Crewmen," available at http://www.Gaspee.org.

Royster, Charles. *A Revolutionary People at War: The Continental Army and American Character, 1775–1783*. Chapel Hill: University of North Carolina Press, 1979.

———. *Light-Horse Harry Lee and the Legacy of the American Revolution*. Baton Rouge: Louisiana State University Press, 1981.

The Saturday Evening Post 8, no. 421, August 22, 1829, Philadelphia.

Savannah Morning News, March 3, 1901; March 6, 1901; and April 23, 1933.

Scheer, George F. and Hugh F. Rankin. *Rebels and Redcoats*. New York: Da Capo Press Inc., 1957.

Silvia, Jack, "Notes on the Possible Construction and Rigging of the Gaspee," available at Gaspee.org, undated.

Smith, Joseph Jencks, ed. *Civil and Military History of Rhode Island, 1647–1800*. Providence: Preston and Rounds Co., 1900.

Staples, Hon. William R. *The Documentary History of the Destruction of the Gaspee*. Providence, RI: Knowles, Vose, and Anthony, 1845.

Stegeman, John F. and Janet A. Stegeman. *Caty: A Biography of Catharine Littlefield Greene*. Providence, RI: Rhode Island Bicentennial Foundation, 1977.

Sterne, Laurence. *Tristram Shandy*. New York: Random House, 1948.

Symonds, Craig L., and William J. Clipson. *A Battlefield Atlas of the American Revolution*. Mount Pleasant, SC: The Nautical & Aviation Publishing Company of America, Inc., 1986.

Tarleton, Banastre. *Campaigns of 1780 and 1781 in the Southern Provinces*. 1787. Reprint, New York: Arno Press, Inc., 1968.

Taylor, Maureen Alice. *The Providence Gazette, 1762–1800*. Vol 1 of *Runaways, Deserters, and Notorious Villains: From Rhode Island Newspapers*. Camden, ME: Picton Press, 1995.

Testimony of Rufus Greene before the King's Commission to Investigate the Destruction of the Gaspee, East Greenwich, RI, January 14, 1773. RI Secretary of State Archives Division, Providence, RI.

Thayer, Theodore. *Nathanael Greene, Strategist of the American Revolution*. New York: Twayne Publishers, 1960.

Williams, Catharine R. *Biography of Revolutionary Heroes Containing the Life of Brigadier Gen. William Barton and Also of Captain Stephen Olney*. Providence, RI: Published by the author, 1839.

Wood, Gordon S. *Revolutionary Characters: What Made the Founders Different*. New York: The Penguin Press, 2006.

Wood, W. J. *Battles of the Revolutionary War 1775–1781*. New York: Da Capo Press Inc., 1990.

INDEX